Deconstructive Subjectivities

SUNY Series in
Contemporary Continental Philosophy

Dennis J. Schmidt, Editor

Deconstructive Subjectivities

Edited by
Simon Critchley and Peter Dews

STATE UNIVERSITY OF NEW YORK PRESS

Production by Ruth Fisher
Marketing by Theresa Abad Swierzowski

Published by
State University of New York Press, Albany

For information, address the State University of New York Press,
State University Plaza, Albany, NY 12246

Library of Congress Cataloging-in-Publication Data

Deconstructive subjectivities / edited by Simon Critchley and Peter
    Dews.
        p.   cm. — (SUNY series in contemporary continental
    philosophy)
    Includes bibliographical references and index.
    ISBN 0-7914-2723-4. — ISBN 0-7914-2724-2 (pbk.)
    1. Subjectivity.   2. Deconstruction.   3. Philosophy, Modern—20th
century.   I. Critchley, Simon, 1960–   .   II. Dews, Peter.
III. Series.
BD222.D43   1996
126—dc20   95-10495
                                                         CIP

                                                    8 -14- 96 doo

10 9 8 7 6 5 4 3 2 1

Contents

Sources and Acknowledgments

Dominique Janicaud's essay was originally entitled "L'analytique existentiale et la question de la subjectivité" and appeared in *"Être et temps" de Martin Heidegger: Questions de méthode et voies de recherche,* Jean-Pierre Cometti and Dominique Janicaud ed. (Marseilles: SUD, 1989). It is translated here by Iain Macdonald.

Rudolf Bernet's essay was first published as "Subject en zelfervaring," *Tijdschrift voor Filosofie* 53, no. 1 (March 1991): pp. 24–44.

Jean-Luc Marion's essay appeared in a shorter version in the journal *Topoi,* (1988), under the title "L'Interloqué." It was translated there by Eduardo Cadava and Annie Tomiche and was reprinted in *Who Comes after the Subject?* E. Cadava et al. ed. (London and New York: Routledge, 1991), pp. 236–45. The French text appeared in a shorter version in *Après le sujet qui vient,* J.-L. Nancy ed. (*Cahiers Confrontation,* no. 20 [Winter 1989]). The present version appeared in *Revue de métaphysique et morale* no. 1 (1991): pp. 77–95. It is translated here by Simon Critchley, who referred extensively to the shorter English version.

Manfred Frank's essay is a shorter version of a text on Schelling, "Identität und Subjektivität," which appeared in his essay collection *Selbstbewußtsein und Selbsterkenntnis* (Stuttgart: Reclam 1991), pp. 79–157. It was originally written as a lecture for a meeting of the Schelling-Gesellschaft in Leonberg in 1989. It is translated here by Peter Dews.

All other contributions appear for the first time in this volume.

Ute Guzzoni's essay was written under the title "Wollen wir noch Subjekte sein?" and is translated here by Peter Dews.

One

Introduction

Simon Critchley and Peter Dews

The central aim of the present collection of essays is to highlight the *variety* of ways in which subjectivity has been interpreted within the Continental philosophical tradition, from post-Kantian idealism (Jacobi, Schelling) to post-Husserlian phenomenology (Heidegger, Levinas), psychoanalysis, Frankfurt Critical Theory, poststructuralism, and more recent developments. However, our title suggests an argument which goes even further than the claim that a certain model of the subject—whether identified as the principle of a totalising reflexivity, as universal ground for epistemic certainty, as self-presence, or as rational self-assertion and mastery—has been allowed, up until quite recently, to dominate the scene even if only by its negation. It implies that, when the full range of what has been thought under the concept of the 'subject' comes into view, and when the possibilities of *genuine* alternatives are assessed, then the subject may appear, in many of its guises, to be one of the driving forces behind—rather than the prime defense against—that unravelling of metaphysics which has come to be known, after Derrida, as "deconstruction." Might it not be the case that the subject appears, disruptive and uncontainable, at the very point of breakdown of the foundational project of philosophical thinking?

If one were to seek the inaugural moment of such a breakdown, then the dramatic interventions of Friedrich Heinrich Jacobi into the debates of the 1780s and '90s would seem an obvious place to start. Two of the essays in this collection are concerned with exploring the—near or remote—consequences of Jacobi's path-breaking arguments within the context of German idealism. In his contribution, Andrew Bowie suggests that Heidegger's generalizations concerning "all philosophizing in the modern period since Descartes," which he describes as knowing "in advance, or [thinking] it knows, that everything can be proven and grounded in an absolutely strict and pure manner,"[1] overlooks the disruption of this project which begins with

1

Jacobi's attack on the consequences of the Enlightenment. Further-more, Bowie argues, Jacobi's contrast between 'truth' and 'the true,' and his celebrated claim that "the greatest achievement of the enquirer is to disclose and to reveal existence *(Dasein),*" point towards Heidegger's own conception of truth as disclosure or unconcealment. In Jacobi's case, of course, this prephilosophical, indeed pretheoretical dwelling in the truth includes an unshakeable sense of ourselves as free and morally responsible beings, a sense which Heidegger—certainly after the *Kehre*—would wish to qualify heavily. At the same time however, what is important for Jacobi in this "subjecthood" is its radical otherness with respect to all worldly entities and relations. As Dieter Henrich puts it: "In grappling with Spinoza's thinking [Jacobi] came to the conviction that in the dimension foundational for acquiring an understanding of ourselves, one must reckon with relations that cannot be mastered in the conceptual structure underlying the knowledge of finite objects . . . once this fact and the reasons for it are appreciated, one is free to give the relation-to-self a constitution hitherto unimaginable, even by those who had recognized the singular, disclosive significance of this relation and the difficulties entangling attempts to master it theoretically."[2]

Andrew Bowie traces the convoluted path of Schelling's efforts to take up the challenge of Jacobi's thinking, his constant struggle to reconcile the systematic requirements of thinking with an acknowledgment of the *resistance* of the subject to theorization. Schelling's fundamental objection to Jacobi is that his appeal to intuition fails to contest rationalism on its own terrain: "If Jacobi maintains that philosophy cannot grant precisely what is most eagerly desired of it, namely an explanation of what lies beyond the border of common experience, then he is in complete agreement and harmony with rationalism, only differing by the fact that he refers, in relation to everything which ought to be the highest prize of philosophy, to non-philosophy, to non-knowledge—to feeling, to a vague idea, or else, particularly in his earlier writings, to belief . . ."[3] At the same time, however, Schelling is profoundly aware of the elusiveness of our fundamental self-understanding. Perhaps most famously, the 1809 treatise *On the Essence of Human Freedom* begins by posing the fundamental question of how our primordial, inarticulate awareness of freedom can be acknowledged without denying the necessary interdependence of conceptual determinations. Here, as throughout the later work of Schelling, freedom functions not as the principle of an objectifying domination but rather as that groundlessness which ultimately under-mines the possibility of a philosophical totalization, whose ineluctable imperative is simultaneously acknowledged. From this standpoint, as Bowie indicates, due consideration of the work of Schelling drastically alters our sense of German idealism as advancing towards the final transfiguration of substance into subject in Hegel.

Manfred Frank's contribution is also concerned with Schelling's thought, although concentrating on the phase of the *Identitätsphilosophie*. Frank seeks to demonstrate that Schelling's concept of identity lies at the heart of an attempt to overcome the model of the world-objectifying subject which is profoundly rooted in the history of West-ern metaphysics. Schelling's subject does not stand autarkically over against a degraded nature but knows itself part of that to which it finds itself opposed, in a complex structure of identity which does not exclude diremption and difference. Although Schelling will ultimately abandon the *Identitätsphilosophie*, because of its inadequate account of freedom, he will never cease struggling to overcome the model of an originary subject surveying the inertness of an objectified reality from its transcendental fastness. Indeed, as Schelling's thinking develops, the subject increasingly becomes a vortex of conflicting forces, perma-nently liable to perversion and disruption: "The subject which is at first a subject which is *pure* and not present to itself—in wishing to *have* itself, in becoming object to itself—is tainted with contingency . . . It admittedly wants itself *as* such, but precisely this is impossible in an *immediate* way; in the very wanting itself *(in Wollen selbst)* it already becomes another and distorts itself."[4]

As Bowie mentions, a subterranean link runs from the thought of Schelling to Freudian theory. A number of commentators, Odo Marquard most prominently, have argued that the irreducible *tension* between nature and history, the insistence on a 'ground' which cannot be conceptually sublated, which demarcates Schelling's thought from Hegel's, clearly anticipates themes which will be central to psycho-analysis. Since nature cannot be eliminated as a force independent of, and in many ways resistant to, processes of logical development, whether individual or collective, "it is crucially a matter of guarantee-ing—or at least of comprehending—that nature in history can and does work, not 'against' reason and history, but 'in the same sense as' reason, history and human 'culture.' To this end, it must be shown that, and shown how, nature is somehow able to operate rationally and historically. This is the problem of *'reason through un-reason,'* of an *indirect reason.'* "[5] This gulf between such a notion of indirect reason and the familiar "postmodernist" target of the rational, autonomous subject can readily be seen from the following remarks of Schelling: "The basis of understanding is therefore madness. Thus madness is a necessary element, which should merely not come to the fore, not be actualized. What we call understanding, if it is effective, living, active understanding, is really nothing other than coordinated madness."[6]

Explicitly psychoanalytical versions of such a perspective on the subject are explored in the essays by Phillipe van Haute and Peter Dews. Van Haute describes the Freudian subject as torn between guilty submission to the transcendent source of authority (in Freud's mythology, the murdered primal father) and an identification with this authority which threatens to produce a totalitarian closure of the social. Not the least valuable feature of Van Haute's contribution is the manner in which it exposes the fantasy of a pure encounter with alterity, the counterpart of a simplifying critique of the subject which powers certain forms of postmodernist discourse. As Van Haute writes, "The incorporating movement has always already started. Consequently, there is no moment when we are confronted with the other in its pure otherness. The process of cannibalistic identification that is directed towards absolute immanence is always already there from the very beginning."[7] Van Haute concludes that the defense against a repressive closure of the social cannot succeed simply through advocating respect for the other, since without a moment of identification the result would be a complete disintegration of political bonds. In this sense Van Haute redescribes subjectivity itself as a constant oscillation and balancing between alienating, guilt-induced individuation and an equally alienating submersion in the collective.

In his essay, Peter Dews looks at the model of intersubjectivity which is implicit in Lacan's rethinking of psychoanalysis and which can be seen as challenging Habermas's conception of the relation between subjectivity and intersubjectivity, as the principles of historically sequential paradigms. In Lacan's thinking, it could be said, each of these principles "deconstructs" the other, revealing a subject of the unconscious which resists and skews the reciprocal structures of intersubjectivity, just as these structures in their turn expose the illusory stability of the "subject" as ego. Focusing on the joker in Habermas's pack of validity-claims, namely, "truthfulness," Dews seeks to show how Lacan's account of a "truth of the subject" which transcends any determinate context parallels the explication of validity-claims in Habermas, while subverting the latter's attempt to theorize the subject entirely in interactive and communicative terms.

The other major source for contemporary Continental debates on the subject is post-Husserlian phenomenology, especially Heidegger. In their markedly different ways, each of the essays by Rudolf Bernet, Simon Critchley, Ute Guzzoni, Dominique Janicaud, Jean-Luc Marion, and Rudi Visker begin from Heidegger's critique of the subject in *Being and Time*, if only to then proceed to a critique of that critique.

For Heidegger, the opening of the question of Being is intrinsically related to the opening of the question of the Being of being human, in ways which do not rush precipitously into a metaphysical determination of the human being as, for example, one often finds in the philosophical employment of concepts like 'subject,' 'mind,' 'consciousness,' 'ego,' 'person,' or 'agent.' Heidegger pursues this question in *Being and Time* by examining the human being under the title of *Dasein*, understood as that being who is defined by the fact that Being is an issue for it, who has itself in question, who can raise the question of its "who." One might say that *Dasein* is the entity who comes *before* the subject, whose existence precedes the epistemological division of entities into subjects and objects. In its everyday, inauthentic existence, Heidegger claims, *Dasein* is *Mitsein*, it is in the world with others before it is with itself. Although, in its authentic existence—through the experience of angst, death, and conscience—*Dasein* becomes individualized and resolute, that is, it becomes a Self, this conception of authentic selfhood cannot be confused with metaphysical conceptions of subjectivity. Or can it?

Such is the question that animates the contributions of Critchley, Janicaud, Marion, and Visker, namely: is *Dasein*, that is, the conception of the human being that is explicitly opposed to the subject, itself free from the traces of metaphysical subjectivity, or is it one of the last heirs to this metaphysical tradition? As a way of exploring the fate of the subject in the phenomenological tradition, Marion takes the example of *Dasein* and asks, "To what extent does the existential analytic exceed the problematic (and thus also the abolition) of the metaphysical subject?" After a discussion of *Being and Time*, Marion concludes that the Heideggerian claim to anticipatory resoluteness *(vorlaufende Entschlossenheit)* as the authentic structure of *Dasein*, and Heidegger's description of the latter in terms of self-constancy *(Selbst-ständigkeit)*,[8] mean that the *Dasein*-analytic rediscovers "the metaphysical avatar of constitutive subjectivity." Marion continues,

> Thus arises the prodigious paradox of 1927: the extasis of care, which radicalizes the destruction of the transcendental subject in Descartes, Kant, and Husserl, nonetheless leads to a miming of the subject by re-establishing an autarky of *Dasein*, identical to itself through itself up to the point where this ipseity stabilizes itself in a self-positing . . . The shadow of the ego falls across *Dasein*.[9]

Similar conclusions are arrived at by Janicaud and Visker. Janicaud critically questions Heidegger's desire to destroy subjectivity, and, after a discussion of the structure of self-relation or self-reflection that emerges in Heidegger's analyses of anxiety, death, and conscience, he concludes,

> If, therefore, the Self is not erased but stripped of its import as soon as the existential analytic is deployed, one must yield to the observation that subjectivity is neither destroyed nor emptied of content by Heidegger. It is metamorphosed, but nevertheless preserved and even revived through the fundamental role of the *Selbst*.[10]

Yet, if the conception of self possessed by *Dasein* does not free itself so easily from the confines of metaphysical subjectivity, and indeed might even remain a prisoner of metaphysical language, then Janicaud does not content himself with passing judgement on Heidegger but rather sketches an alternative approach to subjectivity, as what he calls a *diaphanous* subjectivity. The latter is a conception of the self as a transparent openness to both its own being-in-the-world and that of others, which is prefigured, Janicaud intriguingly suggests, in Rilke's *Sonnets to Orpheus*. Such a diaphanous subjectivity would avoid what Janicaud sees as the *reactivity* (in Nietzsche's sense) of Heidegger's discourse on the subject, in which one must choose between either a metaphysical subject or an ecstatical opening to the truth of Being. As such, diaphanous thought might be "liberated from all reactive gestures with respect to metaphysical *theoria*" and might respond to the "practico-existential radicalism of *Being and Time*."[11]

Is everydayness necessarily inauthentic? Is Heidegger's discourse on *das Man* as the 'self' of inauthentic everydayness, necessarily part of a moralizing critique of the public realm (Arendt) with the instrument of a "jargon of authenticity" (Adorno)? Is what Heidegger says of the falling or "dropping" *(verfallen)* of *Dasein* into *das Man* still subject to the metaphysics of subjectivity, or does it already move beyond it? In his contribution, Visker pursues these questions by investigating the link between Heidegger's discourse on the subject and the themes of authenticity and inauthenticity. He shows convincingly both that *ambiguity* is what Heidegger fears most (it is one of the defining characteristics of *das Man*), and yet ambiguity is what haunts the analysis of *Being and Time* at every turn. In this way, a subtle fissure opens up between the ambiguous structures of Heidegger's text and Heidegger's desire to eliminate ambiguity. The fact that Heidegger fails to keep to his promise of an everydayness that would not be necessarily inauthentic, or the fact that existentials like falling or "dropping" disappear from the existential analytic, follow not, Visker claims, from the logic of Heidegger's analytic, but rather from a *decision* imposed upon that analytic, where everydayness and falling are judged to be inauthentic. The intriguing question that Visker raises for the future reading of Heidegger's early work is whether we could keep the richness and ambiguity of Heidegger's existential analytic and do without his decision to reduce ambiguity.

So, if *Dasein* represents less a break with the tradition of the metaphysics of subjectivity than the latest heir to that tradition, is this also true of Heidegger's work after the *Kehre,* where the call to which *Dasein* responds is not its own voice of conscience but the call of Being itself, the *Anspruch des Seins*? What is the nature of this call? And what is the nature of the being who is called? Such are the questions taken up by Marion in the later sections of his contribution. Although broadly sympathetic to the ambition of the later Heidegger, Marion criticizes him for failing to provide an analytic of the being to whom the call is made, what Heidegger calls simply (perhaps too simply), *Mensch.* Marion gives an original phenomenological analysis of the call and the one called, whom he calls *l'interloqué,* "the interlocuted." The latter is analyzed under four headings—convocation, surprise, interlocution, and facticity—and on the basis of this analysis Marion claims that the selfhood of the being who is called is not autarkically given but received from a call or appeal that gives me to myself. In a claim that is not too distant from the spirit of Visker's analysis, Marion argues for an originary inauthenticity insofar as what is most my own and most proper to me derives from a call that is not mine, that is im-proper; he writes, "Authenticity, far from opening upon an untained origin or leading back to such an origin, dissimulates after the fact the originally inauthentic movement of the gift."[12]

Marion's thesis of an originary inauthenticity produces a picture of the self as radically divided or differentiated within itself, where "authentic" selfhood would be nothing other than the capacity for an inauthentic loss of self—self-experience is self-loss. It is this theme that also motivates Bernet's original phenomenological account of self-experience, where it is claimed that *"Affectivity, or better, the possibility of being touched and moved* is the privileged place for such an experience of self." However, such an experience of the affective loss of self does not entail the traumatic annihilation of the self but, rather, "maintains and reveals the self to the self as a tense, changing and vulnerable self."[13] Bernet pursues this theme of self-experience as division in three moments. First, in moral self-experience, the phenomenon of conscience is precisely that of a division of the self, where the voice of conscience is both that which transcends the self and which is immanent to the self, a claim that Bernet makes good in a discussion of conscience in *Being and Time*. Second, in psychoanalysis, the division of the self is acknowledged in Freud's late notion of *Ichspaltung*, which is elaborated by Lacan as a division that takes place at the level of language itself in terms of the distinction between the speaking subject *(sujet de l'énonciation)* and the subject spoken about *(sujet de l'énoncé)*. Third, in relation to Derrida, far from declaring the so-called death of the subject, one can find in Derrida's work an implicit acknowledgement of the differential structure of self-experience, "There exists no interior self-consciousness without an exterior appearance of the subject in pronouncements, gestures, activities, and so on."[14] However, for Bernet, the most fundamental characteristic of self-experience is its affectivity, a feeling of oneself, an affectivity that is not reducible to the spectre of auto-affection (should such a thing ever be possible) but is rather an experience of self as loss of self. This thesis is then pursued through a discussion of co-affectivity or feeling together, the most powerful example of which is sexuality, that strange dialectic of self-gain and self-loss that characterizes the libidinal body.

This account of the divided self constituted in affectivity presents striking parallels with the account of the subject in Emmanuel Levinas's work, as it is presented in Simon Critchley's contribution. Although subjectivity has been a constant theme in Levinas's work, Critchley focuses on the presentation of the subject in Levinas's second major book, *Otherwise than Being; or, Beyond Essence*, [15] where Levinas explicitly situates his work as a response to the poststructuralist and antihumanist critique of the subject. For Levinas, the subject is constituted not at the level of intentionality or consciousness—such, for Levinas, is Husserl's persistent intellectualism—but rather at the level of sensibility of simple sensing *(le sentir)*, what Levinas also calls *life*. Life, for Levinas, is love of life and love of what life lives from: the sensible, material world. Levinas's work offers what, with Michel Henry, we might call a *material phenomenology* of subjective life.[16] For Levinas— and this is what is persistently misunderstood about his work—ethics is not an obligation at the level of consciousness, where my responsibility to the other is mediated through rationality, the universalization of maxims, good conscience, or some formal-procedural conception of justice; rather, ethics is *lived* in the sensibility and corporeality of a relation to alterity. In a continuation of Marion's and Bernet's arguments (and also, as Critchley shows, with elements of Lacan and the later Merleau-Ponty), the Levinasian subject is shown to be originally inauthentic, that is, the identity of the subject is not available to consciousness or to reflection and is structured intersubjectively in a relation to alterity. The ethical subject experiences itself as a divergence from self, an experience that Levinas describes as trauma, and which, for him, describes the responsible structure of the psyche. As such, the Levinasian conception of the subject does not react conservatively to the poststructionalist or antihumanist critique of the subject by nostalgically trying to restore the primacy of the free, autonomous ego. On the contrary, it is precisely because the discourses of antihumanism and poststructuralism have deposed the subject from its position of sovereignty that what Levinas calls the sanctity *(la sainteté)* of the human can be delineated.

In a final move, Critchley parallels Levinas's conception of the subject with certain of Derrida's remarks from a conversation with Jean-Luc Nancy.[17] After an intriguing, if ambiguous, allusion to the possiblity of "post-deconstructive" determinations of the responsibility of the subject,[18] Derrida remarks, "In order to recast, if not rigorously refound a discourse on the 'subject' . . . one has to go through the experience of a deconstruction." He continues,

> Some might say, quite rightly: but what we call "subject" is not the absolute origin, pure will, identity to self, or presence to self of consciousness but precisely this non-coincidence with self. This

is a riposte to which we'll have to return. By what right do we call this "subject"? By what right, conversely, can we be forbidden from calling this "subject"? I am thinking of those today who would try to reconstruct a discourse on the subject that would not be pre-deconstructive, around a subject that would no longer include the figure of mastery of self, of adequation to self, center and origin of the world, etc. . . . but which would define the subject rather as the finite experience of non-identity to self, as the underivable interpellation inasmuch as it comes from the other, from the trace of the other.[19]

Setting aside the obvious Levinasian echoes this passage evokes and noting Derrida's refreshing openness to the possibility of new discourses of subjectivity, phrases like "non-coincidence with self," "finite experience of non-identity to self," and "the interpellation inasmuch as it comes from the other," find resonance with many of the contributions to this book, whether they approach the question of the subject from the context of German idealism, phenomenology, or psychoanalysis. Indeed, as one surveys the entire volume, one is struck by the surprising similarity of convictions and concerns that span such divergent approaches and traditions:

1. There is a need (at once existential, ethical, and political) to maintain discourses on the subject in the face of a cross-traditional consensus that wants to bring about their overcoming.

2. Such discourses on subjectivity are by no means condemned to be conservative or reactive attempts to refound the subject as a stable identity or substantiality, nor are they attempts to find an Archimedean point from which to relaunch the project of metaphysics.

3. Such discourses on subjectivity need not represent a naive return to a pre-deconstructive, pre-Heideggerian, or, indeed, pre-Kantian position.

4. The subject continues in its deconstruction, and is perhaps first truly glimpsed *as* its deconstruction, in the abyssal foundering of the claims of traditional metaphysics. As Derrida puts it, the recasting of the subject can be achieved only by going through the experience of deconstruction.

5. Deconstruction has a history, that is, it is a name (there might be others, for example, philosophical modernism) for a period in the history of philosophy that is at least two centuries old and which is traversed by a subterranean stream that covertly crosses and connects the diverse landscapes of German idealism, phenomenology, psychoanalysis, poststructuralism, and postmodernism. Deconstruction cannot but be challenged and deepened by a relation to its own (pre)history.

Perhaps it is proper for the last word to go to Ute Guzzoni: "Do we still want to be subjects?" That is, if modern subjectivity consists in a constant struggle against its own self-hypostatization, against a withdrawal into autarky which leads to nihilism, might it not be better if we sought to change terrain and to leave this apparently interminable conflict behind? After a discussion where every word of Guzzoni's initial question in analyzed in terms of the history and possible future of the subject, and a confrontation with the social and impact of subjectivity as a mode of self-relation, she concludes,

Do we still want to be subjects? In my view, no. As subjects Europeans discovered and colonized foreign continents, Christians converted other peoples, men disciplines their wives, and husbands and wives disciplined their children. As subjects individuals have suppressed their own inclinations and needs, while generalities have excluded those elements which could not be incorporated. I believe that we can no longer want to be subjects. But this does not mean that we can renounce questioning ourselves and asking what things would be like, were we to learn to accept ourselves as fallible and not all-determining mortals.[20]

However, can we rest content with a mere acceptance of fallibility and finitude, without stifling the impulse to philosophical reflection, and thus never raising the deepest issues concerning who we are? How is the appropriate balance to be struck between interrogation and affirmation? Whatever our answer to these questions, the poststructuralist critique, deconstruction or genealogy of the subject, or the Habermasian attempt to displace the subject paradigm with an intersubjective model, must not be allowed to become a headlong flight from the standpoint of the experiencing self, with all its conflicts and paradoxes, including the temptation of this flight itself. Wherever possible, the insights of these modes of thinking should be mobilized to render the "subject" more worldly, more concrete, more pluralistic, more differentiated. This is no easy task, of course. For as our title, *Deconstructive Subjectivities*, suggests, there will always remain a simultaneous complicity and tension between philosophical reflection, with its potentially de-worlding and dismantling effects, and the traces of singular experience which are both indelible and yet always being written over, erased by their inevitable interpretation.

Two

Prolegomena to Any Post-Deconstructive Subjectivity

Simon Critchley

The Subject as the Subject of Metaphysics (Heidegger)

What, or rather who, is the subject? Subject derives from the Latin *subjectum* literally, "that which is thrown under." Thus, the subject is that which is thrown under as a prior support or more fundamental stratum upon which other qualities, such as predicates, accidents, and attributes, may be based. *Subjectum* translates the Greek *hupokeimenon*, "that which lies under," "the substratum"; a term which refers in Aristotle's *Physics* and *Metaphysics* to that of which all other entities are predicated but which is itself not predicated of anything else.[1] In a classical context, then, the subject is the subject of predication; the *hupokeimenon* is that which persists through change, the sub-stratum, and which has a function analogous to matter (*hulē*). It is matter that persists through the changes that form (*morphē*) imposes upon it. In remembrance of this sense of the subject, one still speaks of a subject matter (*ē hupokeimē hulē, subjecta materia*) as that with which thought deals, the matter of a discussion or the subject of a book or a painting. Indeed, one immediately here notes the oddity that the word *subject* can also designate an object. As Heidegger points out, during the middle ages the meaning of the words *subjectum* and *objectum* was precisely the reverse of their modern signification.[2] In the context of the English language, lexicographic evidence suggests that from the middle ages until the eighteenth century the word *subject* was used to name independently existing entities: the subject was that which was acted or operated upon, the "object" upon which one exercised one's craft. For example, the dead body dissected for medical experimentation was, and still is, called a "subject." The modern philosophical use

13

of the word *subject* as the conscious or thinking subject, as self or ego, as that to which representations are attributed or predicated (the subject as the subject of representation) first appears in the English language as late as 1796.[3]

Returning to Aristotle, we can see that *hupokeimenon* has the meaning of a foundation, as that upon which all other entities are based, the grounding principle upon which all entities become intelligible. Early in *Sein und Zeit,* Heidegger states that every idea of a subject, regardless of the protestations against the substantialization of the subject (i.e., the subject as a soul-substance or *res cogitans*), in Kant for example, always posits an *ultimum subjectum,* an absolute foundation (*SuZ* 46). Thus, from its context in Aristotle's *Metaphysics,* the subject is metaphysical: it is the very element of metaphysical thinking. To determine the subject as *hupokeimenon* is to make a claim to the meaning of Being, meaning being defined with Heidegger as the foundation or that upon which (*das Woraufhin* [*SuZ* 151]) entities can be grasped as such. Metaphysics is here defined with Heidegger in fidelity to Aristotle as *philosophia protē,* as that science (*epistēmē*) that asks the question *ti to on,* What is an entity? (in German, *Was ist das Seiende?*); or again, what is an entity in its Being (*Was ist das Seiende in seinem Sein*)? Metaphysics does not ask after the Being of any particular region of entities; it is not a regional ontology like biology (the investigation of the Being of living things) or physics (the investigation of the Being of physical things, i.e., matter). Rather, metaphysics asks after what it means for any entity to be as such, and this question constitutes the guiding question of philosophy. Thus, for Heidegger, the question of Being (*die Seinsfrage*) is the guiding question of philosophy, and the history of philosophy, from Plato to Nietzsche, consists in a series of determinations or theses on the meaning of the Being of entities, what Heidegger also calls "words for Being."[4] Heidegger's fundamental historical insight is that, in this series of theses on Being that constitutes the history of metaphysics, the *question* of Being itself is forgotten or passed over. This is how Heidegger can claim that the history of metaphysics is a forgotteness or oblivion of Being (*Seinsvergessenheit*). Modestly stated, the aim of Heidegger's thinking is simply to renew the experience of the question of Being as a question, as a source of perplexity about what it means for entities to be. This is the purpose of the quotation from Plato's *Sophist* on the untitled first page of *Sein und Zeit,* "For manifestly you have been long aware of what you mean when you use the expression 'being' [*seiend*]. We, however, who used to think we understood it have now become perplexed," (*SuZ* 1). Philosophy begins with a movement into perplexity (*aporia*) or questioning about the meaning of the Being of beings, and Heidegger's thinking begins with a certain repetition (*Wiederholung*) of this Greek beginning.[5] However, in order for philosophy to begin, for human beings to be attuned to the philosophical mood of perplexity or wonder, the previous ontological tradition must be submitted to a de(con)struction (*Destruktion*) or what the later Heidegger will call a dismantling (*Abbau*).

Keeping in mind this broad sense of the subject—and I am slightly distorting Heidegger's account of metaphysics—metaphysics is always a metaphysics of the subject, insofar as philosophy has always sought to name the *subjectum*, the ultimate foundation or beginning point for an understanding of entities, or to offer a thesis on the Being of beings. In this broad sense, the master words of premodern metaphysics—*eidos, ousia, causa sui*—are all subjects. *The subject is the subject of metaphysics*, and philosophy deals with the determination of the subject as the ultimate foundation upon which entities become intelligible. The possibility of the subject is the very possibility of philosophy.

Following the Heiddeggerian account of the history of philosophy more faithfully (a narrative which remains illuminating even if one should continually want to question the scope of its applicability, what Gadamer calls its unilateralism, or what Derrida sees as the univocity of its sending of Being[6]), what is particular to modern metaphysics, and this means philosophy after Descartes, is that this metaphysical foundation is no longer claimed to reside in a form, substance, or deity outside of the human intellect but is rather found in the human being understood as subject; Heidegger writes, "Man has become the *subjectum*" (Der Mensch ist das *subiectum* geworden[7]). The *human* subject—as self, ego, or conscious, thinking thing—becomes the ultimate foundation upon which entities are rendered intelligible, that in virtue of which entities are understandable in their Being. As Hegel allegedly shouted to his students during his lectures on the history of philosophy, with the conception of the human being as *res cognitans* in Descartes we have reached the *terra firma* of modern philosophy[8]—although, and this is a massive caveat, one would be hard pressed to find the word *subject* used in its modern sense in Descartes' *Meditations*[9].

The initial task, as I see it, is not to decide *sub specie aeternitatis* whether human beings are subjects or not but to examine historically what happens when the human being is conceived of as a subject, what metaphysical presuppositions are implicit in the application of the philosophical concept of the subject to the human being, and whether we should continue to conceive of human beings as subjects.

In Kantian terms, the turn towards the subject is the Copernican turn, where cognition no longer follows the object, but rather where the object comes to depend upon the subject's constitution of objectivity. Although, for Kant, the ground of the subject, which is the ground of thought itself, cannot be known—for that one would need an intellectual intuition (enter Fichte[10])—the principle of apperception, where I can only grasp the manifold of representations insofar as they are mine, as the "I think" accompanies all my representations, is, Kant writes, "the highest principle in the whole sphere of human knowledge."[11] It is the transcendental unity of apperception, a subjectivity that is, I would claim, logically rather then ontologically entailed as a place-holder in the argument of the Transcendental Deduction, that provides the principle of "connexion" that Hume claimed was necessary to the constitution of personal identity, but which he found was wanting from his own "deconstruction" of the Cartesian subject.[12]

Turning to Husserl's account of the subject, in the *Cartesian Meditations*, he claims that philosophy begins with the turn toward the transcendental subject, that the *ego cogito* is the ultimate and apodictically certain foundation for my world.[13] Phenomenology, at least after the publication of *Ideas I* in 1913, begins with the subjective turn, the reduction or *epochè* of the naïve objectivism of the natural attitude, and the development of transcendental subjectivism; *phenomenology is an egology*. Returning to Heidegger, it is my suspicion that much of Heidegger's critique of the Cartesian subject is largely and parricidally directed against Husserl's Cartesianism. From the appearance of *Ideas* onwards, the phenomenological field is delimited as the field of pure consciousness: consciousness is pure and absolute Being.[14] For Heidegger—and this argument inspired both Levinas's critique of Husserl's theoreticism in his 1930 Doctoral Thesis and Sartre's 1937 *The Transcendence of the Ego*[15]—Husserl's Cartesian turn in *Ideas* is a failure to see through the radicality of the discovery of intentionality in the *Logical Investigations*. Husserl's metaphysical dogmatism consisted in rooting intentionality in consciousness and consequently failing to ask the question of the Being of intentional consciousness and ultimately the question of Being itself. With the publication of *Ideas*, Husserlian phenomenology, "moved into the tradition of modern philosophy," that is, sacrificed radicality for traditionality, falling prey to the tradition's temptation toward decadence and falling (*das Verfallen*).[16] As Merleau-Ponty has elegantly shown in "The Philosopher and his Shadow,"[17] this Heideggerian narrative of Husserl's increasing Cartesianism is, to say the least, somewhat complicated by the analyses of the body, perception, and intersubjectivity given in *Ideas II* (which only appeared in 1952, although Heidegger had a copy of the manuscript on his desk in 1925). In the lecture course of the same year, *History of the Concept of Time,* Heidegger rather precipitously remarks that even given the account of personalistic psychology given in *Ideas II,* "everything remains ontologically the same"[18]. The originality of *Ideas II* is that Husserl engages in an empirical—not transcendental as in the *Cartesian Meditations*—analysis of the human being as a psychophysical unity that is constituted intersubjectively through an act of empathy (*Einfühlung*). Betraying Dilthey's influence, Husserl shows how the naturalistic attitude of the natural sciences is founded upon the personalistic attitude of life. For Merleau-Ponty, *Ideas II* is the shadowy preparation for an ontology of brute or savage Being (*l'être brut, l'être sauvage*), an ontology that would seem to have much in common with Heidegger's ontological critique of phenomenology. The point at issue here is that Heidegger's critique of the Cartesian Husserl is necessarily based upon a partial reading of the Husserlian text and premised upon an oversimplification of the extremely rich and complex history of subjectivity between Descartes and Husserl. In a moment of welcome humility, Heidegger seems to recognize this when he says, "even today I still regard myself as a learner in relation to Husserl."[19]

On a Heideggerian account, any determination of the subject, whether in terms of *res cogitans,* the I think, the I (Fichte), Spirit (Hegel), transcendental ego, Man (Dilthey), or person (Scheler), always remains within the closure of metaphysics, that is to say, within the limits of a traditional ontology characterized by the forgottenness of oblivion of Being. For Heidegger, symptomatic of this oblivion (an oblivion, incidentally, continued in much contemporary philosophy of mind) is the failure to ask the question of the Being of being human and the dogmatic and precipitous determination of the human being as subject or consciousness. Heidegger asks: what does it really mean for a human being to be determined as a subject or a consciousness? As Deleuze reminds us, the subject is a philosophical concept, and the question of the subject is a metaphysical question, *the* question of modern metaphysics, namely, that in order to understand what it means for entities to be, we have to begin with the subject as the principle or ground of philosophy.[20] The subject is, in Descartes's words, "the sticking point" at which the sceptical, hyperbolic movement of doubt ends and philosophy begins: *ego sum, ego existo.*[21] But, Heidegger would ask, what is the Being of the *sum*?

The determinations of the subject that have been discussed above—in Descartes, Kant, and Husserl—would all seem to equate the subject with consciousness, self-consciousness, or reflection; they assume that I am the being who is conscious of having these doubting thoughts, and insofar as I have them it cannot be doubted that I exist at that moment as a thinking thing; or that I am the being who synthesizes these representations and who is self-conscious as the being to whom these representations belong, "for otherwise," writes Kant, "I should have as many-coloured and diverse a self as I have representations of which I am conscious to myself."[22] However, it should be noted that all attempts to break the bond linking the subject to consciousness, or reflection, for example, Lacan's subject of the unconscious, remain profiled upon the same metaphysical horizon.[23] Without minimizing the importance of Lacan's decentring of the subject— what he calls Freud's "Copernican turn"—an unconscious subject, a subject defined in terms of lack at the heart of its Being, a many-colored and diverse self—it is still a subject and ergo a metaphysical fundament, even if it is an unknowable, ungraspable fundament. To determine the subject in terms of a lack of Being (*un manque-à-être*) is still to offer a determination of subjectivity (perhaps this is unavoidable for reasons I shall give below). The same Heideggerian argument could also be proposed with respect to all accounts of prereflective, preconscious or nonidentical subjectivity, achieved through restitutions of Schelling, Schleiermacher, Sartre (for whom the subject or the *pour-soi* is also a lack of Being), or Levinas.[24]

In passing, I would like to turn this Heideggerian analysis onto Heidegger and ask: is Dasein, that is, the conception of the human being that is explicitly opposed to the subject, itself free from the traces of metaphysical subjectivity? Heidegger himself clearly thought this was the case, and Dasein is rigorously distinguished from metaphysical conceptions of the subject. Heidegger sought to demonstrate phenomenologically how the subject/object distinction basic to Kantian (or rather Heidegger's real target of neo-Kantianism, he is particularly critical of Heinrich Rickert, his former doctoral supervisor[25]) epistemology is founded upon the ontological structures of Dasein understood as Being-in-the-world. For Heidegger, to posit the Being of being human in terms of the conscious subject is to reify the human being and to oppose the latter to a world which is understood as an objective realm posited over against the subject. Furthermore, the question of the subject's access to the objective realm, the sole concern of a philosophy that understands itself as a theory of knowledge, is presupposed as a theoretical or contemplative access through, in Husserlian terms, certain objectifying acts. For Heidegger, the subject/object dualism constitutive of epistemology understands both the subject and the world as entities that are *vorhanden*, "present-at-hand," or objectively present to a theoretical regard. The modern philosophical positing of the conscious subject silently and constantly presupposes the massive privileging of *Vorhandenheit* over *Zuhandenheit* and of theory over practice. In his final seminar held at Zähringen in 1973, Heidegger reiterates how consciousness (*Bewusstsein*) is rooted in Dasein and how both presuppose a certain givenness or openness to *das Sein selbst*.[26] The path of Heidegger's thinking moves from *Bewusstsein*, through Dasein, to *Sein*.

In *Sein und Zeit*, Heidegger displaces the Cartesian starting point for philosophy in the *res cogitans* by defining Dasein as *Mitsein* (Being-with). As he writes in the important 1924 lecture, *Der Begriff der Zeit*,

> *Dasein* is that entity which is characterized as *Being-in-the-world*. Human life is not some subject that has to perform some trick in order to enter the world . . . As this Being-in-the-world *Dasein* is, together with this, *Being-with-one-another (Mit-einander-sein)*, being with others: Having the same world there (*da*) with others, encountering one another, being with one another in the manner of *Being-for-one-another (Für-einander-sein)*.[27]

In its inauthentic everyday existence, Dasein is with and for others before it is with and for itself. Who is Dasein? Dasein is the entity *who comes before the subject*, who exists prior to the division or separation of entities into subjects and objects. As an aside, might it not be argued that what is truly novel with regard to the question of the subject in *Sein und Zeit* is the irreducibility of *inauthentic* modes of selfhood; Heidegger writes, "Everyone is the Other and no one is himself" (Jeder ist der Andere und Keiner er selbst [*SuZ 128*]). Or again, in *Der Begriff der Zeit*, Dasein is defined as *Niemand*, "nobody."[28] It should not be forgotten that the inauthenticity of *das Man*, "the they" or "the one," has the status of an *existential* for Heidegger and that authenticity arises as an *existentiell* modification of *das Man* (*SuZ 130*).

However, there are various modes of authentic selfhood in *Sein und Zeit*. The basic-attunement or *Grund-stimmung* of anxiety, where entities withdraw and Dasein becomes uncanny (*unheimlich*), individualizes Dasein and discloses it as a quasi-Cartesian *solus ipse*, a solipsistic self alone (*SuZ* 188). Dasein is also individualized in Being-towards-death, in the call of conscience that addresses the particular Dasein as guilty or indebted (*schuldig*), and the final account of selfhood in paragraph 64—which emerges through a complex double reading of the Kantian "I think"—in terms of the constancy of the self (*die Ständigkeit des Selbst*), leaves an individualized Dasein who is decidedly open or resolute (*ent-schlossen*) in the face of death. The question here is whether these authentic modes of selfhood remain free from the metaphysics of subjectivity. Another way of asking the same question: does the subject or self remain after it has been ecstatically temporalized in division 2 of *Sein und Zeit*? Jean-Luc Marion has convincingly demonstrated how Dasein's authentic selfhood repeats the autarky and auto-affection of the self-constituting ego and thus represents the last heir to the tradition of metaphysical subjectivity.[29] For example, it is Dasein who calls to itself in the phenomenon of conscience (*SuZ* 275), and the voice of the friend that calls Dasein to its most authentic ability—to be (*eigenstes Seinkönnen*) is a voice that Dasein carries within it (*bei sich trägt* [*SuZ* 163]).

Nevertheless, to do justice to the question of subjectivity in Heidegger, one would also have to consider patiently the later Heidegger's account of the essence of the human (*der Mensch*) in, for example, the "Letter on Humanism," where the human is the entity that ek-sists ecstatically in nearness to the truth of Being. The Being of being human is defined in terms of an openness to the claim or call of Being (*Der Anspruch des Seins*), a claim that does not originate within Dasein but does relate the human to the event of an alterity or exteriority that is irreducible to the self.[30] As Heidegger notes in the Zähringen seminar, "The Da-sein is essentially ec-static [*ek-statisch*]."[31] For the later Heidegger, the human is no longer a subjective master of entities but, rather, the shepherd of Being ("Der Mensch ist nicht der Herr des Seienden. Der mensch ist der Hirt des Seins"[32]), and it exceeds metaphysics in its ecstatic openness to the temporal donation of the truth of Being, the appropriative event of *das Ereignis*. *Das Ereignis* is the conjunction in the title *Sein und Zeit*, the "and" that shows the belonging together of both Being and time and Being and the human.[33]

All of the above discussion is leading up to the question, Is there a subject outside metaphysics? On the basis of the Heideggerian argument, the answer would have to be negative. If the question of the subject is a metaphysical question, if it is *the* question of modern metaphysics (it is what makes modern metaphysics modern), then the subject is the subject of metaphysics. However, to take up the question that heads a fascinating collection of French articles on the topic of subjectivity, might it not be asked (and this is a very Heideggerian question), Who comes after the subject? (Après le sujet qui vient). Can one not ask after a nonmetaphysical determination of the subject? Or again, as philosophy is metaphysics for Heidegger, can one not ask after a nonphilosophical account of what it means to be a human being? Now, is this possible? Is this even desirable? To pursue a nonmetaphysical determination of the human being would entail, as Jean-Luc Nancy points out, that the question "Who comes after the subject? also be read as an affirmation: Yes, indeed, after the subject who comes? The "who" that comes after the subject would thus be assumed somehow to stand outside the metaphysical tradition—a gesture which is, to say the very least, problematic. How is it that the "who" should be somehow subtracted from the deconstruction of the metaphysical subject? (*AS* 96 / *WC* 101). Who is "who" such that it should stand outside of metaphysics? Is it Dasein, the being who, in *Sein und Zeit,* maintains a privileged relation to its "who"? Is it the human being conceived ecstatically as an openness to the event of appropriation? Or, following Nietzsche, might one speak of this "who" as the *Übermensch,* as that being who, at the end of *Zarathustra,* leaves behind the superior or highest man, introducing a life free from the metaphysical determination of subjectivity?[34]

Which Subject? What Metaphysics?

It is time to raise some critical questions with regard to the above Heideggerian analysis. The question/affirmation, Who comes after the subject?/Yes, *after* the subject who comes, presupposes that there is an "after" to come after the subject, as if an epochal break in the continuum of history had been achieved and that one could leave behind the epoch of subjectivity. For reasons that one might call "classically" Derridian, all ideas of exceeding the metaphysical closure should make us highly suspicious, and the seductive illusions of "overcoming," "exceeding," "transgressing," "breaking through," and "stepping beyond" are a series of tropes that demand careful and persistent deconstruction.

The above question/affirmation also implies the problematic presupposition that there was such a thing as the metaphysics of subjectivity that began in Descartes. In a discussion of Descartes's *Meditations,* Michel Henry has persuasively shown that the Heideggerian (and not just Heideggerian, although Heidegger does have a particular blindness to Descartes) caricature of the *res cogitans* as the subject of representation is based upon an extremely partial reading of Descartes (*AS* 141–52 / *WC* 157–66). Etienne Balibar claims, with some justification, that the category of the Cartesian transcendental subject is something only retrospectively projected onto Descartes's *Meditations* from the *Critique of Pure Reason* (*AS* 26–27 / *WC* 36). However, and *a fortiori*, it should not be doubted that the same complexification of the subject could certainly be given in a reading of Kant (Heidegger comes pretty close to this in paragraph 64 of *Sein und Zeit*) or Husserl (One need only think of Merleau-Ponty's "The Philosopher and his Shadow" or the penultimate chapter of Derrida's *Speech and Phenomena*[35]).

All of which leads one to ask skeptically: has there ever existed a unified conscious subject, a watertight Cartesian ego? Or is the subject some phantasy or abstraction that is retrospectively attributed to a past that one wants either to exceed, betray or ignore? That is to say, is not the subject a fiction that Kant finds in Descartes without it being in Descartes, that Heidegger finds in Kant without it being in Kant, or that Derrida finds in Husserl without it being in Husserl? However, if my critical suspicions are sustainable—and the very least I am arguing for is a more nuanced account of the history of subjectivity—then with what assurance can one speak of *an* epoch of subjectivity? To what extent can one periodize a "modernity" in terms of a philosophy of the subject, a modernity that must be either supplemented by an intersubjective turn to communicative reason and mutual agreement, a turn, according to Habermas, not taken by the various discourses of modernity, or exceeded by a "postmodernity" in which the subject would be somehow dispersed or fragmented?[36] Does not the periodization of modernity in terms of the philosophy of the subject—whether this prepares the way for an extension of modernity or a postmodern turn—presuppose a radically reduced and violent reading of the modern philosophical tradition? In the light of such skeptical questions, all we seem to be left with is a series of caricatures or cartoon versions of the history of metaphysics, a series of narratives based upon a greater or lesser misreading of the philosophical tradition. Such narratives may well be necessary and unavoidable fictions, but they are fictions nonetheless.

However, does metaphysics matter? If, following the Heideggerian account, there is no subject outside of metaphysics, then should this deter us from thinking the subject? Or might one argue, as Vincent Descombes has done, that the entire debate on the subject is simply *une querelle d'école*, based upon the fiction of a metaphysical subject that is simply not required in order to explain philosophically our sense of individual agency (*AS* 115–29 / *WC* 120–34)? Is not the debate on the subject, and here one rehearses Hume's critique of Descartes, based upon the grandiloquent and unintelligible presupposition of a founding conscious subject that is simply not shared by the English-speaking philosophical tradition, where one might more readily expect debates to focus on concepts of personhood or agency? To my mind, such a questioning would have to begin by thinking through the influence of the Wittgensteinian demolition of the metaphysical subject and those celebrated remarks on solipsism in the *Tractatus*: the subject is nothing in the world or part of that world, just as the eye is not in the perceptual field that it surveys, "The subject does not belong to the world: rather it is a limit [*Grenze*] of the world." For Wittgenstein, solipsism, rigorously followed through, coincides with realism, "the I [*das Ich*] of solipsism shrinks to an extensionless point and there remains the reality coordinated with it"[37]

Seeing the tradition through Heidegger spectacles, one is inclined to see metaphysics as the site of a lack. The history of metaphysics is a history of the progressive covering over of the original sending of Being by the Greeks (Parmenides, Heracleitus) in a series of determinations or theses on Being. The history (*Geschichte*) of metaphysics begins with a sending of Being (*Schickung des Seins*) that sends itself as a destiny (*das Seins-Geschick*) and where the sending holds itself back and undergoes a progressively more profound withdrawal. Heidegger calls this withholding of the sending of Being an *epochè*, and the history of metaphysics is a series of epochal transformations, where the original sending of Being undergoes deepening obfuscation.[38] Metaphysics, that is to say, philosophy from Plato to Nietzsche, is an exhausted series of possibilities that has attained its completion or fulfillment (*Vollendung*) in the thoughtless technological domination of post-Nietzschean modernity, where the will-to-power has become the sheer power of the will-to-will (*der Wille zum Willen*), which is no longer under human control.[39]

On this Heidegger picture, the question of the subject is entirely complicit with the metaphysical forgetfulness of the *Seinsfrage*, and indeed the history of modern metaphysics is the history of the progressive subjectivization of Being (in reading Heidegger, one sometimes feels that Descartes was simply a catastrophic error). Thus, for Heidegger, there is no subject outside metaphysics, and any conception of the subject is metaphysical. My suggestion here is that the *Heideggerian statement of the problem of metaphysics and subjectivity demands a Heideggerian solution,* that is to say, conceiving of the human being nonsubjectively as an ecstatic openness to that which metaphysics is unable to think: the truth of Being, *das Ereignis,* the bivalence of *alētheia.* My skeptical question is, In virtue of what must one give exclusive priority to this Heideggerian approach to the question of metaphysics and subjectivity? What is the nature of its truth claim? (Is it phenomenological? Is it historical? Is it sociological?) Is it not *too reactive* and totalizing a solution to the question of the subject which presents one with an either/or alternative: *either* a metaphysically compromised conception of the subject *or* a *Mensch* or ecstatic Dasein open to the truth of Being? If a defence of subjectivity, say that given by Levinas in *Totality and Infinity* (*TeI* xiv / *TI* 26), coincides with a restitution of metaphysics (albeit a strange metaphysics of exteriority, which, as Derrida writes, is something "new, quite new, a metaphysics of radical separation and exteriority"[40]), then how and why exactly is this problematic? Are we henceforth prohibited from thinking metaphysically about what it means to be a human being for fear of falling into nihilism? Or should we, paraphrasing Adorno, be suspicious at this point, claiming that all acts of overcoming are always worse than what they overcome?[41] Might not the problematic of the overcoming of metaphysics lead paradoxically to a deepening of nihilism? *Contra* Heidegger, do we not need more complex and nuanced accounts of metaphysics and subjectivity and of the relation between subjective experience and metaphysical experience, of the kind that Adorno finds in aesthetic experience and that Levinas finds in the ethical relation to the Other?

My view, broadly stated, is that the ambiguity of thinking the subject after Heidegger must be governed by the double bind of a double affirmation: firstly, by the profound need—ethically, politically, metaphysically—to leave the climate of Heidegger's thinking; and secondly, by the conviction that we cannot leave it for a philosophy that would be pre-Heideggerian[42] (i.e., there is no going back behind

Heidegger and no going forward without him; the break occasioned by *Sein und Zeit* is, in my view, philosophically decisive). In what follows, I would like to employ the critical leverage of Levinas's critique of Heidegger to argue for a conception of the subject that will hopefully acknowledge our sense of self, the fact that I am someone when I speak (thereby retrieving the *hacceity* of the subject, its thisness, its uniqueness), a sense of self that might begin to meet the claims of ethical and political responsibility. Levinas, I believe, presents us with the *possibility* for beginning to think a post-Heideggerian conception of the subject that will hopefully not be metaphysically or naïvely pre-Heideggerian. However, before discussing Levinas, I would like to broaden the horizon of my discussion by sketching another, related line of investigation into the question of the subject.

Subject and Structure: The Double Bind of the Present

To what context does the question/affirmation Who comes after the subject/Yes, after the subject who comes refer? As Derrida notes in a conversation with Jean-Luc Nancy, the question refers to a *doxa*, to an opinion, to something current in our intellectual culture. It refers to the so-called liquidation of the concept of the subject in a dominant strand of recent French philosophy, a strand that one may more or less adequately label as "poststructuralism," "neostructuralism," "structural Marxism," "Freudianism," "Nietzscheanism," or "Heideggerianism" (this list of "isms" could no doubt be extended). We are all to a greater or lesser extent familiar with this *doxa*, and to speak at the level of caricatures, one recalls the grand and prophetic gestures of Foucault when he spoke of the erasure of man like a figure drawn in sand at the edge of the sea, of Lacan's decentring of the subject in his reading of Freud, of Althusser's account of the transformation of individuals into subjects (subjectivity conceived as subjection) through the interpellation of ideology, of Derrida's inscription of the subject within language and the formulation of language as *différance* of which the subject is an effect, of Deleuze's account of the subject as a desiring machine or a body without organs. At the level of *doxa*, it would appear that the discourse of what, in the English-speaking world, is called "post-structuralism"— has proceeded towards, if not a liquidation, then at least a displacement of the subject from the center of philosophical or theoretical activity. Henceforth, thinking begins not with the constituting conscious subject but with the material, historical, economic (both in the Marxist and Freudian senses of the world), discursive, or linguistic structures, practices, and drives that constitute subjectivity and of which the subject is an effect. Regionalized, marginalized, and rendered secondary, one might say that, within this *doxa, the subject is subject*, recalling a widespread meaning of the word in political philosophy (as Etienne Balibar points out, in the wake of the American and French revolutions, it is the citizen of a republic who comes after the subject of a monarch [*AS* 28–29 / *WC* 38–39]). Rather than the subject being the autonomous, independent human agent—whether the monarch of nature, the possessive individual, or the bourgeois citizen endowed with certain inalienable rights—the subject is displaced into a heteronomous relation of serfdom and dependency. Subjectivity is constructed by structures that exceed the individual agent.

Recalling the polemics of Luc Ferry and Alain Renaud, this *doxa* might most conveniently be described as that of *La pensée 68*.[43] Despite the extreme hermeneutic violence that characterizes many of Ferry and Renaud's analyses, it is worth noting that their critique of *La pensée 68* hinges upon a reopening of the question of the subject beyond its Heideggerian (in Derrida), Nietzschean (in Foucault), Freudian (in Lacan), and, most importantly for them, Marxist (the sociologizing of the subject in Bourdieu) determinations. It is a critique governed by an affirmation of the autonomous humanist subject, a subject with human rights living, ideally, in a liberal democracy. As a consequence, it is not difficult to grasp that the question of the subject has a deeply political context: to criticize the constellation of *la pensée 68* is to be against the antihumanistic, antidemocratic legacy of French poststructuralism and in favor of human rights, democracy, and freedom. In brief, what one sees in Ferry and Renaud is a return to the primacy of the subject (and an interesting and interstitial return to Sartre—via Fichte—against what can only be described as the anti-Sartrean consensus of the sixties and seventies) conceived as a *political* reaction against the deconstruction of subjectivity. As Castoriadis wryly notes in a paper given, ironically, in May 1986, it would seem that the subject is once again back amongst us and very much back in vogue.[44] The neoconservatism of '86 inverts the radicalism of '68. However, if the subject is indeed back on the intellectual and cultural agenda and provides the focus for topical philosophical papers, conferences, and books, then is this simply a consequence of the vicissitudes of intellectual fashion? Is the reopening of the question of the subject simply to be understood as a political reaction to a failed radicalism?

This is not, I would claim, the whole truth of the situation. To operate once again at the level of caricature, one can give some examples of ways in which the subject has recently been thought in a radical and novel manner: (1) in Foucault's final work on the practices surrounding the formation of ethical subjectivity in antiquity and the notion of care for the self (*Le souci de soi*) as a practice of liberty and autonomy,[45] (2) in the feminist critique of gender neutral (i.e., male) subjectivity and the introduction of the question of sexual difference into the question of the subject,[46] (3) in the reinterpretation and foregrounding of the subject in Lacanian psychoanalysis,[47] (4) in the turn towards the subject in recent literary theory, where a consideration of German early romantic and idealist aesthetic theory and philosophy is beginning to invert certain simplifications and platitudes prevalent, particularly in English departments, about the death of the subject,[48] (5) and in the growing influence of Levinas's work, which has always defended a novel conception of the subject precisely in order to maintain an ethical responsibility at the heart of political life.

Indeed, on the question of politics, the reopening of the question of the subject cannot be viewed in isolation from the reexamination of questions of ethics and politics, questions very much sharpened in the United States by the Paul de Man affair and in France by *l'affaire Heidegger*. On a wider canvas, the revolutions of 1989 in Eastern Europe and the subsequent collapse of the Soviet Union and civil war in "Yugoslavia," have intensified debates around the question of the political subject who demands individual freedom, human rights, and democratic government and institutions. This problem is expressed discreetly but acutely by Derrida in an annex to the 1983 text *Le Retrait du politique*, where he recounts the unease he experienced when faced with the political demands of the intellectuals associated with Charter 77 in Czechoslovakia: How can one reconcile the latter's demands for individual freedom and autonomy with the claim that these philosophemes must be deconstructed because they belong to a metaphysical or logocentric tradition?[49]

Thus, to put it rather grandly, the "spiritual situation of the age," dangerously poised at the threshold of a New World Order (although it is difficult to discern anything politically and economically novel about it; it seems to be a world order characterized precisely—and critically—in terms of the absence of the new: a neurotic longing for a past that was never present, for traditional values, premodern ethnicities, and theologized nationalities), while being simultaneously plunged into the chaos of war, resurgent nationalism, ethnic conflict, and social fragmentation, seems to demand a radical reopening of the question of the subject in ways which do not simply react conservatively to the critique or deconstruction of the subject by uncritically reconstructing the humanist subject of metaphysics. Rather, the problem that we face, both as philosophers *and* citizens, has the form of the antinomy or double bind sketched above: is it possible to retain what was valid in the deconstruction of the subject, in Heidegger and others, while at the same time maintaining a notion of subjectivity that is adequate to our sense of self and to the actuality of ethical and political responsibility? The problem is more acutely expressed by Manfred Frank in the opening pages of *What is Neostructuralism?*

> How can one, *on the one hand*, do justice to the fundamental fact that meaning, significance and intention—the semantic foundations of every consciousness—can form themselves only in a language, in a social, cultural and economic order (in a structure)? How can one, *on the other hand*, redeem the fundamental idea of modern humanism that links the dignity of human beings with their use of freedom, and which cannot tolerate that one morally applaud the factual threatening of human subjectivity by the totalitarianism of systems, of rules and social codes? (my emphasis[50])

"On the one hand . . . on the other hand"' how are we to think this double-handed double bind? Are our hands tied? Should we choose one side of the antinomy over the other? Should we resolve the antinomy dialectically according to the logic of *Aufhebung*? Should we think the two halves of the double bind as necessary but irreconcilable moments within a deconstruction? Such are the questions that I would like to address in the remainder of this chapter. Basing myself on a reading of Levinas, I shall propose a determination of the subject as the locus of responsibility or, better, responsivity[51]—a minimal, nonidentical, and preconscious subject defined in terms of sensibility, a subject that is ethical to the extent that it is sensibly responsive to the Other's address. This determination of the subject, which I shall eventually define as "post-deconstructive," is not at odds with the claims of the Heideggerian, antihumanist, or poststructuralist deconstruction of the subject; rather, the latter clear the space in which such a conception of subjectivity can be articulated for the first time.

Levinas: the Subject is Subject

Levinas presents his work as a defence of subjectivity, but what is this Levinasian conception of subjectivity? Subjectivity is a central and constant theme in Levinas's work, and in his first postwar writings, *De l'existence à l'existent* and *Le temps et l'autre* (both published in 1947), Levinas describes the advent of the subject out of the impersonal neutrality of the *il y a*.[52] However, I shall sketch the notion of the subject as it is presented in Levinas's second major—and, I believe, greatest—work *Otherwise than Being or Beyond Essence* (1974). I shall privilege the latter work because, in many ways, it is written from out of the context of the poststructuralist and antihumanist critique of subjectivity. It is, in part, a response to the constellation of *La pensée 68*, which Levinas also discusses in two essays: "Humanism and Anarchy" (1968) and the extraordinary "Without Identity" (1970).[53]

In *Otherwise than Being* Levinas begins his exposition by describing the movement from Husserlian intentional consciousness to a level of preconscious sensing or sentience, a movement enacted in the title of the second chapter ("De l'intentionalité au sentir"). From the time he wrote his 1930 doctoral thesis on Husserl, Levinas has been critical of the primacy of intentional consciousness, claiming that consciousness qua intentionality maintains (despite the breakthrough of Husserl's *Logical Investigations*) the primacy of theoretical consciousness, where the subject maintains an objectifying relation to the world mediated through representation: the worldly object is the *noema* of a *noesis*. Such is Husserl's intellectualism. Now, in a gesture that remains constantly faithful to Heidegger's ontological undermining of the theoretical comportment toward the world (*Vorhandenheit*) and the subject/object distinction that supports epistemology, the movement from intentionality or sensing, or, in the terms of *Totality and Infinity*, from representation to enjoyment, shows how intentional consciousness is, to put it simply, conditioned by *life*, by the material conditions of my existence. Life is sentience, enjoyment, and nourishment, it is *jouissance* and *joie de vivre*. It is a life that lives from (*vivre de*) the elements: "we live from good soup, air, light, spectacles, work, sleep, etc. . . . These are not objects of representations" (*TeI* 82 / *TI* 110). Life, for Levinas, is love of life and love of what life lives from: the sensible, material world. Levinas's work offers a *material phenomenology of subjective life*, where the conscious I of representation is reduced to the sentient I of enjoyment. The self-conscious, autonomous subject of intentionality is reduced to a living subject that is subject to the conditions of its existence. Now, for Levinas, it is precisely this I of enjoyment that is capable of being claimed or called into question ethically by the other person. Ethics, for Levinas, is simply and entirely this calling into question of myself—of my spontaneity, of my *jouissance*, of my freedom—by the other (*TeI* 13 / *TI* 43). The ethical relation takes place at the level of sensibility, not at the level of consciousness; the ethical subject is a sensible subject, not a conscious subject.

For Levinas, *the subject is subject*, and the form that this subjection assumes is that of sensibility or sentience. Sensibility is the way of my subjection, vulnerability, or passivity towards the other, a sensibility that takes place "on the surface of the skin, at the edge of the nerves" (*AE* 18 / *OB* 15). The entire phenomenological thrust of *Otherwise than Being* is to found ethical subjectivity in sensibility and to describe sensibility as a proximity to the other, a proximity whose basis is found in what Levinas calls substitution (*AE* 23 / *OB* 19). The ethical subject is an embodied being of flesh and blood, a being that is capable of hunger, who eats and enjoys eating. As Levinas writes, "only a being that eats can be for the other" (*AE* 93 / *OB* 74); that is, only such a being can know what it means to give its bread to the other from out of its own mouth. In what must be the shortest refutation of Heidegger, Levinas complains that Dasein is never hungry (*TeI* 108 / *TI* 134), and the same might be said of all the heirs to the *res cogitans*.

Ethics is not an obligation toward the other mediated through the formal and procedural universalization of maxims or some appeal to good conscience, rather—and this is what is truly provocative about Levinas—ethics is *lived* in the sensibility of a corporeal obligation to the other.[54] It is because the self is sensible, that is to say, vulnerable, passive, open to wounding, outrage, and pain, but also open to the movement of the erotic, that it is capable or worthy of ethics. As Levinas remarks in the autobiographical "Signature," "moral consciousness is not an experience of values but an access to the exterior being, and the exterior being par excellence is the other."[55] Levinas's phenomenological claim—and by phenomenology Levinas means a methodological adherence to the spirit rather than the letter of Husserlian intentional analysis—is that the deep structure of subjective experience, what Levinas calls the "psyche," is structured in a relation of responsibility or responsivity to the other. The psyche is the other in the same, the other within me in spite of me, calling me to respond.

Merleau-Ponty makes similar claims about the intersubjective constitution of subjectivity taking place at the level of sensibility on the basis of his reading of *Ideas II*.[56] He argues that the philosopher must learn to bear the shadow of the sensible world, the pretheoretical core of brute or wild Being (*l'être brut, l'être sauvage*). It is at this pretheoretical level that a phenomenological ontology must show the constitution of the self and the other prior to the formation of the subject: "The idea of the subject, and that of the object as well, transforms into a cognitive adequation the relationship with the world and with ourselves that we have in the perceptual faith."[57] The question here is whether the Levinasian account of sensibility and the intersubjective constitution of subjectivity can in any way be assimilated to Merleau-Ponty's account of Husserl. Although there is much room for proximity between Levinas and Merleau-Ponty on their privileging of sensibility, a certain distance would have to be recognized with regard to their conceptions of intersubjectivity. Merleau-Ponty embraces the Husserlian account of intersubjectivity described in *Ideas II*, where, at the empirical level, my psychophysical unity is not attained at the level of a solipsistic self-experience but is given only through a recognition of unity in the other person, a unity which is then transferred analogically to myself.[58] In Merleau-Ponty's words, the self and the other are intimately related like two hands touching, a handshake, the intertwining of a chiasmus. It is with this experience of the toucher-touched that Merleau-Ponty formulates a relation to the visible world irreducible to the consciousness/object distinction which still plagued the analyses of *The Phenomenology of Perception*.[59] For Merleau-Ponty, the intersubjective relation, conceived on analogy with the chiasmic relation to the visible, is one where the self and the other "are like organs of one single intercorporeality."[60] For Levinas, on the other hand, ethics is not chiasmic; the relation between the self and the other is not analogous to two hands touching—ethics is not akin to a handshake. Levinas asks, "Is the meaning of intersubjectivity at the level of sociality attained while being conceived by analogy with the image of the joining of a persons hands?"[61] For Levinas, the ethical relation to the other cannot be based on the fact that I need the other in order to achieve psychophysical integrity. Ethics is a movement of *desire* that tends towards the other and that cannot be reduced to a *need* that returns to self. Ethical intersubjectivity must be founded on the datum of an irreducible difference between the self and the other. The entire exposition of *Totality and Infinity* is intended to show that the ethical relation is one where the relata remain absolute—an absolute relation offensive to the principle of noncontradiction, what Levinas describes as "formal logic." Thus, although Merleau-Ponty's account of intersubjectivity is based on a necessary retrieval of sensibility, it remains an ontological, or what Levinas calls "gnoseological," relation that reduces the alterity of the other.[62]

In "Without Identity," Levinas concurs with Heidegger's determination of Dasein as an openness to the world, but the openness of the ethical subject is the openness of vulnerability, of sensibility. The subjectivity of the subject is a passivity that cannot be grasped or comprehended, that is beyond essence, otherwise than Being. In a manner similar to that of Lacan, the deep structure or truth of the subject is achieved when the ego opens itself to the Other (capital *O*), that is, to the structure of intersubjective communication that takes place at the level of the unconscious. *The identity of the subject is denied to consciousness, or to reflection, and is structured intersubjectively.* For Levinas, like Lacan, the subject cannot be grasped essentially, in its Being, and any metaphysical statement (*énoncé*) of the form, "the Being of the subject is *x*" fails, by definition, to capture the subject of the *énonciation*. The subjectivity of the subject is *without identity*, because of the divergence or cut (*coupure*) between, in Lacan's terms, ego and subject, or *énoncé* and *énonciation*. The responsible or responsive structure of the psyche cannot be identified by consciousness and the subject is always missing from or lacking itself.[63]

Who is the subject? It is *me* and nobody else. As Dostoevsky's underground man complains, I am not an instance of some general concept or genus of the human being: an ego, self-consciousness, or thinking thing.[64] Levinas phenomenologically reduces the abstract and universal I to me, to myself as the one who undergoes the demand or call of the other. As Levinas puts it, "La subjectivité n'est pas le Moi, mais moi."[65] That is, my first word is not *ego sum, ego existo*; it is, rather, *me voici*! (see me here!), the prophetic word that identifies the prophet as interlocuted by the alterity of God. The subject arises in and as a response to the other's call; this is what Levinas calls "the religiosity of the self" (*AE* 150 / *OB* 117). To put it another way, ethics is entirely *my* affair, not the affair of some hypothetical, impersonal, or universal I running through a sequence of possible imperatives. Ethics is not a spectator sport; rather, it is my experience of a claim or demand that I both cannot fully meet and cannot avoid. The ethical subject is, in the true sense of the word, *an idiot*.[66] No one can substitute themselves for me, and yet I am prepared to substitute myself for the other, and even die in the other's place. For Levinas, I cannot even demand that the other respond responsibly to my response, "that is his affair," as Levinas remarks in an interview.[67] Subjectivity is hostage, both in the sense of being a hospitable host and also in the sense of being held captive by the other; the other is like a parasite that gets under my skin. In is *me* who is hostage to the other, who cannot slip away or escape this responsibility. This is the meaning of the concept of election for Levinas: I am elected or chosen to bear responsibility prior to my freedom. My subjectivity is a subjection to the other.

Antihumanism and Poststructuralism: Clearing a Place for the Subject

What consequences does the antihumanist or poststructuralist critique of the subject have upon this Levinasian conception of subjectivity? Does the former in any way invalidate the latter? In order to illuminate this question, I want to focus on two passages from *Otherwise than Being* and a sentence from Levinas's short article on Derrida, "Wholly Otherwise." Towards the end of the central "Substitution" chapter of *Otherwise than Being*, Levinas writes, amnesically alluding to Heidegger,

> Modern anti-humanism, which denies the primacy that the human person, free and for itself, would have for the signification of Being, is true over and beyond the reasons it gives itself. It clears the place (*il fait place nette*) for subjectivity positing itself in abnegation, in sacrifice, in a substitution which precedes the will. Its inspired intuition is to have abandoned the idea of person, goal and origin of itself, in which the ego is still a thing because it is still a being. Strictly speaking, the other is the "end"; I am a hostage, a responsibility and a substitution supporting the world in the passivity of assignation, even in an accusing persecution, which is undeclinable. Humanism has to be denounced only because it is not sufficiently human (*AE* 164 / *OB* 127–28[68])

Thus, the antihumanist critique of subjectivity clears a place for the subject conceived in terms of subjection, substitution, and hostage. Rather than seeing antihumanism as a threat to ethical subjectivity, Levinas claims that the former entails the latter by abandoning the philosophical primacy of the free, autonomous, autarkic subject. The truth of antihumanism consists in its claim that the subject can no longer support itself autarkically; it is, rather, overflowed or dependent upon prior structures (linguistic, ontological, socioeconomic, unconscious, or whatever) outside of its conscious control. Levinas's point is that the humanity of the human signifies precisely through this inability to be autarkic, where the subject is overwhelmed by an alterity that it is unable to master. The subject is no longer the self-positing origin of the world; it is a hostage to the other. Humanism should not begin from the datum of the human being as an end-in-itself and the foundation for all knowledge, certainty, and value; rather, the humanity of the human is defined by its service to the other. Levinasian ethics is a humanism, but it is a humanism of the other human being.

Indeed, one finds a similar logic at work in Levinas's short article on Derrida, "Wholly Otherwise," where Levinas suggests that the Derridian deconstruction of the subject prepares the way for an understanding of the human being in terms of the *creature*. Levinas writes,

> It will probably be less willingly acknowledged— and Derrida will probably deny it—that this critique of Being in its eternal presence of ideality allows, for the first time in the history of the West, the thought of the *Being of the creature (l'être de la créature)*, without recourse to an ontic account of divine operation, without from the start treating the "Being" ("*être*") of the creature like a being (*un étant*) . . . [69]

Thus, according to Levinas, Derrida would probably deny the most radical aspect of deconstruction, its insight into subjectivity as "creaturality" (*la créaturalité*).[70] However, what does deconstruction have in common with creation, and what is the relation of the latter to ethical subjectivity? In a nutshell, the deconstruction of the autarkic humanist subject, and the claim that subjectivity is an effect of structures outside the conscious control of the subject, is assimilated by Levinas to the concept of creatureliness, which defines the human as that being who is overwhelmed by responsibility. Levinas writes in a note to *Otherwise than Being*, "This freedom enveloped in a responsibility which it does not succeed in shouldering is the way of the creature, the unlimited passivity of a self, the unconditionality of a self" (*AE* 140 / *OB* 195). Thus, creatureliness describes the responsibility that defines ethical subjectivity. The creature is that being who is always already in a relation of dependence to and distinction from the alterity of a creator, and it thus introduces a passivity into the heart of subjectivity.

Traditionally understood, creation is the production *ex nihilo* of entities from nothingness. In the Judaeo-Christian tradition, *creatio ex nihilo* is the summoning of the universe into existence, the emergence of a created temporal order from an eternal and uncreated God. Such a theological conception of creation has two important consequences: (1) the absolute distinction of God from his creation, thereby entailing the separation of the creator and the creature and the transcendence of the former over the latter and (2) the absolute dependence of the creature and the created realm upon the creator for their continued existence. Now, Levinas criticizes this theological understanding of creation because, he claims, it treats the relation between the creator and the creature ontologically; that is, it conceives of eternal Being and temporal Being as a totality of Being (*TeI* 269 / *TI* 293). Consequently, this onto-theo-logical account of creation fails to account for the infinity and alterity of the creator and the dependence and passivity of the creature. One might say that Levinas "de-theologizes" the concept of 'creation' and employs it as a way of thinking the structure of ethical subjectivity. Creation should not be thematized ontologically in terms of totality but approached ethically in terms of alterity; that is, the absolute separation of the creator and the creature implies a complete dependence of the latter on the former. The relation of the creature to the creator, of the temporal to the eternal, is a relation between separated terms which cannot be closed over into a totality. Levinas employs this de-theologized concept of creation as a model for thinking a relation between beings who cannot be totalized and who together form a plurality. Indeed, this account of creation, given through Levinas's radicalization of Derrida, brings to mind Schleiermacher's concept of creation in *The Christian Faith*, where creation is the relation of absolute dependence of the creature on the creator, an absolute dependence that is the core of religious self-consciousness, or what was called above "the religiosity of the self."[71]

I would now like to turn to a second passage from *Otherwise than Being*, one that appears towards the end of the second chapter and deals more directly and polemically with structuralism and the human sciences. Levinas begins by setting out the context for the structuralist critique of the subject.

> In our days truth is taken to result from the effacing of the living man behind the mathematical structures that *think themselves out* in him, rather than he thinking them. For it is said in our day that nothing is more *conditioned* than the allegedly originary consciousness or the ego. (*AE* 74 / *OB* 58)

After going on to argue that a conception of ethical subjectivity can be maintained despite the insights of structuralism, Levinas continues,

> One can, to be sure, invoke, against the signifyingness of the extreme situations to which the concepts formed on the basis of human reality lead, the conditioned nature of the human. The suspicions engendered by psychoanalysis, sociology and politics weigh on human identity such that we never know to whom we are speaking and what we are dealing with when we build our ideas on the basis of human facts. But we do not need this knowledge in the relationship in which the other is a neighbor, and in which before being an individuation of the genus *man*, a *rational animal*, a *free will*, or any essence whatever, he is the persecuted one for whom I am responsible to the point of being a hostage for him . . . One can ask if anything in the world is less conditioned than man, in whom the ultimate security a foundation would offer is absent. Is there anything less unjustified than the contestation of the human condition? Does anything in the world deliver more immediately, beneath its alienation, its non-alienation—its *holiness* (*sa sainteté*)—which may define the anthropological over and beyond its genus? . . . The influences, complexes and dissimulations that cover over the human do not alter this holiness, but sanction the struggle for exploited man. Thus it is not as a freedom—impossible in a will that is inflated and altered, sold or mad—that subjectivity is imposed as an absolute. It is sacred in its alterity with respect to which, in an unexceptionable responsibility, I posit myself deposed of my sovereignty. Paradoxically, it is qua *alienus*—foreigner and other—that man is not alienated. (*AE 75–76* / OB 58–59)

Once again, it must first of all be noted that Levinas does not deny the validity of the structuralist or poststructuralist insights into the conditioned nature of the human being. The claim here is that although it may be true to say that the human being is conditioned in the manner argued by psychoanalysis, sociology, and political theory, *we do not need this knowledge when we enter into relation with the other.* Although the human being is undoubtedly and massively determined by the contexts—sociohistorical, psychobiographical, linguistic, biological—into which he or she is inserted, this in no way negates the unconditional priority of the ethical moment which rends those contexts. Thus, the insights of antihumanism and poststructuralism might well be necessary conditions for the determination of subjectivity, but they are not sufficient to explain the extraordinary event of my responsibility for another, what Levinas calls, in a key word of his later work, the sanctity (*la sainteté*) of the human being. For Levinas, it is precisely this sanctity, defined as the priority of the other over me, that cannot be placed in question.[72]

I have tried to show how the Levinasian account of the self does not react conservatively to the deconstruction of the subject by nostalgically trying to restore the primacy of the free autonomous ego, autarkic and for-itself. On the contrary, it is precisely because the discourse of antihumanism or poststructuralism has deposed the subject from its position of sovereignty that the sanctity of the human being can be delineated. It is qua alien that the human being comes into its own, and what is proper to the subject is its expropriation by the other. Thus, and this is a point also made by Manfred Frank, antihumanism and poststructuralism may be true in their analyses of the ontological, linguistic, psychological, or sociohistorical constitution of subjectivity, but this should not lead one—tragically, prophetically, or cynically—to declare or celebrate the death of the subject.[73] I must never be indifferent to the demand that the other places upon me, a demand which presupposes that I must be me and no one else. The deconstruction of the subject facilitates a novel account of the ethical subject qua me, without identity, an idiot, a creature, a hostage to the other.

Post-Deconstructive Subjectivity

During his conversation on the subject with Jean-Luc Nancy, Derrida makes the following intriguing remark:

To be brief, I would say that it is in the relation to the "yes" or to the *Zusage* presupposed in every question that one must seek a new (post-deconstructive) determination of the responsibility of the "subject." (*AS* 100 / *WC* 105)

An adequate explication of this allusion to the *Zusage* (grant or pledge) would demand a commentary on Derrida's 1987 text on Heidegger, *De l'esprit*.[74] However, by way of summary, *De l'esprit* attempts to show that the primary datum of language for Heidegger is not the experience of questioning—the questioning that opens Dasein to the question of Being and which is characterized by the later Heidegger as "the piety of thinking"—but rather *das Hören der Zusage*, listening to the grant or pledge of language. Prior to the putting of questions to language, Heidegger claims that language has already been granted or addressed to human beings. The significance of the *Zusage* for Derrida is that it shows that all forms of questioning are always already pledged to respond to a prior grant of language. The question and the questioning stance of philosophy is always already a response to and a responsibility for that which is prior and over which the question has no priority. One might say that the "origin" of language is responsibility. As Derrida makes clear in his text on Michel de Certeau, the *Zusage* is understood as a moment of affirmation in Heidegger, "in short, a yes."[75]

Let us return to the above quotation. Derrida, despite his discomfort with the word *subject*—he immediately goes on to say, "it always seems to me to be more worthwhile, once this path has been laid down, to forget the word to some extent" (*AS* 100 / *WC* 105)—claims that it is in relation to the dimension of responsibility prior to questioning opened by the affirmation of the *Zusage* that a new determination of the "subject" is to be sought. The broad claim of my discussion is that the Levinasian account of subjectivity as responsibility to the other provides the framework for the kind of new determination of the "subject" sought by Derrida.[76]

However, what intrigues me in Derrida's remark is the parenthesized adjective "post-deconstructive" (and why parentheses? Does the word risk saying too much or too little outside of its brackets? Indeed, how does one mark parentheses in a conversation?). To my knowledge, this word is a novelty in Derrida's vocabulary. As to what "post-deconstructive" might mean, this is illuminated by a later remark from the same conversation. Derrida says,

In order to recast, if not rigorously refound a discourse on the "subject" . . . one has to go through the experience of a deconstruction. This deconstruction (we should once again remind those who do not want to read), is neither negative nor nihilistic; it is not even a pious nihilism, as I have heard said. A concept (that is to say also an experience) of responsibility comes at this price. We have not finished paying for it. I am talking about a responsibility that is not deaf to the injunctions of thinking. As you [i.e., Jean-Luc Nancy, s.c.] said one day, there is duty in deconstruction. There has to be, if there is such a thing as duty. The subject, if subject there must be, is to come *after* this. (*AS* 102–3 / *WC* 107–8)

The new determination of the "subject" in terms of responsibility, of an affirmative openness to the other prior to questioning, is something that can only be attained after having gone through the experience of a deconstruction of subjectivity, that is, the kind of Heideggerian deconstruction outlined in the first section of this chapter. Post-deconstructive subjectivity would be a determination of the subject *after* deconstruction, a determination that succeeds the duty of deconstruction without lapsing back into the pre-deconstructive or classical conceptions of the subject that we sketched in Descartes, Kant, and Husserl.

Nevertheless, a number of thorny problems arise with this notion of post-deconstructive subjectivity, not the least of which is the presupposition that there is a unity to deconstruction, that deconstruction is a singular and not a plural event. In speaking of the "post-deconstructive," is there not also the implicit assumption of a "before" and "after" to deconstruction that can be specified or periodized in some kind of temporal succession—an epoch of deconstruction that is either preceded or succeeded by other epochs, or some kind of deconstructive *epochè* or withholding from determination or positivity that can be set aside in a return to pre- or post-deconstructive naïveté. Be that as it may, and it would have to be accepted that any post-deconstructive determination of the subject would itself have to be a candidate for renewed and persistent deconstruction, what is remarkable in the above quotations is Derrida's willingness to accept the need for new discourses on subjectivity, for new names and new determinations of the "subject" that will supplement (in the full sense of the word) or succeed deconstruction. In brief, what is glimpsed here is the possible renewal of the "subject" after its deconstruction.

Yet, how might such a post-deconstructive determination of the "subject" be characterized? In a suggestive hint that is sadly not pursued (but upon which the entirety of my chapter might be seen as a commentary), Derrida says,

> Some might say, quite rightly: but what we call "subject" is not the absolute origin, pure will, identity to self, or presence to self of consciousness but precisely this non-coincidence with self. This is a riposte to which we'll have to return. By what right do we call this "subject"? By what right, conversely, can we be forbidden from calling this "subject"?I am thinking of those today who would try to reconstruct a discourse on the subject that *would not be predeconstructive* [my emphasis], around a subject that would no longer include the figure of mastery of self, of adequation to self, center and origin of the world, etc. . . . but which would define the subject rather as the finite experience of non-identity to self, as the underivable interpellation inasmuch as it comes from the other, from the trace of the other . . . [l'expérience finie de la non-identité à soi, de l'interpellation indérivable en tant qu'elle vient de l'autre, de la trace de l'autre . . .]. (*AS 98 / WC 103*)

Look closely at Derrida's formulations in this passage: "Non-coincidence with self," "finite experience of non-identity to self," "the underivable interpellation inasmuch as it comes form the other." Although it would be unnecessarily reductive to read these remarks solely as allusions to Levinas's account of the subject,[77] it is not difficult to see how the Levinasian conception of subjectivity described in this paper, as hostage to the other, or as nonidentical sensible responsivity, could be said to be consonant with the drift of Derrida's remarks. Levinas offers a determination of the subject that is not predeconstructive but which takes place precisely in the space cleared by the antihumanist and poststructuralist deconstruction of subjectivity.

However, and by way of conclusion, I would like to turn full circle back to the train of thought with which I began this chapter and ask, Does not this post-deconstructive account of the subject itself fall prey to the Heideggerian deconstruction outlined above? Is not the Levinasian conception of the subject itself metaphysical? It was claimed above that, on a Heideggerian account, there is no subject outside of metaphysics and that, consequently, any determination of the subject, including any post-destructive determination, would remain within the metaphysical closure. Remaining within the parameters of the Heideggerian problematic, there are two ways, it seems to me, of avoiding such a lapse back into the metaphysics of subjectivity: (1) to maintain a persistent and permanent deconstruction, without attempting to offer any positive theses; a kind of infinite vigilance or modesty that would renounce the attempt at a new determination of the subject or any other classical philosopheme[78] and (2) to embrace the position of the later Heidegger and conceive of the human being nonmetaphysically as an ecstatic openness to the truth of Being. With regard to these two options, I have argued in this chapter that the task of thinking the subject after Heidegger must be governed by the double bind of a double affirmation, that is, both by the profound need to leave the climate of Heidegger's thinking and by the conviction that one cannot leave it for a philosophy that would be pre-Heideggerian. This entails, in John Llewelyn's formulation, the task of avoiding "the metaphysics of subjectivity . . . without falling into the metaphysical denial of metaphysics by positing a power that has at most a contingent need of human or other being."[79] Thus, against the above two options, I would argue that (1) the former merely sidesteps philosophy and perhaps risks conspiring with the very nihilism it seeks to deconstruct (Recall that Heidegger condemns such a position as a false substitute for philosophy, "the mere interpretation of the traditional texts of philosophy, the elaboration and slaving away at metaphysics [*das Ausarbeiten und Abarbeiten der Metaphysik*])[80] and (2) the latter offers an account of the subject that is too dehumanized and "reactive." I would follow Dominique Janicaud in refusing the strictness of Heidegger's opposition between the classical metaphysical subject and the human being conceived as ecstatic openness—"The question is rather: what becomes of subjectivity when it loses its substantiality, its imperial sovereignty, its certainties and perhaps even its will?"[81]

Nonetheless, the claim that the Levinasian subject is metaphysical would indeed seem to be in perfect accord with many of Levinas's own remarks on metaphysics. *Totality and Infinity* begins with a positive definition of metaphysics in terms of desire for the infinitely other: metaphysics is transcendence and the very movement of alterity (*TeI* 3–5 / *TI* 33–35). A few pages further on, in "Metaphysics precedes ontology," Levinas polemically rehearses the anti-Heideggerian arguments first formulated in the 1951 essay "Is Ontology Fundamental?" (*TeI*

12–18 / *TI* 42–48[82]) For Levinas, the primacy of fundamental ontology in the early Heidegger decides the essence of philosophy: "it is to subordinate the relation with *someone,* who is an existent (*un étant*) (the ethical relation) to a relation with the *Being of existents* (*l'être de l'étant*)" (*TeI* 16 / *TI* 45). To maintain this subordination of the human being to the Being of beings is to privilege ontology over ethics, the Same over the Other, power over peace, and freedom over justice. For Levinas, the relation between ethics and ontology must be inverted ("il faut intervertir les termes" [*TeI* 17 / *TI* 47]); that is, it must be shown that ontology presupposes metaphysics, not vice versa, and that the ethical relation with the Other is not grafted on to an antecedent *Seinsverständnis* but is rather a foundation or infrastructure. Ethics is first philosophy. In a letter appended to the 1962 paper "Transcendence and Height," Levinas writes, with an oblique but characteristic reference to Heidegger's politics,

> The poetry of the peaceful path that runs through fields does not simply reflect the splendour of Being beyond beings. That splendour brings with it more sombre and pitiless images. The declaration of the end of metaphysics is premature. The end is not at all certain. Besides, metaphysics—the relation with the being (*étant*) which is accomplished in ethics—precedes the understanding of Being and survives ontology.[83]

Levinas opposes metaphysics to ontology and claims that Dasein's *Seinsverständnis* presupposes a non-ontological relation with the other human being (*autrui*), the being to whom I speak and am obligated before being comprehended. Fundamental ontology is fundamentally ethical metaphysics.

Thus, it would seem that Levinas's strategy with respect to Heidegger is one of reversal, an inversion of the priority of Being over beings and a restitution of metaphysics against ontology. From a Heideggerian perspective, one might object that Levinas simply returns to a classical metaphysics of beingness (*Seiendheit*); that is, a determination of Being in terms of beings and a humanistic privilege of one particular entity, the human being.[84] While still employing the ontological language he seeks to undermine, Levinas defines Being as *exteriority* ("*l'être est extériorité*" [*TeI* 266 / *TI* 290]); that is, what it means to be a human being is to be open to the radically non-comprehensible alterity of the Other. In addition to the performative self-contradiction entailed by employing the language of ontology to undermine ontology, Levinas's determination of Being is metaphysical to the same extent as all previous determinations of Being, from Plato to Nietzsche. What distinguishes Levinas is the fact that he is a retarded metaphysician, still producing theses on Being at the moment when philosophy has ended and we have entered the completion of metaphysics. By failing to see the radicality of the question of Being as a question, Levinas is logically, is not chronologically, pre-Heideggerian.

However, should one accept this "Heideggerian" reading of Levinas? Is Levinas simply engaging in an inverted Heideggerianism? Although this view has its temptations, it does not, I believe, give the whole picture. Levinas is not only engaging in a reversal of Heidegger, which leads him to repeat the language of metaphysics, but also *enacting* a displacement of metaphysical language. This displacement can be seen in Levinas's use of palaeonyms like, *ethics, metaphysics,* and *subjectivity,* ancient words which undergo what Derrida has described as a "semantic transformation" in Levinas's hands.[85] Levinas's language forms *a series of palaeonymic displacements,* where the ancient words of the tradition are repeated and in that repetition semantically transformed: ethics signifies a sensible responsibility to the singular other, metaphysics is the movement of positive desire tending towards infinite alterity, subjectivity is preconscious, nonidentical sentient subjection to the other, and so forth. The Levinasian text is swept across by a double movement or logic of ambiguity, between a metaphysical (in Heidegger's sense) or ontological (in Levinas's sense) language of Being *and* the thought (if it is a thought, if it is not rather the break up of thought before its matter) of the otherwise than Being that interrupts metaphysics or ontology. Levinas's writing, particularly after *Totality and Infinity,* is hinged or articulated around an ambiguous or double movement, between a palaeonymic repetition of the language of metaphysics and a displacement of that language, or between what Levinas calls, with deceptive simplicity, "the Said and the Saying" (*le Dit et le Dire*).

On the question of subjectivity, my claim is that Levinas does not simply engage in an inversion of Heidegger that returns him to a pre-Heideggerian, pre-deconstructive determination of the metaphysical subject. As we saw above, Levinas accepts the Heideggerian deconstruction of the subject insofar as the latter maintains the privilege of theoretical, contemplative, objectifying consciousness. Indeed, if one reads Levinas's 1930 doctoral thesis alongside Heidegger's 1925 lectures on Husserl in the *History of the Concept of Time* (a reading unavailable to Levinas at that time, as the lectures were only published in 1979), then it is clear to what extent Levinas's critique of Husserl's intellectualist and theoreticist concept of 'intuition' is derived from Heidegger. Levinas's early reading of Husserl is "inspired" by "the intense philosophical life that runs through Heidegger's philosophy."[86] For Levinas, "Knowledge of Heidegger's starting point may allow us to understand better Husserl's end point"; that is to say, there is a necessity to follow the movement from transcendental phenomenology to fundamental ontology and to focus on the existential problems of life, freedom, time, and history.[87] As is clear from the 1932 essay "Martin Heidegger et l'ontologie," the move from Husserl to Heidegger entails the deconstruction of the subject and the turn to Dasein.[88]

The persistence of Heidegger's critique of the theoreticism of Husserlian intentional consciousness in Levinas's work can be seen, to pick just one example, in the 1984 paper "Ethics as First Philosophy."[89] After defining metaphysics as that science or knowledge of the Being of beings that is had through theoretical contemplation, Levinas uses the example of Husserl to show how the theoreticism of intentional consciousness that characterizes phenomenology as *philosophia prōtē* in fact presupposes a pretheoretical, preintentional consciousness, the "infinite subjection of subjectivity."[90] For Levinas, the determination of the subject in terms of "the passivity of the non-intentional" precedes "any metaphysical ideas on the subject."[91]

However, although Levinas initially follows the ontological turn in Heidegger's deconstruction of the classical metaphysical subject, particularly with respect to Husserl, he then goes on to reformulate subjectivity in a way that undermines the fundamentality of Dasein and the claim of fundamental ontology to be first philosophy. If Dasein is defined as that being who is open to the question of Being, *das Befragte,* then Levinas understands the ethical subject as the site of responsibility prior to questioning and ontology. Levinas writes,

> The ego is the very crisis of the Being of beings (*de l'être de l'étant*) in the human domain. A crisis of Being, not because the sense of this verb might still need to be understood in its semantic secret and might call on the powers of ontology, but because I begin to ask myself if my Being is justified, if the *Da* of my *Dasein* is not already the usurpation of somebody else's place.[92]

If Dasein is that being whose "essence" (*Wesen*) lies in *Existenz*, then by what right does Dasein exist? If Dasein is disclosed through its *Da*, the "there" of the world that Heidegger defines in *Sein und Zeit* as "the clearing" (*die Lichtung*) (*SuZ* 133), then is this not "my place in the sun," and thus—following Levinas following Pascal—"the beginning and image of the usurpation of the entire earth"?[93] Prior to the mineness (*Jemeinigkeit*) that is the condition of possibility for my authenticity (*Eigentlichkeit*), and an antecedent to the essential propriety that binds the human being to the event of appropriation (*das Ereignis*), it must be asked, *By what right do I exist?* What justification is there for me before the Other? The basic question of philosophy is not Heidegger's Leibnizian question, Why are there beings at all and why not rather nothing? it is, rather, How does Being justify itself?[94]

Abbreviations

AE Emmanuel Levinas, *Autrement qu'être ou au-delà de l'essence*, The Hague, 1974.

AS Jean-Luc Nancy, ed., *Après le sujet qui vient*, Cahiers Confrontation 20, Paris, 1989.

OB Emmanuel Levinas, *Otherwise than Being or Beyond Essence*, trans. A. Lingis, The Hague, 1981.

SuZ Martin Heidegger, *Sein und Zeit*, 15th ed. Tübingen, 1984. All references give the German pagination, included in the margins of the English translation. (Cf. *Being and Time*, trans. J. Macquarrie and E. Robinson, Oxford, 1962.)

TeI Emmanuel Levinas, *Totalité and Infini*, The Hague, 1961.

TI Emmanuel Levinas, *Totality and Infinity*, trans. A. Lingis, Pittsburgh, 1969.

WC Eduardo Cadava, Peter Connor, and Jean-Luc Nancy, eds., *Who Comes after the Subject?* New York, 1991.

Three

The Question of Subjectivity in Heidegger's *Being and Time*

Dominique Janicaud

Why return to subjectivity if *Being and Time* is not a book *about* subjectivity but, on the contrary, the most determined attempt to move away from subjectivity? The argument will unfold gradually; for the moment, suffice it to provide a preliminary indication of the aim: to confront the enterprise of *Being and Time* at its very heart with a question posed from a standpoint itself criticized, questioned, and "destroyed" by Heidegger. Is it not regressive to question the project of *Being and Time* starting from a seemingly limited—that is, historically [*historialement*] condemned—subjectivity? Let us assume this opening objection. We will attempt to step back from Heidegger's book—not to reproduce the famed *Schritt zurück* but rather to catch Heidegger on the wrong foot.

Some initial remarks will help us to articulate the problem. First of all, a stylistic indication of the Heideggerean desire to avoid the arbitrary nature of subjective *pathos* in taking up the question of Being. From the very beginning of *Being and Time*, the tone is impersonal: "Our aim in the following treatise is to work out the question of the meaning of *Being* and to do so concretely."[1] This aim *follows* the "Necessity for Explicitly Restating the Question of Being."[2] As for the content aimed at, in connection with what and by whom is the question posed? What is this *entity* that relates to itself? A *subject*? The word is carefully avoided: "This entity which each of us is himself and which includes inquiring as one of the possibilities of its Being, we shall denote by the word '*Dasein*.' "[3] Putting aside (and between quotation marks) the term *subject* means also the "destruction" of the folding back of that which questions [*le questionnant*] onto that which is questioned [*le questionné*] (or of the one recuperating the other) so common since Descartes. There is indeed a distinguished primacy of *Dasein*, but this primacy relates back to (and is subordinate to) the

47

ontico-ontological primacy of the question of Being; the circular character of the question is referred to the *formal* structure of the ontological question. The opening of the Existent which *Dasein* is called into
question the meaning of Being in such a way that the *Da* is discovered
to be *insubstantial*. Whence the exigency of a new hermeneutics, more
discerning than the all too ontic hermeneutics of the subjectivity of an
ego—be it transcendental.

We are beginning now to touch on the very core of Heidegger's
thesis on the nonsubjectivity of *Dasein* and so must refine the first
massive precept: Heidegger strives to "destroy" subjectivity. What,
then, does it mean to "destroy"?

Not only does Heidegger affirm the *positive* aspect of destruction
(in par. 6)—not to let go of the past but to free it from ossification
(which results from a forgetting of historicality [*historicité*,
Geschichtlichkeit]); he also distinguished between two degrees of this
labor: one, to reconquer the originary ground of Greek ontology (for
example, the redefinition of truth as *aletheia* and of *aletheia* as robbery,
Raub, in par. 44), and two, to critique the history of spirit (that is to say,
the self-constitution of modernity based on the "substantiality of the
subject"), because it reinforces the forgetting sedimented by Platonic-
Aristotelian ontology (*natural* metaphysics, in which time—in particular—is construed in terms of inner-worldly entities).

The reason for distinguishing between two phases of destruction
is given in par. 64: "Substantiality is the vital ontological lead for
determining the subjectivity of the subject."[4] It is because of this *substantiality* of the subject (and of subjectivity) that the interpretation of
the meaning of Being must be undertaken "in the light of the problematic of Temporality."[5] In effect, the meaning of Being is thought by
Plato as presence (*ousia*): "Entities are grasped in their being as 'presence'; this means that they are understood with regard to a definite
mode of time—the '*Present*.' "[6]

It is on the basis of this substantialisation that the "subjectivation"
of Being operates in modernity (the metaphysical placement of the
subject/object correlation as a transcendental horizon). Because
substantialization must be understood as presencing, subjecti(vi)ty
[*subjecti(vi)té*] is presencing redoubled, re-presentation. (This is how,
as the transcendental center of representation, Kant determines the "I
think," the subject of judgement.)

Thus, Heidegger takes on a double deadlock with this *Destruktion*,
which, to attain to radicality, cannot be direct. Moreover, this task (of

destruction) is a prerequisite for the discovery of *Dasein*'s ownmost constitution. Let us return to these two stages.

The Subjectivity to Be "Destroyed"

Let us begin with a revealing passage from paragraph 40:

> Anxiety individualizes Dasein and thus discloses it as a *'solus ipse.'* But this existential "solipsism" is so far from the displacement of putting an isolated subject-Thing into the innocuous emptiness of a worldless occurring, that in an extreme sense what it does is precisely to bring Dasein face to face with its world as world, and thus bring it face to face with itself as Being-in-the-world.[7]

According to this very dense passage, the subjectivity to be "avoided" is characterized by the correlation between a *substantial* ego (thinglike, ontic) and *worldlessness* (in other words, by entities without "references" [*renvois, Verweisungen*] and by a present that is nothing more than present). Let us specify the terms of this correlation (which relates back to the worldly or psychologized subject that Husserl brackets in order to establish the transcendental ego): the subject-Thing "says" "I, I" (*Ich-Ich*);[8] by retracting into its ego, it all at once misses care (and its potentiality-for-Being) and Being-in-the-world in the richness of its involvement, its signs, and its references.[9] It is almost too easy to identify Descartes as the philosophical adversary implicit here, insofar as he "deworlds" matter and nature. In paragraph 19, Heidegger insists on the fact that *res corporea* becomes substantia, that is, extension in terms of length, breadth, and depth. The extended is "that which can change itself by being divided, shaped, or moved in any way." Here one must refer also to paragraph 21, the "Hermeneutical Discussion of the Cartesian Ontology of the 'World.' " Once again, it is the absence of world that is lamented. "Mathematical knowledge is regarded by Descartes as the one manner of apprehending entities which can always give assurance that their Being has been securely grasped."[10] Now, the object of mathematical knowledge is that "*which always is what it is.*" It has the character of a constant "remaining" (*ständigen Verbleib*): *remanens capax mutationum.* "In this way, Descartes explicitly and philosophically carries out the switch-over (*Umschaltung*) from the development of traditional ontology to modern mathematical physics and its transcendental foundation."[11]

Let us add, following the lines of Heidegger's interpretation, that Descartes also applies mechanism to the play of affectivity: exteriority gains self-comprehension as an incarnate entity according to the apportionment of action or of passion. In place of the Being-in (*In-sein*) of the world [*l'articulation au monde*], there is the problematical coexistence of two substances.

The status of the subjectivity to be "destroyed" cannot therefore be understood without its worldly or spatial correlate. The substantial Cartesian ego has nothing more than a mathematized space as its correlate. As a result, the ego that is but an ego is presented by Heidegger as either indurated—excessively solid—or as a "free-floating 'I' " (*ein freischwebendes Ich*). What is found beyond these divergent metaphors (with respect to the involvements of the world) is an indifferentiation [*indifférenciation*]—the indifferentiation of an ego that wants to be sovereign and for which autonomy is self-confirmation, the permanence of a being that is just *its* being.

The (supposedly) sovereign subjectivity of Cartesian modernity makes itself out to be the center of the world, the center of a universe of representations (a perspectival center, as is the case with Leibniz). We shall see that the Existent's ownmost constitution requires rather a *decentring* with respect to itself.

The *Existent*'s Ownmost Constitution

This constitution is marked by an intense tension between the *appropriation* implied by the "mineness" of care and the "expropriation" that follows from the move outside oneself, through the ecstatical character of *Da-sein*.

In fact, "expropriation" strikes the Existent (never purely or substantially self-possessed) immediately. It would be weak to say that the Heideggerean "subject" is all at once *outside itself*. It is outside itself without having been in itself. All at once outside itself as *Dasein*, it is such, however, only in relation to a possible in-itself: "The person is not a Thing, not a substance, not an object."[12] The mode of Being of this entity that takes on (or can take on) its opening is more originary than Cartesian substantiality but also more originary than the anthropological, psychological, and biological determinations of humanity. If it is true that *"[f]rom an existential-ontological point of view, the 'not-at-home' must be conceived as the more primordial phenomenon,"*[13] then it is temporality that finally reveals itself to be the purest source for this origin: *"Temporality is the primordial 'outside-of-itself' (Ausser-sich) in and for itself."*[14] This ecstatical dimension, in turn, is intimately oriented by a wrenching [*arrachement*] of the future.[15] The priority (*Vorrang*) of futurity is the most originary aspect of *Dasein*: the "Being-towards" [*être-à*] that projects me outside myself is more subjective than any subject, or rather transgresses all subjectivity from within.

But how can this originary "outside-of-itself" be "in and for itself"? Is a pure "outside-of-itself" even conceivable? Even as the deconstruction of the metaphysics of the subject renders comprehensible and makes manifest the possibility of a more originary approach to the Existent, so does the existential analytic seem to knock up against a wall, if not a contraction, in its phenomenological journey towards an origin ever more pure. For henceforth, what referent will the wrenching of the future make use of to be grasped as such?

In *Being and Time*'s own terms there is no other response to this question than: the possibility of *appropriation*. "Dasein is an entity which, in its very Being, comports itself understandingly towards that Being."[16] No appropriation without a self-relation. This self-reference is inscribed in every "definition" of *Dasein* and in all variants. For example, at the outset of paragraph 9: "We are ourselves the entities to be analysed. The Being of any such entity is *in each case mine*."[17] From the prerequisite acknowledgment of "mineness" to the thematic identification of understanding and interpretation as existentials, the guiding thread of self-relation—far from being severed—has its indispensable importance confirmed in a dynamic perspective, as a task: the deepening of the ownmost.

This preservation of a relation to the self that no longer has the constancy of the present or the permanence of an ego causes no small difficulty; it reveals an extremely conflictual philosophical situation that is the very site (a site of torment) of *Being and Time*. The analysis of this situation must now be taken up again and pushed forward.

The Preservation of the Self

We have seen that Heidegger, on the subject of anxiety, speaks of an "existential solipsism," an expression that I would not have dared to

use—even in quotations marks—if Heidegger himself had not provided the example. In addition, it is strongly and explicitly emphasized that anxiety individualizes the Existent: the anxious one makes
himself anxious [*l'angoissé s'angoisse*]. Anxiety has—we sometimes have
the difficult privilege of experiencing it for ourselves—the vertiginously
circular character of a maelstrom dragging our edgy freedom over
into the void of its own abyss. But in Heidegger, at least in *Being and
Time*, anxiety has neither the concrete-symbolic connotations of certain
types of neurotic behavior nor the aspect of a terrifying void, the
absence of all meaning, all rejoinder, all possibility. On the contrary, it
is singularly positive. With regard to what? With regard to the future
of the Self, its ownmost potentiality-for-Being, which signifies "*Being-
free for* the freedom of choosing *itself* and taking hold of *itself.*"[18] The
"itself" (*Sich-selbst*) is well worth emphasizing. Heidegger does not
value anxiety ontologically, except in so far as it separates and
reappropriates with regard to the resolute choice that the Existent makes
with respect to *its* world. Consequently, resoluteness (*Entschlossenheit*)
itself would be not the indeterminate opening of pure appearance but
the Existent's waiting for its *own* ownmost possibility. Of the Existent
that has responded to the call of care, Heidegger writes, elliptically
but quite eloquently: "It has chosen itself" (*Es hat sich selbst gewählt.*)[19]

If, therefore, the Self is not erased but stripped of its import as
soon as the existential analytic is deployed, one must yield to the
observation that subjectivity is neither destroyed nor emptied of content by Heidegger. It is metamorphosed, but nevertheless preserved
and even revived through the fundamental role of the *Selbst*. What
Heidegger calls into question is not the *movement* of the Self towards
its freedom but rather its reification, its substantialization, its being
"deprived of its worldhood." The call (*Ruf*)[20] for appropriation is accomplished in a decision that I must make *alone*: only in ontological
solitude (*nur in der Vereinzelung*) can I respond to this call that anxiety
addresses to me.[21]

The "turn" of the later Heidegger ought not to elicit a selective
reading of, nor retrospective corrections to, *Being and Time*. Sartre,
despite his schematism, his admitted deviations with respect to the
role of the *cogito* and *Mitsein*, was not completely unfaithful to the
inspiration of *Being and Time*. But he could not admit that freedom
must take place in the interiority sent from futurity. There is a self-
referentiality of time, always wrenched, always ecstatical, which in
fact supports whoever takes himself to be the *subject* of existence—but

which is such, as it were, only as an addressee and a carrier, as though by proxy. I can be nothing but alone in bearing the burden of time: it is the ecstasis of this burden that articulates *In-sein*, my relation of belonging to the world.

This is, to be sure, a quite paradoxical interiority which *constitutes* me fundamentally, as with every other Existent, but to which I must nevertheless gain access *alone*. An interiority that finds its home only in projection, in the permanent movement of the anticipation of possibility. Is this an interiority without a subject? Without the substantial subject that connects it to its proper ego, hardens it, and isolates it from the world? But this "subjectivity" lacks neither care nor conscience (*Sorge, Gewissen*) nor certainly—it must once again be emphasized—self-reference: "When fully conceived, the care-structure includes the phenomenon of Selfhood (*Selbstheit*)." (*Die vollbegriffene Sorgestruktur schließt das Phänomen der Selbstheit ein.*[22])

Without the foundation (which is really a *Grund*) of a Self more profound than an ego, but immanent to phenomenality and inseparable from the very temporalization of Being, everything put forward in *Being and Time* would collapse: "Dasein *is authentically itself* in the primordial solitude (*Vereinzelung*) of the reticent resoluteness which exacts anxiety of itself."[23] If appropriation is thereby worked out in ontological solitude, it is also worked out in the continuing possibility of disappropriation, the diversion of the Self towards the pseudo-certitudes of the ego. The latter is sure of itself but closes itself off to Being, which is time. A reversal of idealistic "egocentrism": the ego, which thinks itself sovereign, is in fact nothing more than the derivative of a Self more fundamental; far from being the point of appropriation, it offers just the reverse. This self-proclaimed autonomous ego is really much closer to the They-self than it is to the Self. It is defined only on the basis of an ontical indifferentiation (which explains the substantialization of *res cogitans* with respect to *res extensa* in Descartes).

Much later, in the 1973 Zähringen seminar, Heidegger frees phenomenology for its originary meaning: a "phenomenology of the inapparent."[24] *Being and Time* already contributes to such a phenomenology, however, *in the field of subjectivity*. The Existent asks itself about *its* own Being: the process is, from one end to the other, explicitly circular; but, in targeting what the Self has as its ownmost, the process moves towards a secret center (itself decentered), which does not show itself at first glance. (Such is the character of the "phenomenon" analyzed in paragraph 7.) Paradoxically, the shock to which Heidegger submits idealistic and egological subjectivity, far from dislodging the subjectivity *at the root of Being*, reveals an acuity unnoticed by metaphysics (except perhaps by Schelling). In becoming the motivating force of *appropriation*, time remains—although ecstatical—the foundation of an ultimate and intimate self-reference.

For Heidegger (after *Being and Time*), everything happens as though one must not *turn back* to this Self, which is nonetheless close and pressing: the greatest danger, in the remission (*Verwindung*) of metaphysics, seems to be this constancy of self-reference, this subjectivity that follows us like a shade. Eurydice? The thinker, no more than Orpheus, could not avoid turning around.

Are we consigned to acknowledge "defeat" (an issue, at any rate, dealt with by Heidegger himself)? Does *Being and Time* remain a prisoner of the language of metaphysics and, therefore, of metaphysics itself? One would then have to add *das Selbst* to the list of fateful metaphysical snares [*lots-pièges*], along with *Grund*, *Wahrheit* and perhaps *Eigentlichkeit*.[25]

Rather than expatiating in the shadow of this great work by seeking to "strike a balance" between defeat and breakthrough, it seems preferable to sketch out an approach to subjectivity that will both take up Heidegger's interrogation of subjectivity and follow through the critical traversal of this interrogation.

Towards a Diaphanous Subjectivity

Let us begin with a criticism that must be directed towards the Heideggerean interpretation of subjectivity in *Being and Time*. This interpretation tends (this expression is still too weak) to schematize, if not caricature, the subjectivity it rejects, or pretends to "destroy." It presents subjectivity as something substantial, thinglike, tautological, worldless. It fashions thereby a custom-made foil: a reductive subject retracted into itself, a limited and unilateral subjectivity. But Descartes (on the basis of the infinity of the will), Kant (on the basis of the transcendental unity of apperception), and Hegel (on the basis of the absoluteness of Spirit)—not to mention Husserl—would all agree with Heidegger's criticism, in the end to enhance it, *in the very name* of a subjectivity given back its depth.

In effect, it is not true that subjectivity can be reduced to a reified, narcissistic, high-strung ego that repeats: "I, I"; it is not certain that this ego is worldless and that it ends in indifferentiation. On these points, Heidegger seems to be quite smug. However, after *Being and Time*, he is prepared to acknowledge, if not the ineluctability of subjectivity, then at least its ontological and historial depth. (Obviously, without taking up, in his own name, the Hegelian hymn to infinite subjectivity as the principle of modernity.) Heidegger was prepared to acknowledge, in *Hegel's Concept of Experience*, that there exists an insubstantial subjectivity at the heart of which the ontological difference lets itself be deciphered.[26] And his *Nietzsche* shows that he recognized the link that leads from Descartes's infinite will to the optimal intensity of the will-to-power—and to the *differentiation* of perspectival centers of power.

In light of Heidegger's later approach and his epochal interpretation of metaphysics, we can better comprehend that the historial import of subjectivity goes well beyond its substantification or reification (although these are to be criticized as "symptoms" of a metaphysical tendency and come to present themselves head on, as it were, to an analytic of existential structures); correlatively, subjectivity (in this historial sense) is difficult to move beyond, perhaps even impossible to move beyond (like metaphysics itself), in so far as it is the very "sending" of modernity. While this "sending" does nothing but overtake itself in the figure of novelty [*das Neue*], and is thus intensified through the displacement of its limits, it never gets away from itself. Reversals, displacements, and transgressions are perhaps thereby no more than avatars in the lineage of subjectivity that is our lot, from Kierkegaard to Bataille, via *Being and Time*! This book is not to be excluded from this aspect of the play of modernity but should be inscribed therein as its renewed displacement, perhaps even its unexpected confirmation.

Paragraph 64, "Care and Selfhood" (*Sorge und Selbstheit*), would have to be reread closely to understand that Heidegger is seeking a new *mode* [*tenue*] of subjectivity, which he calls *Selbst-ständigkeit* and which he sees consummately deployed in the anticipatory resolve (or the decisive disclosedness) of *Entschlossenheit*.[27] But it is here that one must mark a divergence, whereby the appeased and diaphanous look of a thought liberated from all reactive gestures with respect to metaphysical *theoria* might respond to the practico-existential radicalism of *Being and Time*. This appeasement is lacking in *Being and Time* and is still awaited, despite appearance, at the close of "Time and Being."[28] In fact, in the end, Heidegger allows us—in part despite himself—to

aim for such a diaphanous subjectivity, open to the ontological secret;
a subjectivity that lets difference show through, instead of closing itself off. When Heidegger evokes knowledge of self, he mentions *transparency* (*Durchsichtigkeit*), that "sight which is related primarily and on
the whole to existence."[29] He specifies that the Self does not fold back,
therefore, into its punctuality but rather opens itself simultaneously to
its own Being-in-the-world and to that of the other [*l'autrui*]; it is
diaphanous in its situation of circumspection and considerateness.
However, Heidegger does not go so far as to speak of a "diaphanous
subjectivity," and it is uncertain whether he would have agreed to
include in the possibility of "diaphany" the most reflexive point of
subjectivity offering itself to the look [*regard*] (as I have suggested in
another context, with respect to Rembrandt's last self-portraits).[30]

In putting forward such a reading, one must step away from
what is still *reactive* in *Being and Time*, suspect in turn the suspicion
maintained by Heidegger with respect to subjectivity (as well as to the
human and humanism), and beat the thinker at his own destinal game
(for if the subjective is our sending, can we or should we "leave it to
itself" like metaphysics?).

Although the later Heidegger acknowledges the historial importance of subjectivity, he still attempts to distance himself from it, and
even more radically: the *Lichtung* that offers the world in the fourfold
offers itself: I do not posit it; the mortal (at the heart of the *Geviert*) no
longer says *I*; it is in the space of universal-technological communication that the *I*'s come, go, and interconnect with each other. Thus, does
the question remain unanswered as to whether the later Heidegger
frees up all the destinal profundity of subjectivity, all the lucid diaphany
and Nietzschean irony, as in the poetry of Rilke or Valéry? His fundamental criticisms of Nietzsche and Rilke leave room for doubt.

The interpretation proposed here does not mean to reproach
Heidegger for not having adequately deconstructed subjectivity. Nor
is it a question of going further in the deconstruction. Rather, let us
understand how and in what sense Heidegger went as far as he did
in this deconstruction; let us admit that, along the way, he has taught
us a great deal and has thereby contributed to the "distantiation" of
modernity with regard to itself; but let us not hesitate to criticize what
in Heidegger remains reactive with respect to subjectivity and the site
of rationality. What I call "contiguity" requires that thought be driven
to the destinal reception of the *ongoing sense* [*sens maintenu*] of subjec-

tivity, as well as to the acknowledgement of rational possibilities *possibles rationnels*] still held in reserve.[31]

In conclusion, and to be brief, I refuse the choice: either a subject-Thing or an ecstatical opening. The question is rather, What does subjectivity become when it loses its substantiality, its imperial sovereignty, its certitudes, and perhaps even its will? Can it not grasp and take up its destinal limits? Is there not always within subjectivity something elusive that holds itself in reserve? Let us reflect on the interiority that comes to the fore in Bach's cantatas, Beethoven's sonatas, and the *Sonnets to Orpheus*. A diaphanous subjectivity does not lack a world; it lets itself be transfixed by the face to face of mortality and an absent god. A diaphanous subjectivity is decentred, ex-centric; the enigma is its orient; it is itself and wholly other. The edge of Being, and yet itself.[32]

Four

Dropping—The "Subject" of Authenticity
Being and Time on Disappearing Existentials and True Friendship with Being

Rudi Visker

We can't change the country. Let us change the subject.

James Joyce, *Ulysses*

The philosopher, Heidegger says somewhere, is "the friend of Being,"[1] and he then goes on to explain that precisely because of this friendship the philosopher will have to die. This death, however, need not be a physical death; it need not happen in some forlorn corner of the cave where the poor light of the hearthfire will not betray the cold dagger's steel. Philosophers today are no longer invited to drink the liquor from the poisoned chalice, do not as a rule have to choose between either committing their books or their bodies to the flames. Such a death, violent as it may be, could in principle be prevented: Amnesty International could be alerted, or one could try to influence public opinion in the cave by collecting signatures and handing over petitions, and, as we all found out recently, in the last resort the United Nations could send in its armies to restore the philosopher's right to the freedom of speech. But however effective such interventions might be, they would not restore Heidegger's peace of mind. For what if the poisoning happened in a less spectacular way? What if it had to do with the fact "that those living in the cave get interested in the philosopher? That they tell one another, that one should have read this philosophy; that the cave decides to give awards and bestow honorary titles to the philosopher; that they even print his name on the frontpages of their journals and magazines? In short, that they start to admire him?" (*GA*34: 84). If that is how the poisoning works—not by ostracizing philosophy but by giving it pride of place—the prospects of our

59

interventions could be less bright than they may have seemed at first sight. Then the war to free philosophy from its bonds threatens to be without end. For it is no longer a matter of restoring the freedom of philosophical speech, since it is precisely speech itself which, for all its freedom, condemns the philosopher to be buried alive in a cave from which he may not escape, provided he does not misunderstand both himself and his task.

Such then is the death which, according to Heidegger, no true philosopher ever sought to escape. And this death, Heidegger stresses, is not what supposedly happened to Socrates at the end of his life when he, as Plato tells us, was forced to drink from the chalice. For the poison that killed Socrates was not in the chalice: it was there all along and what Socrates had to "endure" was the permanent confrontation with death during his *Dasein*—with death not as something happening to his body but as the undermining of the strength and power of his *Wesen*, of his essance.[2] That philosophy will always die in the cave, that it will remain powerless in the ruling domain of the self-evident, only testifies, for Heidegger, to the fact that philosophy is, for essential reasons, a lonely enterprise (*GA* 34: 86). It should not try to engage in a discussion with idle talk, but neither can it disengage itself and seek refuge in some ironic feeling of superiority (*GA* 34: 85). At most it can hope to violently grab one or two from the mob and force them out of the cave to which they will eventually have to return and die (*GA* 34: 86).

I did not start off with this section from Heidegger's 1931 lecture course on the essance of truth, to recall how lonely we have been or should have been, since we made friendship with Being and chose philosophy as our "subject." Nor did I simply summarize this passage in order to point to the "obvious" link between what is being said here about the fate of the philosopher and what happened to Heidegger in 1933. What worries me is precisely that on the one hand this link seems so obvious and that on the other hand in one way or another— we will have to come back to that—right here and now, we might ourselves be exposed to the very risk Heidegger warned us about and then fatally succumbed to. What worries me is precisely the possibility that while we are on our way to attack or to defend Heidegger's assessment of the relation between philosophy and the public sphere, we might be ourselves falling prey to just the kind of popularity Heidegger took to be a symptom of the perhaps unavoidable crisis of philosophy. The recent "Farias affair" is there to remind us that we will not make this crisis any more avoidable by laughing away

Heidegger's supposedly doting praise of loneliness or by dismissing his reservations about the power of the "they" and by seeing in his concern about the fate of philosophy a mere expression of his lack of concern for the public sphere, his lack of *amor mundi*, of "love of the world." In saying this, I am not suggesting however that Heidegger got it all right, but I want to defend, at least for the time being, the legitimacy of his worries about the fate of a tradition that would be merely repeated, without any concern for the "original experience" (*BT* 266 / *SZ* 224)[3] behind it, without any attempt at appropriation (*Zueignung*). And if I want to focus on these worries, if I refuse to discard them right away, it is not only because, given the situation we are in, it would be preposterous to do so but also because they take us—indeed, they have already taken us—into the heart of our subject here, into the heart, that is, of *the* subject.

In fact, the whole of the Heideggerian discourse on the subject or on what ontologically precedes it but ontically does not seek to distinguish itself from it first and most of the time (*zunächst und zumeist*), everything *Being and Time* has to tell us on Dasein before or after the subject, rests on the semantic chain of the "proper," the "appropriation," the "authentic," and the "own." Heidegger's worries about the fate of philosophy and of tradition cannot be understood without investigating this chain which leads us from the symptomatological description of a possible, perhaps inevitable, "crisis" (the lack of *Zueignung*, of "appropriation") to an aetiological level (*eigen, selbst, Man-selbst*) and further on to what looks at first sight like a therapeutic discourse on *Eigentlichkeit* and *Uneigentlichkeit*. And this discourse, which was perhaps too quickly dismissed as "the jargon of authenticity," is itself crossed as it were by another semantic chain around such terms as *Zerstreuung* (dispersal), *Verfallen, Abfallen,* and *Zerfallen* (falling, dropping from . . . , decaying), *Schweben* (floating), *Bodenlosigkeit* (groundlessness), *leicht* and *schwer* (light/easy and heavy), and many others. The intertwining of these two semantic chains is, of course, no coincidence, since Heidegger's program in *Being and Time* involves an analytic of Dasein in terms of a fundamental drive or a tendency or a mobility which characterizes Dasein's structure of being and since, as will become clear later on, the reason Heidegger is worried about the dispersal (*Zerstreuung*) to which the ambiguity of idle talk exposes philosophical and any other truth, has to do precisely with this analysis of Dasein in terms of the ontological kinetics which characterizes it. In order to understand this strange movement which links

Heidegger's crisis-symptomatology to a description of its causes in terms of an ontological kinesiology and to a—notoriously difficult and more often than not "misunderstood— therapy, I will concentrate the main part of this essay on the following question: Is what Heidegger says in *Being and Time* on the falling or the dropping of Dasein into the "they" still subject to the so-called metaphysics of the subject, or does his analysis already point to a certain beyond, a beyond the subject or a beyond metaphysics (whatever that could mean)? In other words, is this discourse on the "dropping" of Dasein to be held responsible for that which still chains Dasein to the subject, or does the analytics of Dasein force us to rethink and to rename the "subject" in a decisive way? Is it its "dropping" which turns the subject into a "subject," that is into an *x* which comes to take the place of the metaphysical subject after having burned its last traces? Or is this "subject," Heidegger's quotation marks (146, 150, 323, 418/111, 114, 278, 366) notwithstanding, still a subject in the classical sense? And should we then drop the Heideggerian *subject* of authenticity altogether and look for different strategies to change the subject? As will have been noticed, I have been cautious enough to pick out a title compatible with both possibilities. Instead of giving away the answer before even beginning the analysis, I decided, in good psychoanalytic fashion, to turn it into an affair of the ear. In fact, it will all depend on a colon (Dropping: The subject . . .) which we may or may not (yet) be able to hear. It will all depend on our ears and on the kind of ears Heidegger—or a certain "Heidegger"—would like us to have. For, as we will soon find out, *Being and Time* is a treatise on the ear. To check this, let us first turn to those pages in which Heidegger starts to develop, from section 25 onward, his well-known analysis of the "they" (*das Man*).

An Interpreting Liberation

At first sight, what is at stake here is a phenomenological description of Dasein in its everydayness, of the way Dasein maintains itself in its Being first of all and most of the time (*zunächst und zumeist*). Dasein, Heidegger tells us, is first and foremost fascinated with (*benommen von*) or absorbed into its world. Dasein is busy. It is constantly occupied, always short of time, hustling around (222/177) and understanding itself in terms of that with which it is customarily concerned. As Heidegger puts it: " 'One *is*' what one does" (283/239). And what one does is done in the way others do it: "we read, see and judge about literature and art as *they* [*man*] see and judge [or as "one" sees and judges]; likewise we shrink back from the 'great mass' an *they* shrink back; we find 'shocking' what *they* find shocking" (164/126–27). In everydayness no one is himself. "What one is and how one is, is a no one," and this no one "by whom we are lived in everyday life" Heidegger calls *das Man*, the They, the "One."[4] This anonymous experience is a positive phenomenon (69, 220/43, 176). Its description is part of an ontology of everyday life, and Heidegger stresses that it should not be mistaken for a moralizing critique of everyday Dasein (211/167). And yet De Waelhens[5] is surely not the only interpreter who leaves it to the reader to decide whether this holds true for Heidegger's descriptions of, for example, "curiosity, for which nothing is closed off, and idle talk, for which there is nothing that is not understood" (217/173). Indeed, today, due to the influence of Hannah Arendt,[6] these descriptions are generally considered to be the somewhat embarrassing sign of Heidegger's failure to understand the public sphere, and the sarcastic tone in which he sometimes sketches some of its features[7] is taken to be but the reverse side of the elitist *existential* solipsism allegedly advocated in the remainder of *Being and Time*. In its eagerness to argue its case, this Arendtian reading has of course to neglect important passages in which Heidegger stresses the ontological impossibility of getting rid of the "they" and keeps repeating that proper or authentic (*eigentlich*) existence "is not something which floats above falling everydayness" (224/179), just as this reading, which is the dominant one today, has to neglect that *Being and Time* in more than one passage suggests that although everydayness is first and foremost under the sway of the "they," it need not be: "Dasein comports itself towards its Being in the mode of average everydayness, even if this is only *in* the mode of fleeing in the face of it and forgetfulness there of" (69/44; Macquarrie and Robinson drop the *in*, which I emphasized) or more explicitly: "Everydayness is determinative for Dasein *even when* it has not chosen the "they" for its 'hero' " (422/371; my emphasis). Yet, as these quotes make clear, there can be no doubt that Heidegger considers everydayness, *insofar* as it has been taken over by the "they," to be inauthentic. Or perhaps one should better say: to be improper, while not leaving open the possibility for a properness, an own-ness. "As they-self [*Man-selbst*], the particular Dasein has been dispersed [*zerstreut*] into the 'they' " (167/129).

Commenting on this "dispersion," Heidegger finds himself using such terms as *temptation* (*Versuchung*), *entanglement* (Verfängnis), and even "*alienation*" (*Entfremdung*) (221 ff./177 ff.). He suggests that this dispersion should be seen as a "flight" into "the illusions of the 'they' " (311/266) and even seems to recommend "weaning from the conventionalities of the 'they' " (444/391). The use of the *"Entwöhnung"* in this last quote—a word which also refers to a detoxification process—leaves no doubt that although Heidegger does not underestimate the power of the seducement of the "they," he at the same time thinks its spell can be broken in principle. It should not come as a great surprise then to find Heidegger characterizing *Being and Time* as an "interpreting liberation of Dasein for its utmost possibility of existence" (*interpretierende Befreiung des Daseins für seine äußerste Existenzmöglichkeit*) (350/303). Or maybe it should. For what exactly is meant by an "interpreting liberation"? Does this mean that Heidegger is preparing some kind of deep—or even "very deep"—hermeneutics which, once implemented, will end up with having liberated Dasein? Sadly perhaps, matters are more complicated than our nostalgia may have hoped them to be.

The briefest glance at *Being and Time* will suffice to liberate us from any illusions we might have concerning the ease of such a liberation. The book's strength is precisely that it aims at an *interpreting* liberation. Unlike other theories that operate with the concept of 'alienation' and more often than not fail to explain—or even consider as a problem—the fact that alienation *has* success, that indeed people *can be* effectively alienated, that they are willing to bite the bait of what is—all too rapidly perhaps—labeled as "ideology," that the falseness of consciousness apparently does not seem to stand in the way of the *success* of false consciousness, unlike all such theories Heidegger's in *Being and Time* is acutely aware of the difficulties involved in the concept of alienation, a concept Heidegger himself regularly uses. He knows that the interpreting part of his analysis, the part which is to explain what there is about the Being of Dasein which lets Dasein first and foremost (*zunächst und zumeist*) be alienated from itself—from its self—could end up with showing that in fact there is no alienation at all, that the reason why alienation is so successful is precisely because there is nothing else than that, because, in short, alienation would be original, a supplement to some frailty in Dasein's Being, a suit of armor without which it could not survive. And yet, *Being and Time*, as we have seen, is also a liberation program, and as such it depends on the viability of concepts like alienation. Or so would it seem. For on the one hand, Heidegger tries to show that if Dasein gets "alienated," this is due to the constitution of its Being (*Seinsverfassung*) and has its roots in the fact that this Being is ultimately without grounds, that Dasein's essence lies in its existence, that it is that being which has to be its Being. And this is what turns Dasein's Being "into a burden," and this "burdensome character of Dasein" (*Lastcharakter des Daseins*) (173/134), this unbearable heaviness of its Being, lies behind Dasein's tendency "*zum Leichtnehmen und Leichtmachen*," to take things easily (lightly) and make them easy (light) (165/128). Hence it seeks refuge from the un-homeliness of its Being into the warm and cozy corners of the "they" (233/188). But having said this, it should on the other hand not be forgotten that Heidegger for all his understanding of the fact that Dasein, as he expresses himself in an earlier text, "is bowed under its own burden,"[8] is not willing to consider the "tranquillized familiarity" Dasien gets here, as something else than a "flight into the 'at-home' of publicness," a flight which makes Dasein turn its back to its "*Unheimlichkeit*," to the "not-at-home" which is its proper home. But how can Heidegger reverse things the way he does, calling what we consider to be our home, a hiding-place (*Versteck*) (317/273) and hence not a proper home at all? How can Heidegger still appeal to the "proper," if not by basing this appeal merely on his personal preference for some ideal of existence, or on an elitist tendency that Rorty[9] and other "postmodern bourgeois liberals" are certainly not willing to share? This is, in a nutshell, the problem of *Being and Time*, a problem of which—to a certain extent—its author was acutely aware (358, 360, 361/310, 312, 313).

It is a problem, moreover, which is central to the project: to prepare for the question of Being by questioning the Being of Dasein. For the problem is, of course, that Being is not what occupies Dasein "first and foremost." On the contrary, Dasein tends to live in what Eugen Fink called "ontological indifference."[10] This indifference obfuscates both Being as such and Dasein's Being. It prevents it from realizing that Being is what Dasein is already preontologically familiar with and it is this indifference which is ultimately responsible for the fact that the metaphysics it develops, instead of opening up the question of Being, in fact drops it altogether. If *Being and Time* is to be a phenomenology and if Being is *the* phenomenon par excellence, then of course the covering up of this phenomenon by Dasein and its metaphysics has to be understood and interpreted. If "covered-upness is the counterconcept to 'phenomenon' " (60/36), one will have to analyze Dasein's tendency to cover-up in order to get "*zu den Sachen selbst*," that is, to Being as such. And here the subject—our subject—comes in.

For Heidegger, what lies at the basis of this covering-up by Dasein of the ontological difference, of the fact that it is—to quote Fink again—"only open for things but not for the openness of things,"[11] is nothing else than Dasein's "Being-in-the-world" itself. In its Being, Dasein is, as it were, not closed in upon itself; it is not to be characterized as primarily consciousness and does not face the task of throwing a bridge to the world. Rather, the Being of Dasein is such that Dasein is always already out of itself: with the world (*au monde* as Merleau-Ponty translates), with things and with others. This Being-already-alongside-the world is not "a fixed staring at something that is purely present-at-hand" (88/61); it is a practical familiarity with the world, with things and with others, which engages or absorbs Dasein to such an extent that it tends not to think of itself as a distinct self but rather understands itself "in terms of that which it encounters in the environment and that with which it is circumspectively concerned" (439/387). Dasein does the things it does the way "one" has always been doing it and the way in which the others—any other—are still doing it now. In other words, Dasein is released from the burden (*entlastet*) of having to go through the painstaking process of having to find out everything for itelf (165, 312/127, 268). In falling back upon the world in which it is and in interpreting itself in terms of that world, Dasein simultaneously "falls prey"—the German text which I am paraphrasing, reads "*verfällt*"—to the tradition of which it has more or less explicitly taken hold. This tradition, Heidegger adds, "keeps it from providing its *own* [*eigen*] guidance," "nimmt ihn die *eigene* Führung, das Fragen und Wählen ab" (42–43/ 21; my emphasis). Due to this "falling" into a tradition Dasein can now repeat what others repeated before it, and still others before them. It can become irresponsible in that it lets others respond for it or by responding as others would—in short, others are always involved and this is how Dasein gets deprived by the "they" of its own responsibility: "*Das Man* (. . .) *nimmt dem jeweiligen Dasein die Verantwortlichkeit ab*" (165/127). And thus, as we will see in more detail later, Dasein can forget about the truth and can even become severed, cut off from truth altogether. It can think of truth as correspondence and forget about the fact that at the root of truth there lies a more original truth which is Dasein's own "*entdeckend sein*." its Being-uncovering (*BT* sect. 44).

It is this possibility of a repetition without explicit appropriation which will force *Being and Time* to pick Dasein's ears. For there is something ambiguous about these ears. They are both too powerful and not powerful enough. Helpful, indispensable even as they may seem in any process of appropriation, they have at the same time a tendency to undermine the need for such an appropriation by making their bearer forget his true task and by leading him to believe that mere repetition will do. Untrustworthy allies, then, these ears. And that is why they need fine tuning. For without such fine tuning, repetition will inevitably end up in ambiguity. And ambiguity is what Heidegger fears most.

Fine Tuning Dasein's Ears

Ambiguity then is what Heidegger fears most. It is the sign of a crisis, and it is also for Heidegger, as it was for Husserl—though not in exactly the same way—the crisis of the sign, of the signifying moment. But whereas Heidegger agrees with Husserl on the symptom of the crisis, his existential analysis of Dasein forbids him to share Husserl's optimistic faith in the (teleological) possibility of coping with it. If the crisis for Husserl was due to a loss of contact with the originary and originating experience, and if for Husserl this loss in turn was due, as Derrida reminds us, to "a short-coming, rather than to a defeat,"[12] then for Heidegger the roots of this ambiguity seem to lie deeper. To be sure, these roots do not reach so deeply that ambiguity becomes unavoidable and incurable. Heidegger still opposes on an ontic *existentiell* level the possibility that Dasein either takes hold (*ergreifen*) of its existence or neglects (*versäumen*) it (e.g., 32/12). But from an ontologico-existential point of view, this neglect "is not accidental, not an oversight which it would be simple to correct [*kein Versehen, das einfach nachzuholen wäre*], but [one that is] grounded in a kind of Being [*Seinsart*] which belongs essentially [*wesenhaft*] to Dasein itself" (133/ 100). The "shortcoming" then—for shortcoming there is—seems for Heidegger to be an original element of Dasein's structure of Being. It is a weakness, certainly, but a weakness without which it would be difficult to define Dasein's Being. It is not a weakness of the will and it cannot be overcome by simply willing to overcome it.[13] This is not to say of course that Heidegger thinks this weakness, which is a basic tendency in Dasein, cannot be overcome at all: the fact that it is both embedded in Dasein's structure of Being and that it can *and should* be overcome is precisely the problem *Being and Time* struggles with. At first sight, Heidegger's solution seems both simple and attractive. All that is needed is a certain puncture through "the thin wall by which the 'they' [and Dasein itself as a "they" self] is separated, as it were, from the uncanniness of its Being" (323/278). All that is needed to unblock the road toward ontology and the question of Being is a simple otological operation, a small puncture through Dasein's ears so that it could for a moment at least escape the deafening sounds of the "they" overflowing the question of (its) Being. All that is needed to allow Dasein to let itself be called back from "its lostness in the 'they' " (e.g., 312, 333/268, 287) and to "modify [its] they-self so that it becomes authentic [or proper—*eigentlich*] Being-one's-self [*Selbstsein*]" (312/268) and finally can hear the question of (its) Being, all that is needed to let Dasein pull itself together and turn it into a whole (348ff./301ff.), is a hole, a small puncture. And yet, given Heidegger's views on language and on Dasein's structure of Being, nothing could be more difficult and more risky than unblocking or piercing Dasein's ear. For if Dasein overhears the voice which calls it back to itself, it is ultimately because its ear is directed toward others, because, as Heidegger says, Dasein existentially "as a Being-with which understands can listen to others" (*[weil] Dasein als verstehendes Mitsein auf Andere hören kann*) (315/270–71). Being able to lose itself in the publicness (*Öffentlichkeit*) and the idle talk (*Gerede*) of the "they," Dasein—because its ontological structure necessarily involves *Mitsein*—"fails to hear (*überhört*) its own (*eigen*) self in listening to the [or its] they-self" (315/270–71). The overhearing, the absence of a true or proper hearing (333/287: *das rechte Hören*), the success of idle talk is first of all rooted in the fact that Dasein, as we have seen, is primarily not a proper self but an im-proper *Man-selbst*. In other words, what happened in the cave has to be understood against the background of Dasein's existential rootedness in community, in *Mitsein*. And Heidegger realizes, of course, that if the cave is what it is, philosophers will always have to swallow its poison. Unless the cave could be changed. Unless those who are in the cave, would, instead of sacrificing others, come to terms with their own death. Unless they would become Being-towards-death themselves, by not flying away from death as their "ownmost, non-relational, certain and as such indefinite, not to be outstripped possibility" (303/258–59). Unless, like Tolstoy's Ivan Ilyitch, they would learn to die and become mortals. But again, according to Heidegger, nothing is more difficult than dying, truly dying in the cave. For the cave is the resort of the "they," and as such it is the condition of impossibility for coming to terms with death as "the possibility of impossibility" (307/262). *Mitsein* in the cave cannot but be inauthentic as long as it is ruled by the "they," and yet what makes (or should make) *Being and Time* such an interesting book for political philosophers is that it is not clear whether it is willing to give up the cave and to surrender it to the "they."

What the analytic of Dasein shows to be its prime characteristic—*Jemeinigkeit* or mineness—must be shown (*gezeigt*) to Dasein in its possible authenticity (68/313/42–43, 268). If Dasein is to find itself, the crust by which it covers up its Being-towards-death and under which it seeks refuge in the warm cosy-corner of the "they," must be pierced. That which shows Dasein the possibility of being its "own" or "proper" self cannot, of course, undo the structure of its *Mitsein*. But it should be able to go against the existentiell solidification of this structure. And death cannot do this by itself, on its own. For "they" have always already turned death into something which overcomes others. Like Ivan Ilyitch "they" agree that "since Kaj is a human being, and human beings are mortal, Kaj must be mortal," but just like him, "they" know that "they" are not Kaj, nor a human being in general, and hence conclude that the syllogism only concerns Kaj, or for that matter all other human beings, but not "them." In short, "they" have turned death into something ambiguous that might, and then again might not, end one's life. And this is why Heidegger has to come up with something stronger than this ambiguity, something as unambiguous as possible, a voice perhaps—or perhaps not even a voice. In any case, something that could make the "they" "collapse" (*zusammensinken*) (317/273). Such is the power of "the voice of the friend whom each Dasein carries with it" (*Stimme des Freundes, den jedes Dasein bei sich trägt*) (206/163). Or at least, such is the power Heidegger expects it to have.

A-phonic Voices and Silently Ringing Telephone Calls

Heidegger first mentions this voice in section 34 where he introduces language (*Sprache*) into the existential analysis. Nothing much is said here about this voice; in fact Heidegger tells us nothing more than the one-line remark I have quoted, and he does not say who this friend "whom every Dasein carries with it" is, nor does he tell us why he is a *friend*. However, in his analysis of conscience (sects. 54ff.), Heidegger speaks once more about a voice, and although this voice might not be identical to the voice of the "friend" (the one could be an instance of the other), we might do well to have a closer look at what is being said here about the voice of conscience.

First of all, this voice says nothing. It tells Dasein nothing at all. It only interrupts idle talk, as does the insistent ringing of an urgent telephone call which takes one out of a party or a conference. This telephone call interrupts, and the function of this interruption is to make the otherwise inconspicuous (*unauffällig*) at least for a moment (*Augenblick*) conspicuous. I will later on come back to this conspicuousness when I link the function of this telephone call to Rudolf Bernet's analysis of the phenomenological reduction in Heidegger. But for the moment, let us concentrate on the call itself. In a way, the image of the telephone that keeps ringing is not well taken, for a telephone is the more insistent the louder it rings. But loudness is a qualification Heidegger exclusively reserves for the "they." Since the "they" are always noisy, and always shouting the latest rumors into each other's ears, the call of conscience, however loud it may be, would only add to the overall racket. Hence, it has to call in silence, it can only *silently* interrupt idle talk, it has to be—if one wants to keep the image—an *inner* telephone call.[14] It does not need, as Heidegger says, vocal utterance (*Verlautbarung*); it does not need, as a more literal translation would say, to be put into sound (316, 318, 322/271, 273, 277).

The presence of this voice which does not need *vocalization*—let us agree to translate *Verlautbarung* by this neologism—could not be more disconcerting. And not only because, as Heidegger tells us, it interrupts idle talk, but also because in a way its presence interrupts *Being and Time* and catches it by surprise. The strange thing about this voice is of course not that it is *inner*—we might well be willing to agree with Heidegger's phenomenological description, itself backed up by a whole tradition which tells us precisely that the voice of conscience is an inner voice. It is *not* the *inner/outer* distinction *as such* which should arouse our suspicion but the fact that this distinction is crossed by another one, or even by two other ones: first, by that between *presence or absence of vocalization* and second, by that between *ambiguity or lack of ambiguity*. The inner voice is precisely able to interrupt idle talk because it is unambiguous, and it is unambiguous because it does not need vocalization. This voice which is ontologically prior to the *phonè*, this a-phonic voice called upon by Heidegger to ensure that Dasein is called back from its "alienation" in the "they" and is thrown back upon its *proper* self, can succeed in its task of being a pure self-affection only where Dasein is both the caller and the called

(320/275), because it borrows nothing from anything outside itself, "in the world or in 'reality,' not a single supplementary signifier, not a single substance of expression" that would break its intimacy.[15] As one can expect, the unambiguousness of this a-phonic inner voice is the linchpin which holds together the analysis of *Being and Time* and lets it at the same time dangerously balance on the top of the thin wall which at once both separates *Being and Time* from and connects it with the *phono*logocentric forgetting of Being in metaphysics. I will leave it there, in its precarious balance, for the moment, as a monument to remind the generations to come of what Derrida called "the ambiguity of the Heideggerian situation (*situation*) with regard to the metaphysics of presence and logocentrism."[16] Let me refrain from the foolish urge to push it over, for the stakes are much too high, and our time here is limited. Let us have a look at the consequences of this Heideggerian defiance of the forces of gravity and concentrate on what it does not *with* but *to* the place of language (*Sprache*).

Heidegger explicitly introduces "language" into his analysis in section 34, "Dasein und Rede. Die Sprache," translated for lack of a better English equivalent as "Being-there and *Discourse*. Language." This translation, which renders *Rede* as "discourse," is not without its problems. It is, in fact, very misleading. *Rede*, as Heidegger immediately points out, is not to be confused with language (*Sprache*). It is the ontological condition of possibility for the latter (203/160). *Rede*— Heidegger's translation for the Greek *logos* (208/165)—is what provides for linguistic articulability, but it is not linguistic articulation itself. *Rede* can, but need not, give rise to a process of vocalization, to a *phonè*. Just as the voice of conscience was an inner a-phonic voice, vocal utterance is not essential for *Rede* (208, 316/165, 271). It is not *as such* dependent on it. On the contrary, *Sprache* is but its mundane component, its " 'worldly' Being" ("*weltliches" Sein*) (204/161) and is itself existentially grounded in *Rede* (203/160). It is because *Rede* already articulates Dasein's practical familiarity with the world at a prelinguistic level, because there is already a "totality-of-signification" (*Bedeutungsganze*) for Dasein, because Dasein's world is not without significations (*Bedeutungen*), that there can be *linguistic* articulation (204/161). But as Heidegger remarks, this ontological order of priority between *Rede* and *Sprache* does not entail a relapse into a philosophy of interiority: "Dasein expresses itself [*spricht sich aus*] not because it has, in the first instance, been encapsulated as something 'internal' over against something outside, but because as Being-in-the-world it is already 'outside' when it understands [*verstehend*]" (205/162). This *Aussprechen* however is not to be mistaken for a simple expression in the context of a naive instrumental view on language. Heidegger stresses that it would be wrong to describe what happens in the transition from *Rede* to *Sprache* as a process in which word-things (*Wörterdinge*) get supplied with significations (204/161). Instead "to significations words accrue" (*den Bedeutungen wachsen Worte zu*) 204/161). But if it is clear what this "coming-to-word" (*zu Wort kommen*) of an already constituted "totality-of-signification" (204/161) does not mean, it is less clear what exactly is meant by it. For example, does this "*zu Wort kommen,*" this "*sich aussprechen*" add anything to the already articulated (*gegliedert*) totality-of-signification but its "worldly Being?" But the possibility of it being shared with others? Is its only role that of the indispensable linguistic flesh which has to make its master's *Rede* accessible and attractive? Is it no more than a cloth or a sober gown, destined to remain *einstimmig* (326/281), in unison with its master's silent voice but secretly speculating on the eyes and the ears of the others to deform its unambiguous song? Secretly fostering hopes that it will catch "their" attention and one day become more important than the master himself, free and finally rewarded for the long years during which—to use Husserlian terms—it labored to set free the master's ideality of meaning by tying it to and receiving it into its flesh?[17] Why doesn't Heidegger, instead of holding that "to significations words accrue," take the opposite view that to words significations accrue? Why can't it be the practical familiarity with a language, into which each Dasein finds itself thrown (*geworfen*), that gives rise to significations? For, after all, Heidegger himself points out that language as an entity within-the-world, as the "worldly Being" of *Rede* "becomes something which we may come across as a ready-to-hand (*Zuhandenes*)" (204/161). If language has indeed this characteristic of being ready-to-hand, just like equipment (*Zeug*), if the Being of language is at least in some respect "readiness-to-hand" (*Zeuglichkeit*),[18] wouldn't one then be justified in expecting Heidegger to say that it is to *words* that significations accrue? Just as equipment only gets its practical meaning within a totality of equipment (*Zeugganzes*) (97/68), so words would derive theirs from a *Wortganzheit* (204/161), from a totality of words. Just as, ontologically speaking, "there 'is' no such thing as *an* equipment" (97/68), there would be no such thing as *a* word in isolation, and hence there would be indeed no ontological sense to the idea Heidegger himself dismisses, that word-things get supplied with significations (204/161). In other words, why didn't Heidegger in order to refute a naive instrumental view on language, appeal to the far more subtle 'instrumental' theory of language he himself prepared by introducing readiness-to-hand and equipmentality (*Zeuglichkeit*) into ontological discourse? Why didn't he reckon with language as an always already pregiven symbolic order that is part and parcel of Dasein's facticity (*Faktizität*)? Why didn't Heidegger draw this consequence from his own remarks on the readiness-to-hand of language? Why did he insist on ontologically deriving it from *Rede*? It is clear that part of the answer at least has to do with what Heidegger fears most, with ambiguity.

The Risk of Language

Just as the voice of conscience is not ambiguous because it is not a *phonè* (316, 318/271, 274), so *Rede*, which is not dependent on vocalization, cannot be ambiguous. Ambiguity comes in only with language. And with language untruth comes in,[19] untruth not only in the special sense of a forgetting of a more primordial truth, of a forgetting of Dasein's *entdeckend-sein* (Being-uncovering) (*BT* sect. 44) but also in the narrow sense of *Verdeckung*, covered-up-ness. In fact, as will become clear in a moment, both occur together. Untruth arises as a result of *narchreden*, merely repeating what the others say. And since the possibility of this repetition is inherently inscribed in language, *Rede*, once vocalized, is always under the threat to become *Gerede*, idle talk, and to fall prey to the "they" and become dominated "by the way things are publicly interpreted" (by the *öffentliche Ausgelegtheit*) (264/222). In such repetition, that which is linguistically expressed as such (*das Ausgesprochene als solches*) takes over Dasein's Being-towards those entities which have been uncovered in the original assertion (*Aussage*) (267/224). To be sure, Being towards entities has not been extinguished, but it has been uprooted (*entwurzelt*) by the "they." Entities have not been completely hidden, Heidegger says, but they have been uncovered and disguised at the same time: "the entity shows itself, but *in the mode of semblance*" (*[das Seiende] zeigt sich—aber im Modus des Scheins*) (264/222; my emphasis). *Schein*, "semblance," is the effect of *Gerede*, "idle talk"; and as such it is what constitutes the realm of the "they," that is, *doxa*, life in the cave. *Semblance* is due to Dasein's losing hold of *itself* (its Self) and becoming absorbed and lost in *das Man*. Semblance is a disease *Rede* becomes exposed to by trusting *phonè*, its (un-)faithful servant. But is this disease a fatality, attached to language as such? Would it be wrong to suggest, as De Waelhens did,[20] that language in *Being and Time* stands under the sign of the inauthentic?

At first sight, it seems it would. For Heidegger seems to consider the transition from *Rede* to idle talk (*Gerede*) not as a fall *into* language but as a fall *within* language. He does state that "*Rede* which is communicated [and hence vocalized (*R.V.*)] *can* be understood to a considerable extent, *without* the hearer bringing himself into such a kind of Being towards what *Rede* is about as to have a *primordial* [*ursprünglich*] understanding of it" (212/168; my emphasis), but he does not say that this is what necessarily happens. Or again, we read that "Dasein *need not* [*braucht nicht*] bring itself face to face with entities themselves in an 'original' experience [in *'originärer' Erfahrung*]" and that "it nevertheless remains in a Being-towards these entities" (266/224; my emphasis). Ample evidence, it would seem, for the fact that it is not language as such which is inauthentic but only a way of being in language (first quote), although even that lack of "original" experience might not, as the second quote seems to suggest, be sufficient to call it "inauthentic." But matters are more complicated than that. Immediately after having said that Dasein does not need to have an "original experience," Heidegger goes on to explain that this fact about Dasein's relation to language is what gives rise to the "they": "In a large measure uncoveredness gets appropriated not only by one's own uncovering, but rather by hearsay of something that has been said. Absorption in something that has been said belongs to the kind of Being characteristic for the 'they'" (266–67/224). On second sight then, Heidegger's use of verbs like "need not" and "can" in the foregoing quotes, was plainly descriptive, and the quotes should be read as an attempt to find an answer to the following question: "what is the Being of *Rede* which is expressed and what does this tell us in principle about Dasein's everyday kind of Being?" (211/168). And what Heidegger is telling us is that Dasein's everyday absorption into the "they" has something to do with the vocalization of *Rede*, with language. If there is a fall *within* language, this fall is due first of all to a fall *into* language. For the fall of *Rede* into language is always a fall into the risk of losing contact with the "original" experience. But if language involves such a risk, how involved exactly is language in this risk?

Heidegger tells us that "what is expressed becomes as it were, something ready-to-hand within-the-world [*innerweltlich Zuhandenes*] which can be taken up and spoken again [*weitergesprochen*]" (266/224). And he also tells us, in analyzing equipment (*Zeug*) as an example of readiness-to-hand, that "the peculiarity of what is proximally ready-to-hand is that, in its readiness-to-hand, it must, as it were, withdraw in order to be properly ready-to-hand" (99/69). In dealing with equipment, for example, in using a hammer, Dasein is not confronted with the Being of equipment as such. Equipmentality or readiness-to-hand shows itself as such only when the hammer gets lost or is broken, or is lying in the way, and so forth; only then is Dasein's attention drawn to the Being of its equipments, to the fact that they belong in a wider network of equipment (*Zeugzusammenhang*), and only then can this network reveal to Dasein something about the difference between the innerworldliness of equipment and its own Being-in-the-world (*BT* sect. 16) Dasein's natural attitude is, as it were, corrected by a phenomenological reduction that overcomes it and takes it by surprise. As Rudolf Bernet stresses, it is precisely this feature of Heidegger's use of the reduction—the fact that it "results from an event that imposes itself on Dasein in an unexpected way,"[21] which separates him from Husserl. And as we will see in a moment, this is not a minor feature. For if this reduction is no longer the result of a jump (*Sprung*) which, as Bernet says, is willed and risked by a responsible subject that wants to know all about it, if it comes to Dasein not only as a surprise but as a bad surprise, not as something which it enjoys but as something which it resents, then one can expect Heidegger to have great difficulties in not losing together with the Husserlian subject the possibility of responsibility and authenticity as such. And the least one can say is that Heidegger is not making it easy for himself. Instead of condemning Dasein's clinging to the natural attitude, he seems to defend it: "the self *must* forget itself if, 'lost' in the world of equipment, it is to be able 'actually' to go to work and manipulate something" (405/354; my emphasis). But it is clear of course that this defense cannot be unambiguous if Heidegger does not want to see the tables turned against his own analysis. For if vocalization turns *Rede* into something ready-to-hand, and if the world of equipment *necessitates* a forgetting of the Self, then language as the "worldly Being" of *Rede* not only involves the risk of a certain forgetting *of*, or of a loss of contact *with* an originary and proper-ly (*eigen*tlich) appropriated experience, but is built on it. Language is so much involved in the risk it involves that it presupposes it: "lost" in the world of language, the Self in some way *must* forget itself if it is actually "to go to speech." And maybe this "forgetting" is not really a forgetting; maybe this risk is not literally a risk. For does not Heidegger himself stress that "when we are explicitly hearing another's *Rede*, we proximally [*zunächst*] understand what is said, or—*to put it more exactly*—we are already with him, in advance, alongside the entity which the *Rede* is about" (207/164; my emphasis)? And how could we be, if not because language itself not only articulates an already articulated world but also intertwines with it and opens up a world itself? But this "Heidegger" in *Being and Time* cannot concede. For it would mean conceding not only, as "Heidegger" is willing to do, that "*idle talk* (. . .) is the kind of Being which belongs to Dasein's understanding *when that understanding has been uprooted* [*entwurzelt*]" (214/170; my emphasis), but also that this uprootedness, which characterizes both the mode of Being of the "they" and of *Gerede*, might not be just the result of a fall (*Verfallen*) out of which Dasein can and must free itself, and might not be just the sign of Dasein's alienation or its being-lost in the "they." What prevents Heidegger from following the train of his own thought here is not the concept of authenticity *as such*. It is, as I will try to show, a certain preconception of authenticity, of the self, and of the way they relate to in-authenticity and not-self, which *imposes* on *Being and Time* a decision that is to a certain extent arbitrary.

"Heidegger's" Decision

We have seen how language and equipment, in order to function properly, presuppose a certain forgetting and how the anonymous existence of the "they" thrives on the structure of this inconspicuousness (*Unauffälligkeit*). If the "they" can provide Dasein with an improper self, it is precisely because Dasein, in dealing with equipment and language, "must forget" its proper self (220, 405/176, 354). Put paradoxically, what Heidegger's first reduction shows is that the *proper* functioning of the realm of language and equipment is dependent on the functioning of an *im-proper* (*uneigentlich*) realm of the "they." If this realm is to give way to a proper (*eigentlich*), if the inauthentic (*uneigentlich*) is to be modified into the authentic (*eigentlich*), then a new attempt is needed to make what remains inconspicuous (*unauffällig*) conspicuous (*auffällig*). What has to be made conspicuous is, of course, Dasein's proper self and, as is well known, in order to do that, Heidegger will be looking for a way to tear Dasein's death away from "the inconspicuousness" in which it remains first and foremost—an inconspicuousness, as he reminds us, "characteristic of what is encountered in an everyday fashion" (*die für das alltäglich begegnende charakteristische Unauffälligkeit*) (297/253). In other words, what the analysis of *Angst* and of the voice of conscience, which Heidegger is (re-)introducing here in order to show the existential-ontological and the existentiell possibility of an authentic potentiality-for Being-a-whole (*eigentliches Ganzseinkönnen*) for Dasein, what these analyses will have to do is to undo the inconspicuousness (*Unauffälligkeit*) characteristic for everydayness. In anxiety, Heidegger says, "everyday familiarity collapses" (233/189) or again, the voice of conscience, he tells us, can—by its lack of ambiguity—"make the 'they' collapse" (317/273). The call is to rob (*rauben*) the self of its lodgement (*Unterkunft*) and its hiding-place (*Versteck*) in the "they" by only appealing to the Self of the they-self and passing-over the "they" (317/273).

In fact, this discourse on the "they" is closely linked to what Heidegger has to say on "truth" in section 44 of *Being and Time*. Let me just recall here that at the end of this long, circuitous, and extremely difficult analysis, Heidegger resorts once more to a robbery. After having linked untruth, idle talk, ambiguity (and hence, as we have seen: language), and the "they," Heidegger concludes that truth as *a-letheia* is "a kind of robbery" (*Raub*) and that the *alpha privans* refers to the fact that "Dasein should explicitly appropriate (*zueignen*) what has already been uncovered, defend it *against semblance* (*Schein*) and disguise, and assure itself of its uncoveredness *again and again*" (265/222; my emphasis). Given our preceding analysis of this semblance (*Schein*) and of the way it is linked to a falling (*Verfallen*) that gives rise both to the "they" and to language, it won't take us much effort to show, first that Heidegger's discourse on the "they" is a discourse on truth and second, that this discourse on truth will get *Being and Time* into trouble.

What section 44 suggests is that truth has time and again to be robbed away from untruth. And since truth and untruth, as Heidegger explains, ultimately relate to Dasein's more original truth and untruth, to its disclosedness (*Erschlossenheit*) and to its closedness (*Verschlossenheit*), and since this *Verschlossenheit* is due to Dasein's tendency to fall into the power of the 'they," the fate of truth ultimately depends on Dasein's authenticity, on its "authentic disclosedness" (*eigentliche Erschlossenheit*), on the truth of its existence (*Wahrheit der Existenz*) (264–65/221–22). And so does the fate of untruth, the fate of the "they," the fate of *doxa*, the fate of the cave. And here we have a problem, for what follows is that, because of its conception of truth as robbery, as a-letheia, *Being and Time* seems forced to give up on the cave. Now authenticity itself becomes a robbery, something we have to gain again and again, a perpetual task of appropriating untruth proper-ly (*eigentlich zueignen*) (345/299) in what Heidegger calls "resoluteness" (*Entschlossenheit*), that is, the proper truth of Dasein, its disclosedness in its proper or authentic mode (cf. 264, 343ff./221, 297ff.). Although Heidegger tells us that "even resolution (*Entschluß*) remains dependent upon the 'they' and its world" or that resoluteness notwithstanding "the irresoluteness (*Unentschlossenheit*) of the 'they' remains in power (*bleibt in Herrschaft*), but [that] it cannot impugn resolute [authentic] existence" (345–46/299), it is not at all clear whether what is taking place here could be regarded as a true rehabilitation of *doxa*. For whereas Heidegger tells us that "Dasein is always already (*je schon*) in irresoluteness, and soon, perhaps, will be in it again" (345/299), he does not show us how everydayness itself, how *doxa* itself, could be modified and how *doxa*, on the basis of this modification, not only does but should remain in power. On the one hand, Heidegger is at pains to deny that the authentic Being-one's-self should be regarded as "an exceptional condition of the subject," and he stresses that such authenticity is not "detached from the 'they' " since the "they" remain in power and truth is but the result of a robbery (168/130 and the quotes above). But, on the other hand, he does seem to conceive of authenticity as a momentary escape from inauthenticity and as a robbery which will have to start all over again. First and foremost Dasein is inauthentic, but sometimes it can "escape" the cave. But even when it "escapes" the cave, when "the irresoluteness of the 'they' " no longer is able "to impugn [its] resolute existence," the cave itself, *doxa*, the "they" "remain in power" (345/299, quoted above). Dasein lives, as it were, both in and out of the cave. Better still: the cave turns into a place where an authentic and an inauthentic self are *living apart together*. Authentic Dasein "remains dependent upon the 'they' and its world" but is no longer "impugned" by it (345–46/299, quoted above). The reason why this *L.A.T. model* is so disappointing is because its interpretation of the existential modification of the "they" seems only able to correct Dasein's everydayness by letting Dasein temporarily step out of it. Conceived of in this way, the modification would leave the "they," everydayness or *doxa* as they were. On this reading, then, the philosopher who has to "return" to the cave, could not but be an eccentric, whose sad duty it is to live in a place that goes against the "habits of his heart." He will have to die, but not "after" his own heart. If his resolution is to remain dependent on the "they" and its world, if "the understanding of this is one of the things [his] resolution discloses, in as much as resoluteness is what first gives authentic transparency to [the philosopher's] Dasein" (345–46/299), then *Being and Time* cannot but lead to the apocalypse Arendt and others have associated with it. Then we will have to give up our hopes to get a new "political" philosophy from Heidegger, for *doxa*'s inauthenticity will always remain at odds with the philosopher's authenticity, and the rehabilitation of a public sphere where they could meet will prove to be an impossible project.

Gently Falling . . . into Heidegger's Cave

Is there no way then for *Being and Time* to keep to the promise of its opening pages where it was suggested that everydayness need not be inauthentic (see above section I)? What elements in *Being and Time* are responsible for its apparent failure to stick to this promise, for the fact that throughout the book more often than not everydayness is simply equated with the inauthentic? What if ultimately the responsibility lies with the way Heidegger here conceives of *a-letheia* as a simple opposition between truth and untruth, an opposition in the wake of which all the other oppositions, for example, that between *Eindeutigkeit/Zweideutigkeit* (lack of ambiguity/ambiguity) follow, an opposition moreover which he spent the rest of his life correcting? What would happen if we were to introduce into *Being and Time* the idea that truth is not simply opposed to untruth, that there is an untruth in the heart of truth, that there is a *lèthè* which no *aletheia* can finally overcome?[22] Would this "result" of Heidegger's "Turning" turn us away from the analytic of Dasein? Or would it only do away with a *decision* "Heidegger" imposed on this analytic, *but not with the analytic as such*? A *decision* which, as I suggested, results from a preconception of truth and of language and of the relation between truth and language? A *decision*, finally, which rests on a certain conception of the Self and the way it is related to the they-self, on a certain conception of the authentic and the way it is related to the inauthentic, on a certain conception of Being and the way it is related to covered-upness (*Verdeckung*) as its counterconcept (60/36)?

Being for the Heidegger of *Being and Time* has to be robbed, as it were, of its *Unauffälligkeit*, its "inconspicuousness," and therefore, first of all, Dasein's proper self has to be made conspicuous. But whereas Heidegger's first reduction showed that in "the conspicuousness of the unusable," readiness-to-hand "shows itself a last time" and then "takes its farewell" (104/74), his second reduction through anxiety and the voice of conscience[23] seems to forget the disruptive effects of the first one. Instead of realizing that what the first reduction shows is that Being in some way has to be forgotten, or has to remain inconspicuous, or again, instead of realizing that what it shows is that, in the words of the later Heidegger, "*aletheia* (. . .) has to be overlooked,"[24] the second reduction tries to invert this relationship between the conspicuous and the inconspicuous and to *adjust* it to the concept of truth of section 44. In making death conspicuous, it is the "they," the untruth, which now "shows itself a last time" and then—remember— "collapses" (*das Man sinkt in sich zusammen*; 317/273) in taking its farewell. In doing away with the inconspicuous it is only the inauthentic that is disrupted, and what remains is the authentic, the Self which shows itself for the first time. In other words, whereas the first reduction seemed to lead to a defense of the natural attitude—the Self *must* be forgotten—the second reduction attacks it all the more heavily. But this self which is now made conspicuous, can it do without an inconspicuousness? Is it doomed to succumb again to the inauthentic from which it first managed to set itself free? Can it not fall in an authentic mode? Does falling (*Verfallen*) have to lead to inauthenticity?

Although Heidegger in one place suggests that falling (*Verfallen*) can be either authentic or inauthentic (401/350),[25] *Being and Time* in general considers *Verfallen* to be that essential structure of Dasein's Being which explains why Dasein's Being is first and foremost (*zunächst und zumeist*) inauthentic at an existentiell level. What this means is that, strictly speaking, the existential character of falling/dropping is due to its being a structural *possibility* inherent in Dasein's Being (it explains for the fact that there *can* be inauthenticity), and not to its being a structure *as such*. Although Dasein is always exposed to its tendency to fall, it does not always give in to this tendency. It is not always falling. In other words, as opposed to other existentials as, for example, Being-in-the-world, falling and the existentials related with it, such as the "they," are in a way existentials that can disappear. For example, the "they" is an existential in so far as it refers to a *tendency* which belongs to Dasein's Being, the tendency, that is, to take things easily (*es sich leichtnehmen und leichtmachen*) given the unbearable heaviness of Dasein's Being. Because the "they" constitutes only an existential *structure of possibility*, and not, as Being-in-the-world does, an existential *structure*, it can but need not put itself through to the existentiell level: Dasein can but need not be inauthentic. In other words, the inauthentic is to be linked to fallenness (*Verfallenheit*), whereas the authentic arises only when Dasein manages to free itself from its tendency towards *Verfallen*. If falling would be like the other existentials, it would allow not only for an inauthentic but also for an authentic mode; it would be a structure characteristic of Dasein's Being as such, and not merely a structural possibility.

In pointing out this special status of falling and the existentials related to it, in showing some surprise about the fact that we seem to be dealing here with existentials that can disappear, my aim is not of course to contest that there is a difference between existentials and categorials, and to suggest that the first should be considered in terms of the second, namely as "*vorhanden*" properties of the substance of Dasein. Rather, I wonder if part of the violence we have seen at work in *Being and Time* should not be related to the special status falling seems to get within the framework of Heidegger's existential-analysis, especially since it is this status which will allow him to put the proper (authentic) in an either/or relation to the improper (inauthentic). But is this either/or relationship the only way to think the authentic and the inauthentic? Or does it simply follow from a *decision* Heidegger imposed on his existential analysis? A *decision* concerning the status of falling, a decision motivated by *parti pris* with regard to the meaning of authenticity and inauthenticity and the way they relate to each other? What if the analysis of anxiety reveals not that "Dasein is authentically itself [*ist eigentlich selbst*] in the primordial individualization of the reticent resoluteness which exacts anxiety of itself" (369/322), but only—and here I quote a very different passage—"the *Being-free for* one's ownmost potentiality-for-Being, and therewith for *the possibility of authenticity and inauthenticity*?" (236/191; my emphasis). What if the analysis of death reveals that death—authentic, proper death—is precisely what happens to the philosopher *in the cave*, namely the "permanent con-fron-tation" with the "Nichtig- und Machtloswerdens des eigenen Wesens" (nullification and becoming powerless of his own essance) *(GA* 34:84) and thus gives a final twist to Plato's story and robs it of its dramatic overtones? And what if the analysis of *Rede* and the voice of conscience does *not* reveal a falling into an ambiguity and an inauthenticity that would be due to vocalization itself and from which the voice of the friend would help Dasein recover? What if, since, as Heidegger stresses, "hearing is constitutive for *Rede*" (206/163), and since one can hear either the voice of the others or the voice of the friend, it reveals instead that *Rede* itself is therefore, even *before* vocalization, already *in itself* exposed to the risk of ambiguity? And what if this risk were not really a risk? What if the voice of the friend which comes, as Heidegger says, "from within me and yet from beyond me" (*aus mir und doch über mich*) (320/275), is the voice of the law which cannot be heard without a certain noise? What if a law that would be without noise, perfectly *einstimmig* (326/281), would no longer be a law? To be sure, Heidegger might be right to stress that the voice of conscience tells Dasein nothing at all. But is this "nothing at all" without ambiguity? Is it not ambiguity itself? Is it not the ambiguity of the "do not read me" that turns the law into law and makes my responsibility a responsibility? What if the law would have to be as ambiguous as this: Read me, but do not just read me, it is not sufficient to read me to know what you have to do and how far your responsibility goes?

And yet, whereas this essential ambiguity of the law seems to put a limit on all attempts to turn the voice of conscience into something unambiguous, Heidegger, as we have seen, keeps dreaming of a little hole through which all that legal noise could escape, he keeps looking for a way to reproduce a low-noise, a-phonic voice of conscience; and he is quite prepared to use the violence of his otological puncture, if it can help him to unblock ontology. But in thus turning his back on ambiguity, does Heidegger not at the same time turn his back to death and to true friendship with Being? For what if this friendship cannot do without a certain ambiguity, and what if it is finally this to which the tension between Heidegger's two reductions should draw our attention? Authenticity then would not be that rare state-of-mind (*Befindlichkeit*) in which the self or Being is no longer forgotten and in which truth has momentarily appropriated untruth. To the contrary, only in dropping *from* anxiety, *from* "death," *from* silence into ambiguity, only in the moment of losing its self to the "they"-self, would Dasein be able to experience its self and to find access to an authentic, proper mood (*Befindlichkeit*). Just as the writer, only by losing his thread, discovers he has one, and just as Sheherazade discovers her "own" life in watching it disappear in the "ear of the other," so too might Dasein experience its proper self only when it discovers that its steadiness and steadfastness (*Selbständigkeit*) is not what it gains, by bringing the "movement" (*Bewegtheit*) by which it is thrown to a "stop," but by joining this movement and becoming aware of its powerlessness to escape its dispersal (*Zerstreuung*) (369, 400/322, 348). This "falling" need not make Dasein fall back into the inauthentic again; to the contrary it is only by way of such "falling" that Dasein can reach a state-of-mind or a mood in which it can be authentic.

Anxiety, then, is not what makes the cave collapse (*zusammensinken*) so that it becomes inaccessible forever; *anxiety disrupts life in the cave only in order to show its inevitability*. Never really successful in its attempt to graft the conspicuous onto the inconspicuous, the phenomenological reduction which overcomes life in the cave will not live to see its unknown buds blossom and seems doomed to remain the barren trace of a wound on a stem. And yet, in opening up something which has immediately to be closed again, by showing something which has immediately to be forgotten again, this wound, according to Heidegger, has healing power. Indeed the reduction's most important lesson is not only that it cannot be fully carried through (Merleau-Ponty) but that it must "fail" in order to "succeed" or that its success lies in its failure. Both a failure and a success, the reduction becomes the inevitable chalice by which we experience "das Nichtig- und Machtloswerden" of our own essance. And maybe we should not decline to drink this poison. For it could be a medicine: "das Nichtig- und Machtloswerden" of our *Wesen*, this loss of strength and power of our own Being, is that not the only experience of death we (can) have? If we had more time, I could try to show that such is the experience of a finitude we can only be *finitely* related to and that this experience has a different structure from the one Heidegger was later to describe as "releasement" (*Gelassenheit*). But let us leave that for another occasion.[26] It is time for us to return to the cave. Such was, after all, our agreement. But we need not worry. We will have to die, but "they" won't kill us. Not if we "change the subject."

Five

The Final Appeal of the Subject

Jean-Luc Marion

I

Has phenomenology ever had a more urgent challenge to confront than the determination of what or possibly who succeeds the subject?

Phenomenology has never definitively decided between two ways of thinking this succession: between either definitively abolishing the subject in order to replace it with the very absence of an heir (as Nietzsche claimed he had done) or pausing to repeat, each time, in a mode which is always new, the function of subjecti(vi)ty. On the subject of the subject, phenomenology has never ceased to oscillate from one to the other postulation, between heritage and "new beginning." Such a hesitation doubtless permits us to inscribe phenomenology both within the field of metaphysics and on its margins or even outside of its limits. It remains the case that, from itself, the phenomenological option does not allow us to designate, without further consideration, what or who succeeds the subject. The question of the posterity of the subject will therefore not even find the outline of a response as long as the way in which phenomenology claims to go beyond the subject, and hence the metaphysical subject, has not itself been sketched out. To ask this in another way: Does phenomenology offer a sure route for proceeding ahead, beyond the subject, taken in its transcendence but also in its pure and simple abolition? We shall examine this question through the clearly privileged example of *Dasein*, whose ambivalence Heidegger discerned in *Being and Time*.

As a consequence, we shall ask, To what extent does the existential analytic exceed the problematic (and thus also the abolition) of the metaphysical subject? *Dasein* attains its proper and authentic truth in the figure of care *(Sorge)*, which identifies it as anticipatory resoluteness: "*Dasein* becomes essential in authentic existence which itself is constituted as anticipatory resoluteness *(vorlaufende Entschlossenheit)*."[1]

It is fitting therefore to examine whether this ultimate determination of the meaning of its Being permits *Dasein* to surpass and thus to succeed the subject—or whether we must still await an other.

II

There would be no sense in contesting that *Dasein* definitively subverts the subject, even and especially the subject understood in the sense that Husserl gave it in his transcendental phenomenology. *Being and Time* not only places in question the Kantian transcendental *I* (such as it might indeed still reappear after the *Ideas* of 1913); it places in question the phenomenological *I* in general, in its very foundation understood according to the *Logical Investigations* (against the pious legend of a direct continuity between 1899 and 1927 that one finds in the later Heidegger). In what does this questioning consist? It consists in a radical revolution: subjectivity no longer has as its objective the objectivization of the object, because the ultimate instrument of this objectivization—intentionality—no longer aims, as it did for Husserl, at accomplishing the Kantian project, that is, the constitution of objects, but rather it aims at the opening of a world. The intentionality constitutive of an object remains, certainly, but it is reduced to the status of a particular and derived case of the fundamental determination of the being-in-the-world of the one who from then on renounces the title of "subject," since the objective of the objectivization of the object is abandoned in favor of the title of *Dasein*. One must not be mistaken: the analysis of readiness to hand *(Zuhandenheit)* plays a decisive role in the entire analytic of *Dasein*, because it establishes not only that readiness to hand does not maintain a primarily theoretical relationship to the world, but most of all because that which is worldly is not at first there in the form of an object constituted according to the objectivization exercised by a subject, but according to the mode of a manipulability which, in return, determines *Dasein* itself—handled, as it were, by that which it handles. *Dasein* is no longer in the world as a spectator, even a constituting spectator, *Dasein* is in the world as someone taking part, as a party possibly challenged by that which it meets and encounters. Intentionality accomplishes itself at the same time as it disappears in Being-in-the-world, where the world is substituted for the object and *Dasein*'s existence is substituted for the constituting I. The world no longer amounts to a sum of constituted objects, since it does not consist of anything: it no longer consists at all, but is opened in making a (whole) world. However, this world can thus only open itself insofar as it is *Dasein* that makes the opening in general through its own extasis. The extasis of *Dasein* consists in the fact that, far from founding itself on its own essence or founding its essence on itself (according to the two Kantian and Aristotelian postulations of subjectivity), it is the being for which what is at stake, each time, is nothing less than its Being—even better: it is the being for which, when what is at stake is *its* Being, what is at stake is just as well *the* Being of all other beings. Such an appropriation of Being to the *I*— "the Being of this being is *in each case mine [je meines]*"[2]—should not, moreover, be interpreted as a subjection of Being to the figure of the ego, even to a transcendental egoism (against Levinas's doubtless unjust critique); if Being is each time witnessed as mine, this rather results from the impossibility of other beings attaining their Being and from the impossibility on the part of *Dasein* acceding to Being otherwise than placing itself in play in the first person—in risking itself as it is exposed to death. Being opens itself to *Dasein* in the way in which death affects *Dasein* as a possibility: in person, in the first person, according to the mode of unsubstitutability. The "mineness" of Being no longer indicates that the I subsists in an essentially unshakeable subjectivity, but that Being remains inaccessible to *Dasein* (and thus absolutely concealed) insofar as *Dasein* does not risk itself through exposing itself without reserve and without certainty, as the possibility of impossibility. Being-towards-death, which defines this ultimate possibility, should therefore be interpreted, without any morbid nihilism, as the "mineness" of Being. From intentionality to "mineness," the *I* who is master of its objects and possessor of its Being vanishes in order to let *Dasein* appear, which sets against the subject a double paradox: *Dasein* fails to constitute any object, and thus cannot be assured of any substantiality, but attains its proper being only when it risks itself in the first person.

III

To accomplish its own Being in risking itself in person defines *Dasein* as the one who takes over from the subject. The "mineness," where what is at stake is Being itself, doubtless disqualifies any pretension to the auto-foundation of an unconditional I. This advance does not dispense with the need for a new interrogation: On what condition does *Dasein* accomplish the "mineness" that is characteristic of its proper way of Being? The literal response to this question is contained in a formula: "Resoluteness *(Entschlossenheit)* is a privileged mode of openness *(Erschlossenheit).*"[3] The openness of *Dasein* is displayed according to a privileged mode, that of resoluteness. Indeed, resoluteness, understood as anticipatory, defines the being of *Dasein* as care *(Sorge)* and allows the attainment of the meaning of being from the perspective of the future. It is therefore a question of determining how the ecstatic structure of care is accomplished phenomenologically: briefly stated, what does resoluteness resolve? To what does resoluteness resolve itself for *Dasein*? Towards what does the decision bear? Resoluteness prepares itself and concretely locates itself in several phenomena which are ordered around it in a constellation: it is a question of anxiety, of the guilty or indebted conscience, and of Being-towards-death (as anticipation). All of these phenomena offer a common and essential character to resoluteness; it remains for us to elucidate it.

Anxiety leads to the phenomenological ordeal of the nothingness of all beings, that is to say, all manipulable or ready-to-hand beings and all subsistent or present-at-hand beings: "in that before which one has anxiety, the 'it is nothing and nowhere' becomes manifest."[4] That this nothingness may and even must be understood as the world does not modify the fact that anxiety opens onto nothingness, without anything more than this nothingness itself. The conscience which experiences its debt there perceives an appeal or call, whatever that appeal might be; yet this appeal does not evoke or demand any response, any reparation or any ontically assignable price: "What does the conscience call to him to whom it appeals? Taken strictly nothing. The call asserts nothing, gives no information about world events, has nothing to tell."[5] The indebted conscience therefore opens *Dasein* not onto whatever innerworldly beings there may be but rather to its own transcendence in the encounter with beings in general, a transcendence which alone opens a world. Strictly speaking, the conscience of fault opens nothing for *Dasein* except itself insofar as it transcends beings. And finally, Being-towards-death: at first glance Being-towards-death marks an exception; never, to our knowledge, has Heidegger indicated that Being-towards-death would open onto nothingness, but yet the entire analysis seems to intend this—indeed it opens onto the possibility of impossibility. The anticipation of (or rather in) Being-towards-death finally opens *Dasein* to the absolute possibility—absolute since the impossible is here being attained—which alone qualifies *Dasein* as the ontological being par excellence; here therefore *Dasein* fully experiences its transcendence towards all beings and therefore experiences itself as such. If therefore "in Being-towards-death, *Dasein* comports itself towards itself as a distinctive potentiality-for-Being,"[6] one must conclude from this that *Dasein* does not comport itself towards anything other, to any being, and therefore comports itself towards nothing. Thus, strictly speaking, the three phenomena which determine the Being of *Dasein* as care only define anticipatory resoluteness as an open extasis towards nothing. *Dasein* discovers itself and experiences itself at the very moment of risking itself as that being for whom Being is an issue, an identity which is in itself empty.

For, if it leads to nothing, that does not mean that anticipatory resoluteness leads to nothing at all; through this nothing anticipatory resoluteness "isolates" *(vereinzelt) Dasein* by returning it to the ontico-ontological transcendence which sets *Dasein* apart form innerworldly beings. Such an isolation does not only or primarily signify that *Dasein* acedes to its final form (in the sense that Aristotle speaks of "*ē gar entelecheia korizei*"[7]), or that *Dasein* should *in se redire* (following the Augustinian theme taken up once again by Husserl). Isolation does not purely and simply lead *Dasein* back to itself, but rather to its fundamental determination: being without any possible substitution, itself, in person without another person, at play within Being as within what is its own. That which was formulated at the beginning of the *Dasein* analytic as "mineness" *(Jemeinigkeit)* is stated at the end of the analysis as "ipseity" *(Selbstheit)*: "the ipseity of *Dasein* has been formally determined as a way of existing."[8] *Dasein* therefore exists qua itself. Resoluteness does not resolve anything, because it should not resolve anything, since what is at stake is the possibility of *Dasein* risking itself for that which is its own: namely, to be the being in whose Being what is at stake is Being itself. If resoluteness leads *Dasein*, beyond any ontical relation, to be itself, then ipseity must be understood resolutely as a constancy of self in person, or as a self-constancy *(Selbst-ständigkeit)*—and it is thus that Heidegger does not hesitate to name resoluteness in a development at once strange and capital:

> Ipseity *(Selbstheit)* can be discerned existentially only in one's authentic Being-able-to-be-oneself *(Selbstseinkönnen)*, that is to say in the authenticity of *Dasein* "understood" *as care*. The constancy of the self *(Ständigkeit des Selbst)*, as the supposed permanence of

the subject, gets clarified in terms of care. But at the same time the phenomenon of authentic-inability-to-be opens our eyes to the constancy of a self *(Ständigkeit des Selbst)*, in the sense of its having achieved some sort of position. *The constancy of the self (Ständigkeit des Selbst)*, in the double sense of solidity and "constancy," is the *authentic (eigentliche)* counter possibility to the absence of constancy *(Unselbst-ständigkeit)* or of irresolute falling. The *self-constancy (Selbst-ständigkeit)* does not signify anything else existentially than anticipatory resoluteness."[9]

Thus, ipseity prolongs itself in a constancy of the self, which offers two characteristics: on the one hand, ipseity is prolonged as a self-constancy which confirms that care leads back the self to itself and leads *Dasein* back to a manner of self-identity; on the other hand, the constancy of the self permits us not only to comprehend an evidently metaphysical figure (the "supposed permanence of the subject") but again to understand it from the perspective of authenticity. The analytic of *Dasein* thus rediscovers, in a way that is familiar, but is yet derived from the care which is distant from familiarity, the metaphysical avatar of constitutive subjectivity. Thus arises the prodigious paradox of 1927: the extasis of care, which radicalizes the destruction of the transcendental subject in Descartes, Kant, and Husserl, nonetheless leads to a miming of the subject by reestablishing an autarky of *Dasein,* identical to itself through itself up to the point where this ipseity stabilizes itself in a self-positing. *Autarky,* however strange it might sound, is the suitable term, for resoluteness only opens the world in the ectasis of care through eventually disclosing that the self of *Dasein* leads back to itself. Even if the autarky and self-positing of *Dasein* do not regress back to the self-constitution and permanence of subsistence or the present-at-hand, they mime the latter. The shadow of the ego falls across *Dasein.*

IV

The ipseity of the self positing itself as such, absolutely unsubstitutable by virtue of care and through anticipatory resoluteness, defines *Dasein* through an autarky which is existentially proper to it and supposedly authentic. The entire analytic of *Dasein* is concentrated into this result. Assuming it is actually achieved, this result gives rise to two interrogations, both of them directly linked to the enterprise of surpassing the subject and to the choice of its successor.

The first interrogation points to an aporia that is exterior to the project of *Being and Time:* if the autarky of the Self still essentially defines *Dasein,* whatever the phenomenological or existential justification might be for this autarky of constancy of the self *(Ständigkeit des Selbst)* or self-constancy *(Selbst-ständigkeit),* to what extent does *Dasein* still "destroy" the metaphysical project of a transcendental *I* which is unconditioned because it is self-constituted? Doubtless, *Dasein* challenges the permanency of the *ousia* or the *res cogitans.* Yet the autarky of the Self goes as far as toying with the strange title of *ständig vorhandene Grund der Sorge:* "if the ontological constitution of the Self is not to be traced back either to an Ego-substance or to a 'subject,' but if, on the contrary, the everyday fugitive way in which we keep on saying 'I' must be understood in terms of our *authentic* potentiality-for-Being, then the proposition that the Self is the basis of care and constantly presence-at-hand is one that still does not follow."[10] Beyond the fragility of this denegation, how does one explain this proposition if the metaphysics of a "constantly present-at-hand foundation" is only rejected as premature *("noch nicht"),* and not absolutely? How, moreover, is one to distinguish so clearly between such a constant presence-at-hand *(ständig vorhanden)* of the foundation and the constancy of the self *(Ständigkeit des Selbst)* which is going to follow? In fact, the reflexive character of the verbs, to decide for oneself, to exhibit oneself, to precede oneself, to anguish oneself, and so forth, which are each time enacted for nothing other than the self (for the nothing and for the Self) appear to always mime the hitherto self-founding reflexivity of the transcendental subject and, indeed, of all subjecti(vi)ty. It might well be that *Dasein*'s confrontation with metaphysical egology (from Descartes to Hegel) will remain incomplete and even undecided, like a battle that is suspended before the winner is known.[11] Most importantly, it might well be that *Dasein* does not completely surpass the thematic of the subject that the project of a "destruction of the history of ontology" nevertheless expressly implied in the proposed second section of *Being and Time.* We shall therefore risk the following hypothesis: the analytic of *Dasein,* rather than designating that which succeeds the subject, is the last heir of the subject itself, to the extent that *Dasein* offers not so much an overcoming of the subject as a path by which one may eventually come to the subject. To the extent that the over-coming of the subject can only be envisaged by passing through *Dasein*, and therefore in destroying *Dasein* as well.

Hence the second interrogation, which designates an aporia internal to *Being and Time:* If the autarky of the Self still defines the proper constancy of *Dasein*, how might this autarky be concerned with the question of Being in general? The imbalance, powerfully visible if not always repeated, between the question of Being in general and the analytic of *Dasein*, which traverses the entirety of *Being and Time* and which almost necessarily implies the incompleteness of the book, does not stem from a fault in *Dasein*'s demonstration. On the contrary, it is precisely the exemplary accomplishment of this demonstration that installs *Dasein* in the autarky and the constancy of the Self, without any other opening than itself—to the extent that if the existential analytic definitely leads, in the two sections of the published part of *Being and Time*, to the identification of *Dasein* with the self of anticipatory resoluteness and therefore to itself, the analytic does not, to our knowledge, even sketch the goal, which was explicitly fixed in the introduction, of connecting the Being of *Dasein* to Being in general and of finally reducing the existential analytic to fundamental ontology. Moreover, the final paragraph 83 of *Being and Time* might perhaps be read as the confession *in fine* of the final impossibility of passing from the existential analytic to fundamental ontology: "Can one provide *ontological* grounds for ontology, or does it also require an *ontical* foundation? And which being must take over the function of providing this foundation?"—it is thus that the "fundamental yet still 'veiled' problem"[12] is finally acknowledged. The aporia of fundamental ontology appears all the more radical to the extent that it arises from the very success of the existential analytic: the Self, through positing itself autarkically in its proper constancy through anticipatory resoluteness, no longer admits any extrinsic relation—neither the world (which it opens and precedes) nor entities (which it transcends) nor time (to which alone its authenticity accedes) can lead *Dasein* to evoke Being. Far from exercising its neutrality, Being here finds itself obfuscated. The neutrality of the Self disqualifies any transition from *Dasein* outside of itself towards Being.

Therefore, *Dasein* would not accede to the question of Being in general by virtue of its most authentic determination as an autarkic self. Indeed, *Dasein* cannot appeal or call to Being, since in anticipatory resoluteness *Dasein* calls only to itself: "*Dasein* is the one who calls or appeals and, at the same time, the one who is called or appealed to."[13] Heidegger only found the solution to this paradoxical aporia at the price of the *Kehre,* which, in a sense, sacrifices everything that *Being and Time* had succeeded in making manifest (the analytic of *Dasein*) in order to manifest what was lacking from *Being and Time* (Being in general). And moreover, this heroic reversal is immediately marked, among other innovations, by the disqualification of the autarky and constancy of the Self. Since anticipatory resoluteness, as a self-calling or auto-appeal, fails through neutralizing the question of Being, it must be opened, from the outside, to an appeal or call that it no longer controls, decides, or performs; in the postface to *What is Metaphysics?* and then in the *Letter on Humanism,* this appeal is named as the *Anspruch des Seins,* which is the appeal by which Being claims the human being (rather than *Dasein*) as the phenomenological instantiation of its manifestation. Contrary to *Being and Time,* where the appeal always comes down to an appeal to itself, here the appeal claims the human being in the name of Being, from the outside and in advance. One must choose between anticipatory resoluteness and the claim [*la revendication*] of the human being by Being: Heidegger finally chose to "destroy" the constant autarky of the Self by a recourse to the claim that Being exercises over the human being. By "human being" it is therefore necessary to understand, contrary to any humanism, that which comes after the subject but also after the Self, since the human being lets itself be instituted through the *Anspruch des Seins.* Claimed before allowing itself to be resolved, the human being should thus be named *der Angesprochene*—the one who is claimed [*le revendiqué*].

This thesis marks the second advance of Heidegger beyond subjecti(vi)ty, a more decisive although less often realized advance. And yet, this thesis gives rise to a question that is still more redoubtable than the preceeding difficulties it has managed to vanquish. For, while *Dasein* indeed received an analytic, the one who is claimed [*le revendiqué*] does not, explicitly at least, receive any. And this is indeed why no other Heideggerian term comes to replace that of *Dasein.* Now if it is as the one who is claimed, and not as a constant and resolute Self, that the "human being" gives itself up to the question of Being in general, then the "new beginning" remains suspended over an analytic of the claiming call (*l'appel revendicateur*) in general—which is precisely what is missing. Furthermore, the interpellation that Being exercises over the human being discovers itself to be subordinated to the very possibility of determining the human being as the one who is interpellated or claimed through and through. To break with the subject? To hear the call of Being? This is of little importance in the final analysis: in both cases it is first of all necessary to determine how, why, and up to what point I can hear a call or appeal in general.

V

The claim, then, interpellates me. Before I have even said "I," the claim has summoned me, named me, and isolated me as myself. Moreover, when the claim resounds, the claim that hails me in my name, it is only appropriate to respond—and perhaps respond as silently as the call was silently intimated to me—and to respond by saying, "Here I am!" or, "See me here!" (*Me voici!*), without saying or claiming to advance the least "I." The claim gives rise to a "Here I am!" and thus delineates a *me* without leaving any place to an *I*. The nominative gives way decidedly to that which—provisionally at least—appears to be an accusative case. Contrary to all appearances, it is no longer a question here (as in previous analyses) of a classical critique of the transcendental *I* by and through an empirical and constituted I/me (*je/moi*) in the manner of Kant, Husserl, and Sartre. For this critique finally and much more radically reestablishes a transcendental *I*, which is not constituted but constituting, and which is always originary precisely because it remains unknowable and unconstitutable as an object; indeed, within this metaphysical regime, the relativity of the empirical *I* all the more clearly underlines the absolute primacy of the transcendental and constitutive *I*. Here, on the contrary, in this regime where the claim interpellates *me*, the *I/me* that the claim imparts to *me* and where it assigns *me*, does not designate a return to any transcendental, constitutive, or absolute *I*. The claim, in claiming *me*, refers, across this effect, to its originary interpellation. The experience of the *me*, namely that I hear *myself* speaking, does not offer any proof of some transcendental *I*, an I which comes from some world behind the scenes, but rather, as this pure and simple experience, affects me by its claim and its status as interpellation. The pole to which I must refer *myself*, or more exactly to which the *I* must henceforth refer itself as a *me*, does not lead back to any *I* behind the scenes—an *I* which remains in an invisible reserve as a more originary pole which would open and command the phenomenological horizon—but rather designates an inconceivable, unnameable, and unpredictable instance or agency exercised by the claim itself. Doubtless, to hear *myself* thus interpellated, I experience myself as claimed and, therefore, called in or summoned like some suspect whose identity needs to be verified. But, precisely, this identity no longer returns to me as my own: I cannot produce it as if I were my own master, and were this identity ever to become accessible to me, I would owe this to a speech uttered from elsewhere. I experience *myself* (or more exactly, the *I* experiences itself) as a *myself/me (un moi/me)*, that is to say, as the pure and simple identification through the passive experience of a *myself* which is submissive and receptive: In the experience that the claim imposes on it, the *I* does not duplicate itself in a *myself*, which would rather underline it; it transmutes itself into *himself (lui)* and loses itself. The interpellated *me* ratifies the disappearance of any *I* under the irremediable empire of the claim. The disaster of the *I* marks the accomplishment or completion of the claim.

Here then, this *myself/me* that is assigned to *me* in the claim arises from the disaster of the *I*. Henceforth we will designate the *me* as the interlocuted *(l'interloqué)*. We shall determine the interlocuted by four characteristics: convocation, surprise, interlocution itself, and, finally, facticity. Firstly convocation: when the claim has taken place, the interlocuted experiences an appeal which is powerful and conscriptive enough for it to be obliged to render itself, in the double sense of displacing itself and submitting itself. Thus, the interlocuted should renounce the autarky of every self-affirmation and self-effectuation: It is only insofar as it is altered by an originary relation that the interlocuted recognizes itself as eventually identified. The pure and simple shock *(Anstoss)* of the claim identifies the *I* only by transmuting it immediately into a *me*. This mutation of the nominative case into the accusative case also marks the inversion of the hierarchy between metaphysical categories: the individualized essence (the *ousia protè*) (as the *todē ti*), no longer precedes the relation *(pros ti)* and no longer excludes it from its ontic perfection; here, on the contrary, the relation precedes and produces individuality. And moreover individuality loses it autarkic essence by being derived from a relation which not only is more originary than it but is half unknown; for, the claim delivers up to evidence only one of its two poles—*myself* or rather *me*—without necessarily or for the most part delivering up the other pole, namely, the origin of the call or appeal. Indeed, the call or appeal is perfectly well able to exercise itself as such without displaying itself or placing itself in evidence. Individual essence undergoes a double relativization: it results or derives from a relation and, moreover, from a relation whose origin is unknown. Thus, a fundamental paradox: through convocation, the interlocuted identifies itself, but this identification escapes it straight away by affecting it and rendering it ecstatic in relation to any self-producing autarky of the *I*. Convocation annuls subjecti(vi)ty to the benefit or an originally altered identity.

Surprise: the interlocuted, which results from a convocation, recognizes itself to be taken and covered over (taken over) by an extasis; but this extasis determines the interlocuted because it remains indeterminate with regard to its pole of origin. Such an extasis, imposed on the *myself/me* without its knowledge, contradicts every epistemological extasis, where the self-constituted I displays or shows the constituted object which stands before it in an evidence which is in principle transparent. Surprise is obscure extasis which is somehow undergone: it contradicts intentionality, which is itself a known and knowing extasis displayed by the *I* and derived from itself; far from covering over the clear terrain of knowable objectivity, when the *I* is transmuted into a *myself/me* it recognizes itself as covered over by an unknowable claim. The inversion of this covering over (*sur*-prise) is at once with the disqualification of the grasp *(prise)* of epistemology (sur-*prise*). The one and the other are confounded in the same loss of knowledge, in the double sense of the loss of any original self-consciousness and of the incapability of knowing the original pole of the claim as if it were an object. Descartes can here serve as a guide in his definition of admiration or wonder: "when our *first* encounter with some object *surprises* us and we find it novel, or very different from what we formally knew or from what we supposed it ought to be, *this causes us* to admire it and to be astonished and because all this may happen *before we know* whether or not this object is beneficial to us, it seems that admiration or wonder is the first of all the passions."[14] According to Descartes, the surprise of admiration is nothing less than the first passion of the *ego* and therefore of the subject. In distinction from this, we are here describing here a more originary affection, which precedes metaphysical subjectivity; and even if this subjectivity might eventually proceed from this affection, surprise would render the subject destitute rather than instituting it. Surprise arises before the metaphysical admiration of the subject, it is more original than the *thaumazei,* from which philosophy is born.

Interlocution: of course, it is not at all a question of a situation which would already be dialogical, where two interlocutors would converse in an equal relation, but rather of that which is designated under this name in the ancient French judiciary language: "to ordain that a thing will be proven or verified, before one pronounces on the essence of a state of affairs," "to interrupt the legal procedure by an interlocutionary sentence."[15] Juridically speaking, to launch an interlocutionary appeal amounts to the suspension of an action, insofar as the facts have not been established, and therefore to suspend the question of right in favor of fact; in phenomenological terms, one would say that interlocution operates a reduction: no longer a reduction of the given by a constituting consciousness (Husserl) or *Dasein* (Heidegger) but a reduction of the purely given understood as such. To determine the given as pure given demands the suspension within the *I* of everything which does not directly result from the claim itself, and therefore to reduce the *I* to the pure giving or donation of a *myself/ me*. It is no longer a question of comprehending this giving according to the nominative case (Husserl) or according to the genitive case (of Being: Heidegger) nor even according to the accusative case (Lévinas), but rather according to the dative case—I receive *myself* from the call or appeal which gives me to myself. It would almost be necessary to suppose that this strange dative case was not here distinguished from the ablative case (as in Greek), since the *myself/me* accomplishes, insofar as it is the first gift which derives from the appeal or call, the opening of all other donations or gifts and particular givens, which are possibly ethical. As a given dative, an ablative giving, one might say that the *myself/me* is played out in the manner of the oblative. Receiving itself from the call or appeal which summons it, the *myself/ me* undergoes an interlocution—defining the fact of its pure donation—by reducing every other possible phenomenon to pure donation according to interlocution. Interlocution thus marks the ultimate phenomenological reduction.

Facticity: the interlocuted endures the appeal or call and the claim as if it were a fact always already given, and therefore received de facto; the given fact of the appeal or call lets one infer the irremediable facticity of the interlocuted. None amongst mortals has ever lived for an instant without having received a call and being disclosed as interlocuted by facticity. Or, which strictly comes back to the same thing, no mortal has ever lived for an instant without discovering itself to be preceded by a call or appeal that was already there. The paradigm of this irremediable facticity is derived from the fact, always already attained, of speech itself: the first speech for any mortal was always heard or understood before being able to be uttered. Speaking is primarily and always equivalent to hearing or understanding speech;

to understand speech is always and primarily equivalent to passively hearing or understanding a speech that comes from an other, a speech that is primarily and always incomprehensible, which announces no sense and no signification, except the very alterity of the initiative which the pure fact gives us to think about for the first time. It is not only that the first speech is not said by the *I* who can only undergo it by receiving it, nor is it only that the first speech does not give any knowledge of an object or of reason. It is rather that the first speech opens onto the fact that a gift originally comes to *me* or befalls *me*, because this gift precedes me to the extent that I must recognize that I proceed from this gift. The human being merits the title of the mortal (or, to say the same thing, the animal) gifted with speech, on the condition that the phrase "gifted with speech" be understood in its strict sense: "endowed with speech," that is, having received the gift of speech. Therefore, to express this with phenomenological rigor, endowed by the gift of speech as it is heard or understood, heard or understood as a given. A decisive consequence follows from this: since the call radically precedes the interlocuted which proceeds from it, the one who calls can never coincide with the one who is called, precisely because, however it occurs and whatever its eventual meaning, the call or appeal accomplishes the separation of the two. The facticity of the call precludes the possibility that the one who is called may perfectly understand the call, in whatever sense one gives to this. To suppose, moreover, that the one who is called attains complete understanding of the one who calls forgets the fact that the one who is called can recognize this call only by admitting that it comes from elsewhere, by recognizing the antecedency of its donation or giving— to the extent that any identity (which is impossible de facto) of the call, would de jure reinforce the immemorial originality of the one who calls over the one who is called. Far from the call or appeal guaranteeing that the one who is called can take possession of its property in the figure of the one who calls, and therefore becoming the matrix of authenticity, it rather indicates that the one who is called can come to itself only by receiving (itself) (as) a *myself/me* and, therefore, by also receiving through the same gesture an infrangible separation from that which assures or guarantees the self. The call or appeal gives *me* to and as *myself*, because, through its facticity, it separates me from all propriety, property, or possession of the proper and of what is my own. It is not only necessary to say that the call or appeal, through its facticity, imposes inauthenticity as the original posture (or rather as the originally nonoriginal posture) of the *myself/me*. It is much rather necessary to admit that the facticity of the call or appeal produces a strict equivalence between the access of the one who is called to itself as a *myself/me*, and thus its ipseity, and its original difference from and with itself as an *I*, and thus its inauthenticity. The original and irreducible posture of the *myself/me*—its ipseity—is thus accomplished in inauthenticity. From which follows a paradox: authenticity, far from being de jure primary, rather masks or covers over the fact of the call—the fact that it is the call alone which always already gives (me) (as) myself. The call, and not the *I*, decides upon the *myself/me* before myself—as that for which I precisely am myself; or, better: the *I* is as such only insofar as the call or appeal has always already claimed it and therefore given it to itself as a *myself/me*. Authenticity, far from opening upon an untainted origin or leading back to such an origin, dissimulates after the fact the originally inauthentic movement of the gift. For, the fact of the call or appeal—calling to *me* before *I* even hear anything—makes me originally differ from this origin and from whatever *I* might be.

Summoned outside of my autarky, according to an originary relation, surprised in itself before any knowledge of the one who calls, but reduced to the pure given, the interlocuted, which is claimed by an anterior fact, differs essentially from itself, because it arises from this very call.

VI

However, the thesis that the interlocuted alone succeeds the subject exposes itself to a major and indeed massive objection: the claim can install the interlocuted as such only if some agency performs it. It is necessary, then, that the claim ultimately be referred to a pole whose initiative rends or tears subjecti(vi)ty, by its silence or by its sound. Therefore, it is unavoidably necessary to ask, who or what claims the interlocuted? As to that which could exercise the claim, rival candidates are not lacking: God (by revelation), the Other (by obligation), Being (by the event), Life (by auto-affection), and so forth.[16] But these various candidates permit us only to define a difficulty but not at all to confront it. For, more than the problem of the identity of the one who calls, the difficulty consists in the consequently devalued status of the interlocuted: in all the above cases, when the interlocuted is placed as a derived, regional, and thus contingent agent, does it not necessarily regress to the humble status of an anthropological given (or even a prosaically psychological or subjective given), without any de jure necessity, purely factual and empirical describable, but conceptually indeterminate? The difficulty of designating exactly what or who calls leads, then, before receiving the least solution, to the following difficulty: that the interlocuted is interpreted as phenomenologically fallen. The anonymous indeterminacy of the one who is called. However, this objection, as strong as it may seen, does not hold. It is not only that the anonymity of the one who calls and the facticity of the one who is called do not in any way oppose the interlocuted; they rather positively confirm its disposition.

The anonymity of the one who calls (what or whom?) does not invalidate the concept of the claim but rather confirms it: since I recognize *myself* as interlocuted before any consciousness of my subjecti(vi)ty, which precisely results from this convocation, any eventual knowledge of the one who calls would be added to the claim after the fact, rather than preceeding it as if it were a presupposition. At the origin, the claim is accomplished, and not the consciousness of this claim by the interlocuted, still less the knowledge that would permit the identification of the one who calls in the call or appeal. Moreover, the surprise character of the call forbids the interlocuted from comprehending or knowing its convocation as if it were a determinate, permanent, and named object. To discover *myself* summoned would have no rigor if the surprise did not definitively deprive *me* of knowing, for a time at least, in the instance of the convocation, by what and by whom the claim is exerted. Without the anonymity of the what and the whom, the convocation would not surprise us. Reciprocally, if I knew in advance that Being, or indeed the Other, or indeed God, or indeed life, summoned me, then I would immediately escape from the full status of an interlocuted, since I would be free of any surprise; and thus, knowing in advance (or at least immediately) to what and to whom I was related in the speech that I heard, I would know (what) or I would respond (who) by way of a covering over of a constitution or the equality of a dialogue, that is to say, without the interlocuted passivity of a surprise. In brief, I would become once again an *I* who would be delivered from the status of a *me*. Thus, anonymity belongs strictly to the conditions of possibility of the claim, because it defines the unconditional poverty of the latter: in conformity with the principle of insufficient reason, the claim does not have to become cognized in order to become recognized, nor does it have to be identified in order to be exerted. Only this poverty is sufficient to wound subjecti(vi)ty and exile it outside of any authenticity.

But there is more: the anonymity of the one who calls can be deduced absolutely from the characteristics of the claim. Indeed, the call or appeal resounds first of all prior to any understanding and any hearing, since it surprises—or takes by surprise—a consciousness which was not previously awakened. The call or appeal thus produces the original difference: at the origin, in the fact of the origin, no coincidence, no identity, and no authenticity are found, but rather the separation between the call or appeal and the *myself/me* that it surprises. The delay of *my* surprise with respect to the appeal or call which is always already launched, marks the unique origin of difference, or rather the origin as difference. That which differs is derived from the claim: prior to the partition between Being and beings, also more ancient than the delay between the intuition and the intention (or between the sign and presence), the claim differs. This difference produces the separation between the summoning call or appeal and the understanding of that appeal. Indeed, the interlocuted can do justice only to the convocation from within this surprise and following this essential delay. Surprise says that the appeal or call has already begun to summon, or indeed has already ceased to resound, and that the interlocuted has not finished or indeed has not yet begun to understand it. The facticity of the call or appeal, which rightly implies its anonymity, bears the traces of this difference: effect without cause, fact without reason, the call or appeal comes to an understanding only belatedly awoken, after having already begun to finish, already in the twilight of its dawn. The call or appeal surprises the interlocuted not so much because of its facticity but rather because it remains in origin unknown. The anonymity of the call or appeal, which is implied by its facticity, essentially surprises the interlocuted by its archetypal difference. Deferred through the differing call or appeal, the interlocuted—latecomer, belatedly awoken, originally orphaned by the movement which opens it—thus defines itself by this very delay.

The interlocuted is delayed. It is delayed from its birth, precisely because it is born; it delays its birth, precisely because it must first of all be born. Any living thing must first of all have been born, that is to say, have arisen after or in a delay from its parents, in the attentive circle of an anticipation of the words which would summon it, before the living thing can itself understand or guess; in brief, already surprised by the summons. This latter statement is not at all trivial, since it inscribes the interlocuted, before and more essentially than its mortality, in a difference with respect to the call or appeal. It follows that the interlocuted bears the stigmata of the differing call or appeal, and the full intimacy of its originary inauthenticity, in the very proper name that it bears. Each person has one, two, or sometimes three names, which are, in principle, sufficient to designate a person without any confusion in their ultimate individuality (*haecceitas*). And yet, these names that each one of us bears insofar as we are interlocuted—if it can be supposed that they fully identify us—would not ever be equivalent to a proper name. Or rather, no "proper" name merits this title de jure or de facto. The "proper" name is the result par excellence of an appeal or call: it was given to *me* before I could choose it, know it, or even understand it; it was given to *me* because in fact *I* was given (interlocuted) as and to *myself* (literally: the *I* has been given as and to *me/myself*) by the fact of this name. My right to be me results from the fact that others, without and before me, have given and are giving rise to *me*. I can never say that "I call myself by this (proper) name" (*je m'appelle de ce nom (propre)*); I should always say that *I* have been preceeded by a *me*, namely, as that which others have always already called *me*. In other words, I am only called by that name that others (and *myself*) recognize as such, through launching the syllables like a call or appeal (for better but also for worse). It is they who recognized me first of all (surprising me) in and by this name. And they can only do this and should only do this because it is they and not me (I am delayed in advance) who have given *me* this name. Thus, I am called "myself" only insofar as others have always already appropriated me to a name which, without their convocation, would never have been able to name me properly. My proper name has been given to *me* by those who have appropriated *me*: what is proper to me or my own results from an improper appropriation and thus only identifies *me* through an originary inauthenticity—namely, the difference of the claim. Before the supposedly proper name—which is de facto and de jure improper—might be appropriated to me by others (in convocation), it was necessary that the call or appeal preceded it. From whence arises a first consequence: the anterior and thus differentiating call or appeal constitutes the forename (*le pré-nom*) of the name; the fore-name anterior to the name; and which is proper, while the "proper" name in fact marks an inappropriation; a fore-name which does not itself constitute any name, since it gives, announces, and instigates the name. The fore-name—and it alone—silently satisfies the conditions of possibility for the appropriation of the name that is called "proper" through the convocation. The fore-name precedes the name in the same way as someone calling my name precedes me. The name, by which I alone accede to myself, or more exactly by which *I* accede to the self as a *me*, precedes (and surprises) me only on the basis of the call or appeal (fore-name) which gives it to me (interlocution) and which thus purely and simply gives me to myself as deferred from myself. From whence arises a second consequence: The *myself/me* is born from the appeal or call whose origin is essentially unknown; what is proper to it resides not in its name but rather in the mute fore-name which inauthentically calls it and appropriates it to itself. *I* is called "me" (*Je s'appelle moi*)—henceforth *I* appears only as a differed neutralization of originary difference (that of the convocation), a surface abstraction, a tactical denegation of the diffentiating claim. As a consequence, what is truly proper to a name—the fore-name without name—resides in the very movement of recognizing oneself as called, of admitting the inauthenticity of the surprising convocation, that is to say, in vocation. The only proper name of the interlocuted lies not in such and such a series of names which are by definition improper but in the confession of the call or appeal—that is, in vocation. *Vocatus,* in itself invoked and provoked as a *myself/me*, the interlocuted admits itself to be preceeded by a call or appeal from which it proceeds. Convocation delivers vocation into the appropriating fore-name of all the appropriated names (said to be "proper"). From this arises a third conclusion: the uniquely proper, that which may still respect the differentiating gap of the fore-name, consists in the response [*répons*]. By "response" we understand[17] the resumption of the appeal or call (convocation) by the interlocuted, to the extent that what comes to the interlocuted in the mode of difference (surprise) finds itself acknowledged, admitted, and repeated by the interlocuted as something all the more authentic because it has come to it through an essential inauthenticity. Indeed, the response literally says nothing other and nothing more than that which the call or appeal said in the first place; it thus repeats the originary inauthenticity; but in this way it makes it its own and therefore acknowledges it as paradoxically authentic. At this second level, authenticity does not consist in claiming to produce the equal appropriation of "*I* to *I*," or of leading back the *myself* to the *I*; authenticity consists in taking for itself, that is, for myself, the original and differentiating inauthenticity of the claim; taking it for itself as if it were a charge or a burden, a weight, or perhaps a danger, in the sense that, during a battle, I might cry out, "the next bullet has my name on it!" There is no authenticity in this appropriation but rather the recognition, often forced but at least admitted, and therefore free, that inauthenticity, alienation, and alteration concern me despite myself, to the point where they are more *myself* than I ever am. Thus the response transmutes the claim into its *"interior intimo meo."*[18]

What succeeds the subject is the very movement of irremediable difference which precedes it, insofar as the subject is given to itself as a *myself*, to which any I claiming authenticity only offers a mask, doubly belated and radically secondary, or even originally deceptive. More essential to the I than itself, the gesture that interlocutes appears, freely but not without price, in the figure of the claim—as that which gives the I as a *myself* rendered to *itself*. Grace gives the *myself* to *itself* before the I even notices itself. My grace precedes me.

Six

Rethinking the History of the Subject
Jacobi, Schelling, and Heidegger

Andrew Bowie

I want in this essay to reconsider one key source of the recent critiques of the role of subject in modern philosophy, Martin Heidegger, by looking at him in relation to some of his precursors. My aim is not just to rectify some of Heidegger's misleading claims about the history of modern philosophy, but also to suggest that the approaches of these precursors still offer resources for our contemporary self-understanding. These resources can help explain why it is that philosophers should regard self-consciousness with suspicion, as well as showing that much of this suspicion is based on a very limited conception of what is at issue. The arguments I shall outline here have been largely neglected by those concerned to escape one conception of subjectivity—that of René Descartes—which has too often been assumed to be the only one on offer in modern philosophy until Nietzsche and Heidegger began the work of deconstructing it. If my account is correct this deconstruction, which Lyotard and others are so concerned to continue, becomes somewhat otiose, because what is to be deconstructed is only one facet of a much more complex picture. Descartes's conception has been linked to pathologies as diverse as the ecological crisis—via his assumption that we can become "lord and master of nature"—and the aporias of modern epistemology that result from the subject-object schema. Clearly, therefore, it is vital to establish whether the conception has been as dominant as its opponents maintain. It is Heidegger, above all, who is responsible for the diagnosis that Cartesianism lies at the root of these problems. Heidegger was, though, hardly the first to worry about what might be implicit in the Cartesian model of the subject.

The initial reason for looking at Heidegger in relation to Friedrich Heinrich Jacobi (1743–1819) and Friedrich Wilhelm Joseph Schelling (1775–1854) is simply that Jacobi and Schelling propose related non-Cartesian models of subjectivity of the kind which Heidegger effectively claims do not exist in Western metaphysics. The basic model that is shared in varying ways by Jacobi and Schelling will, once recognized, prove to play a bigger role in modern philosophy than seems possible if one assumes that the Cartesian model is the dominant model of subjectivity.

To begin with, let us briefly reduce two models of subjectivity to simplified outlines, which we can refine in the course of the discussion. The most obvious way of characterizing the positions is expressed in two propositions: the Cartesian "I think, I am" and its inversion, "I am, I think." The inversion of Descartes's *cogito* can be squared, for example, with "eliminativist" materialism, which claims that what I am is really a physico-chemical, law-bound entity, so that my thinking is merely an epiphenomenon of the scientifically establishable material processes of which I consist. The obvious alternative, which is roughly compatible with the position of Descartes and with Kant's transcendental idealism, is to maintain that our ability to establish scientific laws is conditional upon our very ability to think at all, so that this thinking is epistemologically the only certainty we can invoke. It is possible to see both positions as involving the assumption of an absolute ground. In one case the I is grounded in the scientific explanation of its real physical substrate (of the kind one now finds in evolutionary epistemology); in the other scientific explanation itself is grounded in the I. Clearly the debate, stated in this way, is another version of the conflict between materialism and idealism that has played differing roles in much of the history of Western philosophy. At this point one must begin to consider historical manifestations of the question: otherwise we will end up repeating moves which have already been made in very sophisticated ways in the traditions we are about to consider.

Dissatisfaction with one historically specific version of the dichotomy between the mental and the physical is at the root of German idealism. Descartes's revelation of the irreducible dimension of self-consciousness in the *cogito* led, as is well known, via Spinoza's attempt to restore monism, to Kant's much more sophisticated dualism between the phenomenal realm of natural laws and the noumenal realm of freedom and things in themselves. German idealism took this dualism as its starting point in order to try to overcome—or even "deconstruct"—it. The complexity and subtlety of the idealist and romantic responses to the question of self-consciousness have often been ignored, usually by reducing the analysis of German idealism's reflections on subjectivity to a schematic version of Hegel's brilliant but flawed account of self-consciousness as reflection in the other in the *Phenomenology of Mind* and in his system as a whole.[1]

Once this reduction is undertaken it becomes easy for Heidegger to suggest that, despite all claims to the contrary, Hegel, the key representative of "Western metaphysics," overcomes what was in his time termed the "realism"/"idealism" divide on the side of idealism, thereby remaining within an essentially Cartesian perspective. This perception of German idealism is what permits Heidegger to make statements like the following from *The Basic Concepts of Metaphysics*:

> *Descartes* had the basic tendency to make philosophy into an absolute cognition . . . Here philosophy begins with *doubt* and it looks as if everything is put into question. But it only looks like this. Dasein, the I (the ego), is not put into question at all . . . A Cartesian basic attitude in philosophy cannot at all fundamentally question the Dasein of man . . . It, and with it all philosophizing in the modern period since Descartes, risks nothing at all. On the contrary the Cartesian basic attitude knows in advance, or thinks it knows, that everything can be proven and grounded in an absolutely strict and pure manner.[2]

Heidegger obviously includes the materialist and idealist positions sketched above in this characterization, which means that we cannot just see his argument as about failures in idealism which could be overcome by the physicalist inversion of the *cogito*. If physicalism is included in this verdict, it is, then, because it tries to prove and ground things in a strict manner, albeit from the other end of the divide between idealism and realism. Furthermore, however unfair it may be to Hegel to suggest that Heidegger's verdict applies to him as well, there is a case for maintaining that in one respect at least Heidegger's view may be valid, in that Hegel wishes to find a new way of grounding things absolutely by avoiding presuppositions which are not legitimated within the system as a whole. At the same time it is evident that Heidegger's view is clearly invalid for other strands of the development of German idealism and of German romantic philosophy, which cannot be subsumed into a Hegelian paradigm. It is here that Jacobi plays a vital initiating role.

Like the targets of Marx's and Engel's polemic in *The German Ideology* (who have tended to remain unread on the false assumption that they had been finally refuted by their antagonists), Jacobi has generally been assigned a very minor role in the development of modern German philosophy, as someone whose insights were only the prelude to others' more significant ideas. He was in his lifetime the target of often quite vicious attacks by Friedrich Schlegel, Schelling, and others. These attacks had some foundation, in that Jacobi was an inconsistent thinker who did not present his case systematically. The lack of system is, however, actually inherent in what he wished to argue anyway. Like Fichte, Jacobi had, in Dieter Henrich's phrase, an "essential insight."[3] The degree of vituperation directed against Jacobi should perhaps more appropriately be construed as an indication that he had glimpsed something very significant.

Jacobi makes it very clear where he stands with regard to Cartesianism by his declaration, in the introduction to the second edition of *On the Doctrine of Spinoza in Letters to Herr Moses Mendelssohn* (1789) that

> The decisive difference of my way of thinking from the ways of thinking of the majority of my philosophical contemporaries lies in the fact that I am not a *Cartesian*. I begin like the Orientals *(Morgenländer)* in their conjugations with the third, not with the first person, and I believe that one simply should not put the *Sum* after the *Cogito*. I needed a truth which was not *my* creature, but whose creature *I* would be.[4]

He had already claimed in a letter to George Forster in 1788 that Kant's system was "the carrying out to the extreme of the Cartesian statement *cogito ergo sum,* which I would prefer to invert."[5]

The "Pantheism dispute," the dispute occasioned by Lessing's avowal to Jacobi that he was essentially a Spinozist, which is documented in the *Letters to Mendelssohn*, is a key moment in the philosophical history of subjectivity. In this dispute the Enlightenment conception of the subject was abruptly confronted with arguments which made manifest key alternatives in the understanding of the subject in modern philosophy. Heidegger basically projects one side of this understanding—the rationalist side, which was represented by Moses Mendelssohn in the debate—onto the whole of modern philosophy, thereby failing to see the tension that already emerged in this period. The strand of modern philosophy that Heidegger underplays, and which was already becoming evident in aspects of the work of

Pascal (who was one of Jacobi's main points of reference), is linked in a complex manner to that strand of Western theology which rejected the key tenets of Enlightenment theology, such as the ontological proof of the existence of God, in favor of a creator-God who was not finally intelligible to our thinking.[6] One suspects that the ultimate philosophical failure of such theology, documented most obviously in the failure of Schelling's later *Philosophy of Revelation* to establish a philosophical religion, led to its philosophical arguments being forgotten, even though they do not require the theology for their force. In Jacobi's case, his unconvincing advocacy of a *"salto mortale,"* a leap of faith, as the appropriate response to his key philosophical argument should not lead us to dismiss the rest of what he says.[7]

Jacobi's rejection of Cartesianism relates to his general attitude to Enlightenment rationalism, which he sees as fundamentally flawed. Rationalism, as is well known, sees the necessities of thought evident in mathematics and logic as imbued in the very nature of things, so that the task of thinking is to construct the whole pattern of reality on the basis of these indisputable a priori foundations. Descartes's philosophy relies on establishing the link between the one certainty in thought he believed he had established—the fact that even if I doubt the reality of my thoughts I must yet exist in order to doubt that reality—with the "ontological" proof of the existence of God. This proof results from the claim that God's essence as "necessary being"— how could *God*'s existence be contingent?—must coincide with his existence, so that, as Mendelssohn put it: "I cannot separate existence from the ideas of the necessary being without destroying the idea itself. I must think concept and thing or drop the concept itself."[8] In both cases, therefore, necessities within *thought* are used to establish absolute foundations for the truth about the *world*, including the existence of what gives rise to or is the ground of the world. Clearly Kant was aware of the untenability of these arguments, as is evident in his refutation of the ontological proof. Jacobi, though, opens us another dimension of this issue in his account of Spinozism and elsewhere.

Against Spinozism's post-Cartesian claim to establish a complete philosophical system, Jacobi suggests that the claim rests on a "misunderstanding, which always has to be *sought* and artificially *produced* if one wishes to explain the *possibility* of the existence of a universe in any manner," which "necessarily ends by having to discover *conditions* of the *unconditioned*."[9] Cognitive explanation relies upon finding a thing's "condition," but such a procedure generates the problem that the explanation leads to a regress where each condition depends on another condition *ad infinitum*. By the way he makes this point Jacobi already establishes a version of what Heidegger will term "ontological difference," the difference between an account of something in terms of a particular science (in which the thing is seen as what Heidegger terms "*Seiendes*"), and the fact of that something's existing prior to its being subsumed into an explanatory account (which leads to what Heidegger terms "*Sein*," the very fact of the world's being intelligible at all). Jacobi's phrase concerning the "*conditions* of the *unconditioned*" signals his key thought in relation to Spinozism.

Henry Allison maintains that Spinoza conceives of "the causal relationship between God and the world in terms of the logical relationship between ground and consequent. God functions in Spinoza as the logical ground of things. The latter flow from his nature in precisely the same way as the conclusion of a valid argument follows from its premises."[10] Jacobi regards this as mistakenly seeking the "*condition* of the *unconditioned*," in that the ability to assert that there *is* such a relationship between the world and its ground fails to acknowledge a crucial difference: that between what he (inverting the more usual meanings) terms "ground" *(Grund)* and what he terms "cause" *(Ursache)*. The word *ground* derives for Jacobi from Leibniz's "principle of sufficient reason," the principle that *Nihil est sine ratione*, "nothing is without reason/cause/ground," which Jacobi reformulates as "'everything *dependent* is *dependent upon* something.'"[11] A ground is, then, a cause in a chain of other causes, which is therefore itself dependent on other causes and belongs to what Heidegger terms "*Seiendes*," in the sense of that which is explained in a theory. One uses grounds for "explanation," but this is not all we do in understanding the world, because *what* it is that we explain cannot be accounted for by theoretical judgements alone. Jacobi suggests, therefore, that "In my view the greatest achievement of the researcher is to disclose [*enthüllen*] and to reveal [*offenbaren*] *existence* [*Dasehn*] . . . Explanation is a means for him, a path to the goal, the proximate, but not the final purpose. His last purpose is that which cannot be explained: that which cannot be dissolved, the immediate, the simple."[12] Eventually this will lead Jacobi to his conception of a personal creator-God, who is understood as being the ultimate "cause," but it is the moves which he makes on the way to this conception that still matter in understanding the role of the subject in modern philosophy.

Jacobi claims that there is a necessity circularity involved in all truth claims: without this circularity all knowledge claims would be subject to the endless regress entailed in the world of "conditioned conditions." For Spinoza this regress leads us back to the grounding necessity of God and thence to the reconstruction of the totality of conditions in the system of the *Ethics*. Jacobi argues, though, that the fact of scientific knowledge means we must always rely on something immediate in order to make knowledge claims at all, rather than being able to understand the nature of God by understanding how everything is interdependent.[13] Jacobi terms this immediacy *"Glaube,"* "belief" or "faith." Belief, which Jacobi defines as "holding-as-true" *(Fürwahrhalten)*, cannot itself, therefore, be demonstrated, in that the condition of demonstrating conditions cannot itself be a condition in the same way as what it demonstrates.[14]

The function of "holding as true" in Jacobi has not always been adequately understood.[15] Frederick Beiser claims, for example, that Jacobi's notion of *Glaube* rests on a confusion of what we *know* to be true, such as the a priori axiomatic truths of geometry, and what we *believe* to be true.[16] Jacobi, though, like Heidegger, thinks "holding as true" *(Fürwahrhalten)* is prior even to axiomatic truths, in that the possibility of truth cannot be *demonstrated*. The idea that truth involves an "intuitive" aspect, as suggested in Jacobi's notion of 'belief,' is becoming more and more current in contemporary philosophy, forming a link of insights from the tradition at issue here, which are developed by Heidegger and others, to recent analytical (or postanalytical) philosophy. Donald Davidson, for example, talks of our "general and preanalytic notion of truth"[17] and of an "intuitive grasp we have of the concept,"[18] which means we cannot finally give a theoretical description of truth, because we always already rely upon it in order to describe or understand anything at all.

The real question for Jacobi, then, is the relationship between demonstration and what cannot be demonstrated, which is apparent in the problem of demonstrating the relationship of a priori truths to the world. We can generate an infinity of necessary mathematical truths from axioms, but this does not tell us how these truths relate to the world outside those axioms. In Jacobi's view "all the things which reason can bring out by dissection, linking, judging, concluding, and grasping again are simply things of nature, and reason itself belongs as a limited being with these things,"[19] or, as he puts it in his essay "On Transcendental Idealism" (where the stress is on "knowledge," in the sense of that which is *"Seiendes"*), "all our knowledge is nothing but a consciousness of linked determinations of our own self, on the basis of which one cannot infer to anything else."[20] One can logically assess the coherence of these determinations but this gives one no way of demonstrating how they correspond to what cannot be included within the system itself. This kind of argument has recently recurred as an objection to correspondence theories of truth. Davidson claims that all attempts to state a correspondence theory must invoke a frame of reference which can only finally legitimate itself via another frame of reference, not via a direct access to the object to which the truth is supposed to correspond. One is thereby led again to the question of how to escape another version of the regress which Jacobi identifies and which he, like Davidson, thinks can only be avoided by the intuitive prior fact of our understanding what it is for something to be true. Davidson suggests that

> The real objection to correspondence theories . . . is that there is nothing interesting or instructive to which true sentences might correspond. The point was made some time ago by C. I. Lewis; he challenged the correspondence theorist to locate the fact or part of reality, or of the world, to which a true sentence corresponds. One can locate individual objects, if the sentence happens to name or describe them, but even such a location makes sense relative only to a frame of reference, and so presumably the frame of reference must be included in whatever it is to which a true sentence corresponds.[21]

In Jacobi's view we do, though—and this is the crucial point for his subsequent influence—arrive at the fact that there must be more than the world of conditions (or frames of reference), when we realize the necessarily self-contained nature of any system of reason.[22] The attempt to come to terms with this fact is the basis of German idealism.

The history of German idealism can be understood as the attempt to find a way of philosophically articulating the "unconditioned," which is usually given the name of the "Absolute." Jacobi makes clear his relationship to the first major attempt to arrive at this articulation, Fichte's *Wissenschaftslehre*, in the public letter he wrote in 1799 to Fichte, on the occasion of the latter's having been accused of atheism in 1798 (an accusation which led to Fichte losing his academic job). Whereas Fichte can be seen as continuing the Cartesian model in his attempt to ground philosophy in the I, Jacobi goes so far as to say that his own position is no longer philosophy—he terms it *"Unphilosophie"*—because it has renounced the idea that knowledge can be finally grounded within a system. His conception of "philosophy" is, then, that of the self-grounding system, which he sees as inherently narcissistic:

> In everything and from everything [*In Allem und aus Allem*] the human mind, by making concepts, only seeks itself to find itself again; continually tearing itself away from the momentary, determined existence which, so to speak, wants to swallow it, in order to save its being-itself and being-in-itself, in order to carry on this being via its own activity and to do so with freedom.[23]

Whilst Jacobi agrees with Fichte that the "science of knowledge" should strive to be complete, he thinks the completion of the science of knowledge will reveal that what really matters lies outside the domain of "knowledge,"[24] whereas Fichte wishes it to be within "knowledge."

Jacobi's argument may end in a reversion to theism, but the basic move involved cannot be dismissed for this reason, in that it constitutes a critique of the "metaphysics of presence" of the kind which has played such a role in recent attacks on subjectivity in modern philosophy. Jacobi claims that

> A *pure*, that is a *thoroughly immanent* philosophy; a philosophy made only of *One* piece; a true *system* of reason is only possible in the Fichtean manner. Obviously everything must only be given in and through reason, in the I as I, in *egoity*, and already be contained in it, if pure reason alone should be able to deduce everything from out of itself alone.
>
> The foot of reason is listening [*Vernehmen*].—Pure reason is a listening which only listens to itself. Or: Pure reason listens only to itself.[25]

His view has been echoed, almost verbatim, by Jacques Derrida in his Heidegger-influenced critique of Hegel. For Hegel the metaphysical system is completed by the subject's realization of its final identity with what seemed other to it, the object world. The truth of the world turns out to be the world's thinking itself—hence the dictum that the "substance is subject." In Hegel's "Absolute Idea" thought and the world are finally shown to mirror each other via the explication of the moving structure of what he terms *Geist*. Such a realization will overcome both the apparent externality of the signifier to the mind and the problem of the signifier's relation to the signified. Language, which Hegel termed the "existence of *Geist*," would itself be revealed as the product of thought's "*self*-reflection." Derrida, echoing Jacobi, therefore terms metaphysics in the Hegelian sense the "absolute desire to hear oneself speaking."[26] Derrida's work can be read as an exploration of how this exteriority subverts the philosopher's desire for the demonstration of the identity of subject and object, for "self-presence." Clearly, then, Jacobi already undermines the notion of self-presence in a way which, if Derrida is right about Hegel, already provides some of the conceptual means to refute Hegel even before Hegel has developed his system.[27] It is this aspect of the history of modern philosophy which has too rarely been included in the attempts to understand the role of the subject in that history. A crucial aspect of that history is the understanding of the subject's relationship to truth, and here Jacobi makes a further significant move.

Jacobi distinguishes between what he terms *"Wahrheit,"* "truth," and *"das Wahre,"* "the true": Fichte seeks the former, he is interested in the latter. The distinction is a statement of ontological difference, which is very close to Heidegger: "truth" is "ontic," *Seiendes,* that which can be theorized within a science (or a "frame of reference"); "the true" approximates to *Sein,* the "ontological," in the sense suggested by Ernst Tugendhat, which interprets *Sein* as meaning "being true," which can be said of "disclosed" states of affairs but not of objects. Tugendhat suggests that the basic meaning of *Sein* in Heidegger is the "happening of clearing as such [*das . . . Lichtungsgeschehen als solches*]," the temporal disclosure *(Erschlossenheit)* which is the condition of possibility of the manifest world.[28] Thus Jacobi:

> I understand by the true something which is *before* and *outside* knowledge; which first gives a value to knowledge and to the *capacity* for knowledge, to *reason.*
>
> Listening presupposes what can be listened to; reasoned presupposes the *true:* it is the capacity to presuppose the true. A reason which does not presuppose the true is an abomination [*Unding*].[29]

Whereas Fichte famously maintains that "It is . . . the ground of explanation of all facts of empirical consciousness that before all positing in the I the I itself must previously be posited,"[30] thereby giving the I the founding role which he thought Kant had failed to demonstrate, Jacobi, in characterizing his theological notion of the "higher Being," already invokes a notion of "alterity" that will become familiar in the work of Rosenzweig, Levinas, and others who belong in the tradition which emerges from the work of the later Schelling.[31] Jacobi claims, "my motto and the motto of my reason is not: *I*; but, *more* than I! *Better* than I!—a completely *Other* [*ein ganz* Anderer]."[32] Running through all Jacobi's arguments, then, are the beginnings of a break with the notion of truth as correspondence or representation, and a break with the idea of a complete philosophical system which could reflect its truth back to itself.

The effect on his contemporaries of Jacobi's self-confessedly unsystematic insights was greater than has usually been appreciated. It will be clear when we now come to Schelling that the deconstructive work of Jacobi was often a point of reference for Schelling, even when he rejected Jacobi's conclusions. It should already be clear that the sense in Heidegger and his successors that they are inaugurating a wholly new philosophy beyond subjectivity can be relevant only to those aspects of modern philosophy which do not take on board the insights of Jacobi. This leaves open the space for a different conception of the subject in modern philosophy, which does not see it as an absolute epistemological foundation. Let us now therefore turn to Schelling, whose contribution to this different conception has rarely been appreciated.

Schelling, who was thoroughly aware of Jacobi's arguments, uses the same inversion of Cartesianism as Jacobi in 1795, albeit while still explicating the "I am" in a Fichtean manner.

> *I am!* My I contains a being which precedes all thinking and representing. It is by being thought and it is thought because it is; the reason for this is that it only is and is only thought to the extent to which it thinks *itself*, and it only thinks itself because it is. It produces itself by its own thinking—by an absolute causality.[33]

Schelling will equivocate for a long time over his relationship to Fichte, but he will eventually reject Fichte's position for reasons already apparent in the views of Jacobi we have already examined.[34] This conception of the I, which transfers a theological determination, in the form of the *causa sui*, into the nature of the I, confirms Heidegger's diagnosis of Cartesianism which we considered at the beginning. In this view the I regards its own projections as revelations of being, and the world becomes merely an object present to a subject. Heidegger's objections to this kind of conception should now sound very reminiscent of Jacobi:

> [E]ven if we wanted to allow that the world means the subjective form of the human conception of being in itself [*des Seienden an sich*], so that there is no being in itself and everything is played out in the subject, then, along with many other things one would still have to ask: How does man arrive at all even at just a subjective conception of being [*des Seienden*], if being were not previously open [*offenbar*] for him in order for him to do this? What about this openness of being as such?[35]

As is well known, the question of the openness of being leads Heidegger to language and to conceptions of subjectivity which contemporary philosophy has rethought variously in terms of formal semantics (Tugendhat), intersubjectivity (Habermas), the subversion of the subject through its insertion into the symbolic order (Lacan), or the subject's being an effect of the "general text" (Derrida). The common target is the kind of philosophical narcissism we saw exposed by Jacobi.

I have shown in much more detail elsewhere how Schelling moves away from the narcissistic paradigm of the subject.[36] Here I want to emphasize certain aspects of Schelling's exploration of subjectivity which are relevant to the Heideggerian critique of metaphysics.[37] The significance of Schelling's objections to Fichte, which lead him away from a Cartesian model, can be suggested by the fact that they contain startlingly "green" pronouncements of a kind later to be found in Horkheimer and Adorno's *Dialectic of Enlightenment*. In 1806 Schelling attacks Fichte in the following terms, suggesting an evident change of perspective with regard to the nature of the subject:

> [I]n the last analysis what is the essence of his whole opinion of nature? It is this: that nature should be used . . . and that it is there for nothing more than to be used; his principle, according to which he looks at nature, is the economic teleological principle.[38]

Schelling makes the reasons for linking Cartesianism to such issues clearer in his claim that: "The *I* think, *I* am, is, since Descartes, the basic mistake of all knowledge [*Erkenntnis*]; thinking is not my thinking, and being is not my being, for everything is only of God or of the totality."[39] The point is that we cannot define our relationship to nature in terms of nature as the object which is opposed to ourselves as knowing subjects, because this leads back to the kind of regress we have already seen criticized by Jacobi—how can we encompass our relation to the Other of nature without it just becoming a projection of our thinking? This is not just a metaphysical conundrum, as the links of these ideas to the most diverse areas of modern thought can suggest.

Such thinking has, for example, recently even appeared on the agenda of modern physics. Schelling's basic thought has recurred in recent reflections on the "Anthropic Principle," as Barrow and Tipler suggest:

> [T]he Anthropic Principle shows that the observed structure of the Universe is restricted by the fact that we are observing its structure; by the fact that, so to speak, the Universe is observing itself.[40]

Wolfram Hogrebe makes the basic problem most clear when he says in relation to Schelling and the anthropic principle:

> However plausible it initially seems to be that the world which has produced a knowing being [Wesen] has to be thought in such a way that the producing forces are in the last analysis also capable of such a result, it is still problematic that these forces are supposed to be of the same kind as what they have produced.[41]

A systematic scientific view can provide no way of understanding how to move conceptually from differentiated natural forces to that which can be *aware* both of natural forces and of itself. The scientific theory cannot give an explanation of the identity of such forces because what is required for that identification would need to be of a higher order than the two aspects which are identified. This leads to the demand for what Jacobi called the "unconditioned," or *"Seyn,"* which Schelling usually terms the "Absolute," and which Fichte, as we saw, tried to locate in the I. As Schelling realized, though, how could the Absolute then know *itself* if it is divided from itself, in that it must include both sides of what is divided if it is to be absolute at all? Once the dominant Cartesian subject has been undermined, the subject-object relationship cannot be understood from the side of the subject alone, and the subject cannot be thought of in isolation from the nature of which it is an aspect. The universe of the early Schelling

is not, therefore, as is usually assumed, essentially spiritual or vitalis-
tic: it is neither "ideal" nor "real" but the link of the two. The real
question is how this link could ever be articulated in philosophy. It is
Schelling's ultimate failure to do this which takes him beyond the
purview of Western metaphysics, conceived of in terms of the model
of "reflection," of the self-grounding system.

Related questions seem to concern Heidegger, at least until the
Kehre: the missing third part of *Being and Time* was to have shown how
one can move from the understanding of Dasein to the understanding
of being, given the fact that Dasein is always already "in the world"
and thus not enclosed in a Cartesian interiority of consciousness.
However, Heidegger begins to turn away from the notion of Dasein
and increasingly sees the main obstacle to the understanding of being
in the dominance of subjectivity in modern philosophy. Heidegger's
move is mirrored, as we shall see in a moment, in the different read-
ings of Schelling he gives between the 1936 lectures on Schelling's
Philosophical Investigations on the Essence of Human Freedom and lectures
on the same text he gave in 1941. The intraphilosophical reasons for
his differing views are apparent when, in the work on Nietzsche of
much the same period, Heidegger claims the problem with *Being and
Time* was that it failed to understand the question of being:

> The basis for the non-understanding lies . . . in the ineradicable,
> increasingly fixed habituation to the modern way of thinking:
> man is thought of as subject . . . the question of being as such
> stands outside the subject-object relationship.[42]

Once again this is congruent with Jacobi's reflections on Fichte's system, in that the ground of the subject-object relationship cannot be
established from within that relationship. Metaphysics now culminates
for Heidegger in the *"absolute subjectivity of the Will to Power"*[43] "only
with the beginning of the completion of metaphysics can the complete, absolute domination of being [*das Seiende*] which is no longer
disturbed and confused by anything being."[44] The vital issue is his
understanding of ontological difference:

> The difference of beings and being shows itself as the same from
> which all metaphysics emerges, which admittedly metaphysics
> also eludes simultaneously in emerging, that same which it leaves
> behind itself and outside of its territory, as what it no longer

specially thinks about and no longer needs to think about. The difference of being and beings makes possible all naming and experiencing and grasping of beings as such . . . The difference of being and beings is the unknown and ungrounded, but yet always assumed, ground of metaphysics . . . all criticism of ontology within metaphysics only testifies to the always increasing *avoidance* of this unknown ground.[45]

As we have seen, though, such questions were not unusual, even within the metaphysical traditions to which Jacobi and Schelling belong.

Here is Schelling in 1804, discussing the statement of identity, A = A,[46] in which the identity of the subject and the object term in the proposition is seen as dependent upon the prior ground of "absolute identity," which cannot be known in the sense that a particular determinate aspect of the world can be known, because it is the ontological condition of possibility of such knowledge:

> The *sameness* [*Gleichheit*] does not exist via the subject and the object, but rather the other way round, only insofar as the sameness is, *that is, only insofar as both are one and the same,* are subject and object as well.[47]

The concern with what Heidegger terms the "unknown ground" even begins to appear, for example, in 1800 in Schelling's Fichte-influenced *System of Transcendental Idealism,* when he claims:

> The question how our concepts agree with objects is meaningless from a transcendental perspective, to the extent that the question presupposes an original difference of the two. The object and its concept, and, conversely, concept and object are one and the same beyond consciousness, and the separation of the two only arises simultaneously when consciousness arises. A philosophy which begins with consciousness will therefore never be able to explain that agreement, nor can it be explained at all without original identity, whose principle necessarily lies beyond consciousness.[48]

Schelling will continue to think he can give an account of this principle in some manner, though he will ultimately fail to do so. In the case of the *System of Transcendental Idealism* he tries to reveal the "unknown ground" via the work of art, which shows what philosophy cannot say.[49] Most significantly, though, he only briefly entertains the Hegelian way of overcoming the problem within philosophy, which for thinkers like Derrida is essentially coterminous with Western metaphysics.[50] Even in the identity philosophy, where he at times comes closest to Hegel, Schelling often regards the Absolute as the ground of the temporality of the world, not as that which will sublate all the negations of particular knowledge into itself at the end, within the philosophical system. The "absolute identity" of the "real" and the "ideal" prevents the particular from being in an absolute way *qua* particular: "the totality posits or intuits *itself*, by not-positing, not-intuiting the particular."[51] This, though, is the ontological basis of temporality, in that "time is itself nothing but *the totality appearing in opposition to the particular life of things*,"[52] rather than the route, via the "negation of negation," to the "Absolute Idea."

Well before Heidegger Schelling, like Jacobi, rejects all "subjectifying" (*Subjektivieren*) of philosophy.[53] Like Heidegger he rejects philosophy which operates from a division of subject and object and which leads to domination via the subject's one-sided attempt to overcome that division. He thereby shows ways towards the refutation of the conception of thought as representation which gives rise to all the insoluble problems involved in establishing a place from which it is possible to say how the mental representation relates to what it represents or how a proposition corresponds to "reality." In many ways, then, Schelling, while ultimately trying to remain within Western metaphysics, and while generally using its vocabulary, is, like Jacobi, already located outside its most prevalent structures.

Heidegger himself engages directly only with the next phase of Schelling's philosophy after the identity philosophy, which is instigated by the *Philosophical Investigations on the Essence of Human Freedom and Connected Subjects* of 1809 (FS), on which Heidegger lectures in 1936 and again in 1941. Heidegger's analysis is based on the tension that develops during this phase of Schelling's philosophy, between "freedom, as the beginning which needs no grounding [i.e., which is itself the "ungrounded" ground], and system, as a closed context of grounding/justification [*Begründungszusammenhang*]."[54] Schelling's initial target in the FS is pantheism, which he sees as entailing fatalism. The conflict between the system and that which cannot be grounded within the system was, as we saw, at the heart of Jacobi's work: it was, of course, his opposition to the Spinozist system which led him to his view. In the 1936 text on the FS Heidegger regards Schelling as having moved beyond idealism, which Heidegger defines in terms of the I: "Egoity is all being [*alles Seiende*]; and all being is egoity," so that being is interpreted via thinking, as Jacobi suggested of Kant and Fichte. The basis of Schelling's essay, which takes him beyond idealism, is the notion of "will" *(Wollen)*, which is "primal being" *(Urseyn)*. Central to the FS is the freedom to do good *and* evil.[55] This freedom is not Kant's practical reason, which postulates our higher purpose as the higher aspect of nature, but rather freedom to take on all that we are as beings who are always already driven by the same forces as nature, the ground, and have the capacity for good and evil. For Schelling freedom means having to come to terms with that in which we are grounded: "will" therefore plays a similar structural role to Freud's id. The sense that the subject is fully transparent to itself, which is necessary for a Cartesian metaphysics is, therefore, clearly undermined, which is why Heidegger initially has a favorable view of Schelling's text.

However, in the recently published 1941 text on the FS, and in the notes on Schelling from the same period published in his Schelling book, Heidegger comes to see the FS as the "culmination [*Gipfel*] of German idealism." The attention to evil in the FS is an "implicit" attempt "via evil to take the negativity developed in Hegel's *Phenomenology* beyond the "ideal" consciousness-based essence of the distinction between subject and object."[56] Negativity in Hegel still remains within the scheme of self-presence, as that which depends upon the movement of the subject, because it is itself negated at the end in the positive Absolute. The fact that evil in the FS is spirit, because of its inextricable relationship to freedom, means "spirit cannot be the Highest. (Against Hegel; the ground cannot be sublated [*die Unaufhebbarkeit des Grundes*])."[57] Schelling's idea of evil relies, as we saw, on the notion that what impels thinking is grounded in nature. The activity of "reason," which itself initially depends upon the ground, can become the (ultimately futile) attempt to overcome that in which it is grounded by subordinating it to itself.[58] Schelling claims in the *Stuttgart Private Lectures* of the same period as the FS that "Evil is in a certain respect completely spiritual *(das reinste Geistige)*, for it carries on the most emphatic war against all *being*, indeed it would like to negate [*aufheben*] the ground of creation."[59]

What Heidegger does not seem to contemplate is that if in the FS the relationship between subject and object is not reflexive, in that the ground cannot finally be *"aufgehoben"* into reflexive identity in the dialectic, then the straightforwardly metaphysical understanding of a subject which is mirrored in the world's intelligibility, that he sees as still present in the Schelling of the *FS* and beyond, becomes hard to sustain, even though Schelling himself may make great efforts to sustain it. Heidegger claims the way subjectivity is understood by Schelling makes subjectivity into the precursor of Nietzsche's "will to power," the will to overcome the other in the name of the same. Schelling's argument can surely be read, though, as a *warning* against the potential for domination of subjectivity, which as "evil" tries to obliterate its relationship to the ground upon which it is dependent. The manifestations of this domination in modern science and technology's relationship to being—of the kind Schelling warned against in his critique of Fichte—are, after all, aspects of what Heidegger uses to suggest how far modern metaphysics has gone in the forgetting of being. In this way Schelling's "evil" could, in Heidegger's terms, more accurately be equated with metaphysics itself.

In the 1941 notes on Schelling, Heidegger claims that traditional ontology "exhausts itself by considering the essence of being to be already established and unquestionable,"[60] which means that in idealism being is thought of simply as "absolute subjectivity," which is reflexively present to itself. According to Heidegger subjectivity in Schelling always has within it the sense of a return to an essence that is achieved via its returning to itself. Being thus becomes merely "Idea."[62] Schelling therefore becomes incorporated into the history of Western metaphysics, which Heidegger now equates with the subjectification of being that begins with Descartes, and Schelling therefore belongs together with Hegel. Heidegger insists that "despite all, basically the same passion for the same"[63]—the "passion" for self-presence, for a reason which, in Jacobi's phrase, "listens only to itself"—is supposedly there in both Hegel and Schelling. In Schelling "being [*das Sein*] itself is such that what is there [*das Seiende*] differentiates *itself*."[64] The question is how to understand the differentiation, the disclosure of being, without enclosing it in an a priori philosophical system which, like that of Hegel, can be complete because it is constituted by *self*-differentiation. Thinking being in terms of "willing," Heidegger claims, fails to understand what he now terms the "*Ereignis*," the "event" or "appropriation," which cannot be understood from within a metaphysical system. Despite the massive increase in depth, sophistication, and cogency, the basic thought of Jacobi once again appears in Heidegger's destruction of metaphysics. Is this, though, an adequate account of Schelling's conception of the subject's relationship to being? Heidegger's interpretation of the idea of 'primal being' as willing is already problematic, as Dieter Thomä suggests,[65] because it conceals the fact that the relationship of "willing" to the human subject may not be transparent to that subject.

The obvious way to assess this question is to examine Schelling's own extended account of Descartes metaphysics in the Munich Lectures of probably 1833–34, which form the keystone of Schelling's later attempts at a philosophical system, but to which like the rest of Schelling's later work, Heidegger seems never to pay any attention.[66] The following analysis of the *cogito* should already suffice to indicate how far Schelling has moved beyond a straightforwardly Idealist paradigm:

> [T]his *Sum cogitans* cannot . . . mean that it is as though I were *nothing* but thinking, or as if thinking were the substance of my being . . . Thinking is, therefore, only a determination or way of being . . . The *sum* which is contained in the *cogito* is, therefore, only *sum qua cogitans*, I am as thinking, that is, in that specific way of being which is called thinking . . . The *sum* that is contained in the *cogito* does not, then, have the significance of an absolute I am, but only of an "I am *in one way or another*" namely as just thinking, in that way of being which one calls thinking.[67]

The argument can be taken a stage further: the *cogito* itself is, as such, no more absolute than the ideas I have of things, which, even if they do not exist absolutely, are *"not not at all,"* in that they must, in the same way as the *I, be* in thinking if they are to be doubted: "For what is not at all in any way also cannot be doubted."[68] As we have already seen, then, Schelling make it clear that neither the idealist nor the realist account is adequate to the understanding of subjectivity.

Schelling further "decentres" the Cartesian subject by exploring one of the key insights into subjectivity at which Fichte was probably the first to arrive, and which was developed by the Romantics:[69]

> I think is, therefore, in truth in no way something immediate, it only emerges via the reflection which directs itself at the thinking in me, this thinking, by the way, also carries on independently of the thinking that reflects upon it . . . Indeed, true thinking must even be independent of the subject that reflects upon it,

in other words, it will think all the more truly the less the subject interferes with it.[70]

Schelling, like Fichte and Novalis before him and Sartre after him, is aware of the problem of how the subject could recognize itself in reflection, either upon itself or in an other, if it did not already have a pre-reflexive familiarity with itself which is prior to any kind of cognitive self-*re*-cognition. It is this kind of ontological priority which, Schelling realizes, is the real challenge to idealist philosophy, in that the self cannot even make its own being transparent to itself. Throughout his reflections on ontology in this period Schelling rejects the Cartesian model of subjectivity, but he equally rejects the Spinozist fatalism which Jacobi had made so central to the self-understanding of modern philosophy. He rejects Spinozism precisely because it gives no way of understanding how and why it is that the world becomes intelligible to us as subjects, but he does not therefore assume that he can adopt Hegel's version of the "substance is subject," which was intended to get over the Spinozist problem. As I have shown elsewhere, Schelling thinks that Hegel's position is ultimately another version of the self-contained model, which fails to account for the open-ended nature of historical reality.[71]

Heidegger's historical judgement on the question of subjectivity is, then, clearly untenable. There is no space here to consider whether Heidegger himself arrives at an adequate account of subjectivity before or after the *Kehre*.[72] What is clear is that it is no longer appropriate to work with the historical model Heidegger proposes. The question is how it is to be replaced. To conclude I want to suggest that Schelling's accounts of the subject may offer resources which Heidegger's increasing repression of subjectivity as an issue for philosophy, in favor of the history of being, has often obscured. Once one has given up the notion of the subject as any kind of absolute metaphysical ground, it becomes vital that one's account of the subject be adequate to the density and complexity of our modern self-understanding. The destruction of the metaphysics of presence, which, as we have seen, is already substantially undertaken in the most powerful philosophical arguments of Jacobi and Schelling, does not obviate the need for a metaphysics of subjectivity which would, for example, be an adequate response to the liberation of subjective expression characteristic of the greatest modern art, for example, from Beethoven to Mahler to Schönberg and beyond. Neither does revealing the failure of the Cartesian or Hegelian understanding of the subject free us from the duty to confront the ethical problems of subjecthood in modern secular societies. Even the question of truth cannot simply be divorced from the question of subjectivity, once one assumes, as key traditions in post-Kantian hermeneutics (and some recent American philosophy does), that all judgements of truth values inherently involve interpretation.[73] This is especially the case if Heidegger's and Gadamer's conceptions of the role of the subject in interpretation cannot be sustained, either historically or methodologically.[74]

Productive thinking about subjecthood must attempt to find ways of coming to terms with finitude and suffering which do not revert to the illusions of self-transparent subjectivity. What Schelling offers, at an admittedly high level of abstraction, turns out to be surprisingly productive at a more immediate level of self-understanding, which can feed into new developments in psychoanalysis, aesthetics, and other areas of contemporary theory. Schelling's subjects have always been preceded (what he terms *"präveniert"*) by a being which they must assume, but which can never be absolutely their own. The basic structure with which Schelling comes to work is of a being which must be conceived of as *"unvordenklich"* (unprethinkable, being before all thinking) which must yet move beyond this being if the openness of the world is to be understood: "The nature of this necessary existence . . . brings with it that it exists *actu* before it knows itself," it "can do nothing about it being."[75] This works both at the level of the question of being and of the individual subject, though the two should not be simply reduced to each other in the manner of some of his earlier philosophy. The crucial fact about subjectivity is its ability to tear itself away from *"unprethinkable* being" and to "begin a free being. The higher the power of this self-relinquishing and externalization (making objective of involuntary being), the more productive, more independent, the more divine man appears. *Freeing oneself from oneself* is the task of all *Bildung*."[76]

Lest this sound like a return to the omnipotent subject of the metaphysics of presence, it should be stressed that Schelling repeatedly insists that "primal being" can never by finally overcome. This is the challenge to the subject: namely, to come to terms not only with its own sense of potential but also with the ground it can never finally leave behind. Though the subject attempts a narcissistic self-identification it must always fail to achieve it.

But the subject can never grasp itself as what it Is, for precisely in attracting itself [*im sich-Anziehen*] it *becomes* an other, this is the basic contradiction, we can say the misfortune in all being—for either it *leaves* itself, then it is as nothing, or it attracts itself, then it is an other and not identical with itself. No longer uninhibited by being as before, but that which has inhibited itself with being, it itself feels this being as alien [*zugezogenes*] and thus contingent. Note here that correspondingly the first beginning is expressly thought of as a contingent beginning. The first *being*, this *primum existens*, as I have called it, is, therefore, at the same time the first contingency (original coincidence). This whole construction therefore begins with the first contingency—which is not identical with itself—it begins with a *dissonance*, and must begin this way.[77]

Though Schelling is unsuccessful in his attempt to show via his theology how the subject's life and struggle for identity can be finally understood, his account of how nonidentity is inescapable for the individual subject suggests the challenge of this prototypically modern thinker to any postmodern attempt to deconstruct the philosophy of subjectivity.[78] In the perspective I have tried to establish via the analysis of Jacobi and Schelling, the evident complexity and diversity of thinking about subjectivity in the traditions of modern philosophy makes the radical break with the past claimed by much recent Heidegger-influenced theory appear more suspect. It begins to look like a repression of those aspects of self-consciousness which resist being reduced to the larger story of "Western metaphysics" than a liberation from past illusions of omnipotence. The most obvious contemporary necessity, given the inescapability of each individual's struggle for identity, is to avoid the assumption that the search for forms of self-understanding which enables us to live with our inherent divisions, of the kind most notably apparent in the greatest modern art and in theorists of that art like Adorno, is necessarily an attempt to restore the metaphysics of presence. Retracing the history of the largely forgotten critical responses to subjectivity in modern philosophy can help construct a different philosophical agenda, which can begin to do justice to the subject's inevitable "lack of being" from which, as Schelling shows, there is no final escape. Such a reconsideration of ourselves may turn out to be politically as well as philosophically vital.

Seven

Identity and Subjectivity

Manfred Frank

I

One of the fundamental features of modern philosophy is the wide-spread conviction that philosophy is a form of thought which begins from the certainty of self-consciousness. This form of thought, which was introduced by the path-breaking work of Descartes and universal-ized by Leibniz, is said to have reached its highpoint—after an empiri-cist intermezzo—in the philosophy of Kant and especially in that of Fichte. For in these thinkers subjectivity becomes the principle of a de-ductively established system of knowledge, which gains its distinctive kind of objective groundedness through its derivability from the self.

Heidegger and, following him, many thinkers within the spec-trum of poststructuralism, have claimed that one can view this "seizure of power" by subjectivity as the culmination of the forgetfulness of Being or of *différance* which characterizes the West. But what does this seizure of power consist in? It consists in the fact that subjectivity, as the locus of a transparency accessible to itself, is also the origin of all those rules and laws through which the objective world becomes intelligible to us. The mastery of rules guarantees the predictability of future prop-erties of the domain of objects, with the result that—as Descartes says—by means of this knowledge drawn from the subject "we would be able to make ourselves masters and possessors of nature."[1] This viewpoint makes clear to what extent natural science, which is supposedly a value-neutral knowledge of the rules which make nature intelligible (in other words, domesticated through prognosis), derives from the same genea-logical source as technology—the effective use of such knowledge with a view to the domination of nature. The celebrated formulations of Francis Bacon, which identify scientifically acquired knowledge with power, simply ratify the inner connection between scientific progress and the violence of an ever-increasing domination of nature.

The origin of this connection can be traced to the epistemological turning-point which Heideggerians describe as "metaphysics," an expression whose meaning can be given a preliminary gloss as "objectifying thinking." According to this type of thinking, the subject is related through "re-presentation" (*vor-stellend*) to that which is opaque and different from itself—the world of objects. Whatever is intelligible in objects is merely a fulguration of the subject's own transparency. "Nothing is more comprehensible than the concept [*Nichts ist begreiflicher als der Begriff*]," says Schelling mockingly of rationalistic philosophy. "The incomprehensible first begins with that which is opposed to the concept. But precisely for this reason it is only in the incomprehensible that philosophy finds the means of its own more intense development."[2] In this way nature as a whole takes on the status of an indifferent material available for theoretical unveiling and practical use and exploitation.

Current assumptions (which, as we shall see, are not entirely unfounded) make Fichte the chief scapegoat for this trend. And since early Jena romanticism, Schelling included, is widely understood in terms of its relation to Fichte, it has become common to include all the thinkers concerned under the heading of the "philosophy of the subject" (*Subjektphilosophie*) and to consider them as complicit with the culminating blindness of metaphysics.

However this is in many respects misleading. For if subjectivity must be considered a major theme of early romanticism, this is only in the sense that the first generation of Fichte's pupils (to whom Hölderlin also belonged) shared the conviction the subjectivity must be denied the status of an absolute. Subjectivity should rather be grasped as a phenomenon which becomes accessible to itself only under a condition over which it has no control. At the same time, however, this dependency of self-consciousness must itself be explained in terms of the structure of self-consciousness. What we normally call "self-consciousness" is the result of a turning back of consciousness on itself. The technical philosophical term for this turning back is *reflection*. In reflection one and the same thing is subject and object of a self-mirroring process. But how am I supposed to acquire knowledge of the fact that I am—in an irreducible sense—*one* from this duality of image and reflection? And yet on the other hand how can I doubt that this unity is an essential feature of my conscious life? To resolve this dilemma self-consciousness must be seen as deriving from a seamless (or irreflexive) identity which is no longer dissolvable into conceptual relations and which the generation of the early Romantics, following Friedrich Heinrich Jacobi, refer to as "*Seyn.*"

Once this conclusion has been drawn, then identity, rather than subjectivity, becomes the cornerstone of philosophy. But since identity was meant to imply not simply the trivial self-identity of a single thing but rather an authentic relation between different things, it became necessary to anchor the subject, in the equation constituting its identity, in a foundation which would not merely have the form of the subject once again. For Schelling this foundation is nature, and nature as such continues to be an object for the subject. But, in contrast to previous metaphysical thought, nature comes into view in Schelling's work as the subject's *own* other. Nature is bound to the subject through identity, and because of this the subject can indeed becomes alienated from it, through historical processes which Marx and Heidegger merely described in different ways. However, the subject never finds itself opposed to anything other in nature than its own fundamental and indestructible identity with nature. The utopia of the young Marx, the thought of the humanity of nature and the naturalness of humanity finds its model in Schelling's striving "to demonstrate both the objectivity of mind and the subjectivity of matter."[3] This indeed was the "candid thought of the young Schelling."[4] A mode of thought which views nature itself as subject, and subjectivity as naturelike, has transcended the oppositions of objectifying thought and can simultaneously render these comprehensible as abstracted forms of a conceptuality which has not yet secured its own true principle. This principle is no longer that of the subject alone, but rather of its identity with the object. This identity now becomes the real challenge to thought.

II

The challenge arises from the fact that the thought of identity is weighed down by powerful traditions. In working our way through them, it appears that an initial pause should be made when we get to Leibniz. For it was Leibniz who first grasped the problem of identity as the fundamental question which indeed it is and provided two answers to it which belong to different discourses—the first logical, the second metaphysical (or ontological). In the first, reflection focuses on the form of the proposition, in the second on objects in the real world. Following the first approach, Leibniz claims that two expressions are identical which can be substituted for each other in a proposition without impairing its truth value (*salva veritate*).[5] The second approach, based on what is known as the "principle of indiscernables," is ontological and is concerned with substances in the world. The principle declares that "il n'est pas vray que deux substances se ressemblent entierement (c'est-à-dire selon toutes leurs dénominations intrinsèques, et soyent différentes *solo numero*."[6] These two applications of the principle of identity—the logical and the ontological—must be kept carefully disentangled; indeed it is even doubtful whether we have here two versions of the same law, as many assume.

David Hume was the first to express doubts about this when he insisted that, in the expression "identical with itself," the object referred to by the reflexive pronoun must differ in some respect from that referred to just before (otherwise the judgement would say the same thing twice). Kant drew significant consequences from this objection—which eventually results in the undecidability of identity—for the status of the "numerical identity" of the principle of his theoretical philosophy, namely, self-consciousness. Both Hume and Kant suggest that the principle of identity should be separated from the principle of contradiction, the former of being of an ontological and the latter of a logical character. The latter states that one cannot simultaneously affirm and deny something (or that one cannot posit something at the same time as its opposite); the former asserts that something cannot be called "identical" when its properties alter. The logical rule is self-explanatory, but according to the ontological rule identity is a true relationship between two things which are not obviously one and the same. In this case, to identify something with something means to acquire a genuine item of knowledge, whereas judging without contradiction is something self-evident. Thus identity—in contrast to the logical absence of contradiction—appears to include a kind of difference. And here lies the problem which will concern us in this chapter.

This problem is first expressed, in the modern tradition deriving from Leibniz, as a paradox. On the one hand, in order to speak meaningfully of identity, we must be able to distinguish between distinct states of affairs. On the other hand, the meaning of "identity" is taken in the strongest possible sense, with a consequent elimination of all differences between states of affairs. Accordingly, the paradox can be described in the following way:

It is obvious that propositions of the form "A = A" are trivial and uninformative, whereas propositions of the form "A = B" ("Monte Cervino is the Matterhorn," "Everest = Gaurisankar," "The evening star is the same planet as the morning star," etc.) are nontrivial and extend our knowledge when they are true. But if A and B are identical, and if identity is taken as a relation which holds between something and itself, then it becomes impossible to explain how the obvious difference in the cognitive content of the two sentences is possible. There seems to be only one escape from this paradox, which Leibniz took when he declared, in effect by fiat, that all true sentences are analytical sentences.[7]

The "awkward consequences which escape brings with it," as Michael Wolff calls them, can be avoided if the over-strict criterion of identity is loosened up. Frege had something similar in mind when he understood identity, not as the sterile self-relation of one relatum (of a thing "merely" with itself), but rather as a relation between different names for a thing. Quine considers this solution to be the only possible one. According to this view the two characterizations "morning star" and "evening star" would have the same relation to an object or reference (*Bedeutung*), but different meanings (*Sinn*). However this solution is in turn unsatisfactory, because it results in an infinite regress:

> Identity is explained as identity of reference: if A = B, then according to Frege it is, not two different things, but rather the *references* of "A" and "B" which are supposed to be identical. But this has the result that the-reference-of-A = the-reference-of-B. The identity of the reference of "A" with the reference of "B," however, can now in turn only be explained through the identity of the references of the expressions "reference of A" and "reference of B," and so on *ad infinitum*. Furthermore, the infinite regress cannot be avoided through an altered interpretation of the word *reference*. It comes about regardless of whether we understand the reference of the expressions "A," "B," "the reference of A," etc. as the thing indicated in the relevant expression, or whether we understand by this an entity *sui generis* which is located in the intermediate domain between signs and things signified.[8]

Thus the conception of identity as a connection of two relata seems to fail in the same way as the view that it consists "merely" in the connection of one relatum to itself. And yet we seem unable to do without assumptions of identity in our everyday living and speaking—for our acts of predication are directed towards identified things (otherwise we would be speaking of "nothing"), and their identity over time—for example, that of our own person—is a central focus of our concern and our reflective lives. In other words, we abstractly presuppose that every object is identical with itself, but in our speaking, which contains a superfluity of descriptions, we very often cannot tell if these descriptions stand for the same thing (the identity of things is very often unknown to us).

The problem arises when one tries to chose between the relational and irrelational conception of identity, finding the first contentless and the second paradoxical. As far as I am aware, Schelling was the first thinker of the modern period to suspect that this perplexity might have a *fundamentum in re*, which would then make it an appealing option to assume both oneness and difference, and thereby something like *self-differentiation*, in the thought of identity. By this route we find ourselves confronted with the logico-semantically opaque formulation "identity of identity and nonidentity," which Hegel introduced into the discourse of philosophy in the *Differenzschrift*, in order to bring out what was specific to Schelling's approach. But is this formula any less paradoxical than its (relational and irrelational) predecessors?

Schelling's philosophy of identity (*Identitätsphiosophie*) was centrally concerned with removing this suspicion. This philosophy seeks to grasp 'identity' in such a way that it becomes a relation in which two contrary, and indeed contradictory, predicates (A and not-A) apply to the same thing. In this way it takes up the Humean challenge, which suggested that to identify a thing with itself presupposes that it has altered. But whereas Hume's argument results in a sceptical denial of the possibility of identity being ascertained at all, Schelling tries to show that the thought of alteration can emerge at all only against the backdrop of the thought of the unity of the selfsame. Only of that which *could be* something *else* does it make sense to say that it is the *same* as itself. "Concealed beneath self-identity," says Schelling in the *Einleitung in die Philosophie*, "is the capacity to become different from oneself."[9]

There are indeed precedents for this apparently speculative thought-experiment, one of which was considered by Leibniz, while the other was put forward by Karl Leonhard Reinhold and then systematically exploited by Fichte in 1794, in section three of the first *Wissenschaftslehre*. Space, or rather the lack of it, prohibits me from exploring these precedents here, but they do provide the basis for Schelling's mature philosophy, which becomes recognizable from around 1800. Although the conception of identity at work here has resulted in this phase of Schelling's philosophy as a whole being referred to—from very early on—as the "system of absolute identity" (*absolutes Identitätssystem*),[10] the structure of this conception has never really been clarified, or even thoroughly investigated. This is all the more surprising when one considers that Schelling's "System of Philosophy" is conceived entirely in terms of this conception and that it was only on this basis that he could hope to render more fluid the rigid forms of the nature-subjectivity dualism bequeathed by earlier European philosophy.

III

Although I attempt in what follows to make these interrelations more perspicuous, I do so in the regretful knowledge that I will be able to convey only a little of the unique atmosphere of freshness and energy, often also of provocation, which pervades Schelling's bold speculations. Without this, one might easily regard them as having lost all contact with so-called concrete reality. Schelling was indeed convinced that his *Identitätsphilosophie* prepared the way for a break with a fundamental prejudice of modern thought, and perhaps of Western thought in general—the paradigm of the subject opposed to the object, or of the mind which holds nature at a distance and believes itself entitled to mould it according to its own plans, to violate its secrets, and to exploit it as spiritless raw material. For Schelling nature is, not the other of mind, if we understand by "mind" the absolute identity of the real and the ideal, but rather only the other of a *relative* difference from the subject, which is always already subsumed by *absolute* identity. This conception implies neither a *humiliation of nature* nor a *reduction of the subject*, of the kind which was practiced by the positivist discourse of the later nineteenth century, or—in a particularly jarring way—in the programs for the liquidation of subjectivity proposed by a self-styled "postmodernism."

Schelling's identity is absolute in the sense that it alone exists without further conditions, whereas everything else, which owes its being to its relation to another, has only a relative or conditional existence. If we assert correctly of such a conditioned thing that it nevertheless *is*, then we are considering the bond which is at work within it and abstracting from its relatedness to something else, since every existing thing, regardless of its finitude, completely embodies the whole, in the same way that each part of an organism does. But parts of an organism cannot be eliminated or reduced. The decentering of the subject to the status of an organ of the absolute also endows it with the distinction of being a moment of the world as a totality (*Weltganzes*). For Kant described those structures as organisms which bear the purposive orientation of the whole inscribed in even their smallest part, intracellularly as it were. It is precisely for this reason that Schelling's *Identitätsphilosophie* could continue to be understood as the philosophical expression of a nonalienated, radical-democratic idea of nonviolent, harmonious communication—or indeed communion—between *citoyens* by Moses Hess, Prosper Enfantin, Heinrich Heine, and Pierre Leroux. These connotations occur many times in the *Critique of Judgement* (e.g., para. 59 and 65), and it is scarcely surprising therefore that Kant's description of the structure of the organism acquired paradigmatic status for Schelling's conception of identity.

From the second half of the nineties onwards Schelling had begun to speculate that, in the organism, matter and mechanism (also described by Schelling as the "dynamic process") are subsumed within the idea of a whole: mechanism ceases to operate with relative indifference to substance (or matter); it becomes its own other or the other of itself. In the thought of the self-reflexivity or self-regulation of the organism, we find the notion of an other which, as part of the organism, is itself the whole. As Schelling (from 1801 onwards) likes to say, we find "identity as though doubled" (*Identität gleichsam doubliert*) in the self-relation of the organism—two disparate things are compared, each of which already reveals a relation to its other which is subsumed within a bond of identity. We will examine the logical structure of this double relation of identity in more detail at a later point. For the moment it is sufficient to observe that Schelling identifies such organic self-relations with the original "character of mind."[11]

> Here no relation is possible except through a third, to whose idea both matter and concept belong. Such a third however can only be an intuiting and reflecting mind [*ein anschauender und reflektierende Geist*] (and thus an intellectual intuition). Thus you

cannot help but admit that organization is possible only in relation to a *mind*.[12]

The structure of mind is developed from that of the organism, which—in an analogous way—includes that which is opposed to it, namely, mechanism. As we saw, mechanical relations are distinguished from organic ones by virtue of the fact that the elements described as causes are *not* identical with the elements described as effects. The finite world as a whole, in its relativity, is characterized by the noncoincidence or difference of its parts. This difference is as if bent or reflected back on itself in the organism, the distinctness of cause and effect is canceled in their "indifference," as Schelling puts it. Both cause and effect, far from being external to each other, turn out to be moments of a single structure, that of the *self-determination* of mind, which transforms effects into purposes. These effects are final causes which in turn trigger efficient causes, which can thus no longer be distinguished from effects, but are rather woven together in the absolute effectivity of the highest being. This being is simultaneously cause and effect of itself, but not of anything external to and other than itself—and is thus the common denominator of absolute mind and the organism of nature.

IV

The reverse movement of our reconstruction has now reached the systematic site of the identity of the real and the ideal. Although many details of Schelling's philosophy of nature and mind are completely outdated (and speculative in a bad sense), I consider his reflections on identity and difference to be one of the great beacons of Western thought. There are lines of influence which run from Schelling via his pupil Lorenz Oken to Fechner and from thence to the contemporary theory of the identity of mental and physical phenomena.[13] This theory maintains, as Schelling does in paragraph 270 of his Würzburg *System of Philosophy*, that the fact that every mental event is always accompanied by a physical one (a process in the brain) does not entitle us to conclude that one of these is the cause of the other:

> No causal connection is possible between the real and the ideal, between being and thought, which means that thought can never be the cause of a determination of being, nor being conversely the cause of a

determination of thought.—For real and ideal are merely different views of the same substance, and thus they can no more bring something about in each other than a substance can bring something about in itself.[14]

This thought, an exciting one in my view, vividly anticipates a perspective which has been discussed with undiminished intensity over the last twenty or thirty years under the titles "theory of identity" or "nonreductive materialism."

An eliminative materialism of the kind defended by Dennett or Rorty maintains that, strictly speaking, there are no mental phenomena, in other words, that supposedly subjective knowledge-perspectives or "inner experiences" are in fact neurophysiological events which are not recognized as such—and nothing more. In this case, the term *mental event* would be empty, and its true meaning would be "physical event." But an idealist position would be just as eliminative if, like those of Berkeley or Schopenhauer, it declared the material world to be merely a modification of our senses, and—since the senses belong to our subjective equipment—thereby reduced the material to the subjective. In both cases, the task of rendering comprehensible the connection of the mental and the physical is supposedly solved by denying the independent existence of one of the levels and limiting description and analysis to one of the descriptive systems (very broadly, either to materialism or to idealism). However, if the existence of one of the relata whose connection was in question is denied, then the connection falls away also— and the idea that this connection could be made intelligible through the thought of an identity which reigns between them becomes objectless. Reduction of one relatum to another cannot be subsumed under the title "identity" without turning this concept into something trivial. This can be avoided only when sentences like "Mental states are identical with neuronal states" say something which is not self-evident, and this implies that the semantics of the mental does not include analytically the semantics of the neuronal (or the reverse). This is obviously the case. No one would maintain that it is our nervous system or our brain, or parts of the brain (neurones) which think, perceive, will, or have feelings. Even less would anyone maintain that chemical reactions in the ganglia *as such* are accompanied by that subjective perspective on what is experienced which Jean-Paul Sartre or Thomas Nagel hold to be an essential feature of the psychical (or of the life of consciousness). Conversely, neither would we say that the sorrow of love is something essentially characterized by electrical and/or molecular-biological features (even if we subscribe to the view that it *never* occurs *without* something material also taking place—a *conditio sine qua non* is not a *causa per quam*).

In other words, if we take the phrase *characterized by* to mean "identical with," then everything depends on the use of the term *identity*. If we follow Saul Kripke's argument concerning the incoherence of talk about "contingent laws of identity" and also share his conviction that necessity is the only modal category which can be meaningfully applied to relations of identity, we will be forced to conclude that mental and physical processes are identical only when they are *necessarily* identical with each other. At this point, however, we encounter the following problem: mental events have their necessary and sufficient criterion of existence in the fact that they are subjectively experienced. This experiencing is not necessarily articulated in linguistic terms as propositional knowledge (when I am in a particular conscious state, I do not have to be in possession of an accurate interpretation of this state; it is, however, impossible for me to have no consciousness of it, since my consciousness is the only criterion for my being in a specific state at any given time).

By contrast, the statement that my mental state is a C-fiber firing is propositionally structured and—like all knowledge claims—it could be false. In this case I have no Cartesian certainty, such as that which I possess in relation to mental experiences such as pain. Consequently the reductionist or eliminative interpretation of the identity formula ("mental phenomena are *nothing other than* certain physical phenomena") seems to be undermined. But we can also assert, at a more fundamental and formal level, that theories of the identity of the physical and the psychical become completely empty when they establish the identity formula through the elimination of one of the relata. I am convinced that this insight—which lives on in contemporary attempts to establish a "nonreductive materialism"—was also the original driving impulse behind Schelling's operations with an identity formula which includes difference.

V

I now want to open up the parallels, which up to this point have only been asserted, between the nonreductionist versions of contemporary identity theories and Schelling's *Identitätsphilosophie*. This will involve looking in more detail at what Schelling tells us about the remarkable intertwining of the notions of identity and difference at the heart of the structure which mind and organism share.

This structural homology is nowhere explained more luminously than in the *Stuttgart Private Lectures* of 1810. Here Schelling speaks of three characteristic states of absolute identity (which is symbolized as such by the traditional formula A = A). Identity, which can exist only as a symmetrical *relation* of something with something semantically distinct, comprehends "A" first of all as an object, which is *affirmed* in and by the self-affirmation of absolute identity. Secondly, "A" is also included as (*affirming*) subject in itself (since the thought of self-affirmation requires an affirmed and an affirmer). And finally it articulates the *identity* of the two previous moments.[15] However, all this takes place within a pure virtuality, without any *real* difference occurring ("but this is all indistinguishable from the standpoint of the real"). But now we want to posit the merely virtual or conceptual difference as such in its *reality*, in other words, set one moment over against another in a position of externality. This "differentiation" (*Differentiierung*), as Schelling calls it, necessarily modifies the original formula (A = A) into A = B (for now B *really* differs from A, in comparison with the initial situation). But since the essential (or as Schelling says, "substantial") unity of both persists, the original formula $\frac{A}{A=A}$ must be replaced by the following: $\frac{A}{A=B}$. In this new formula, A = B represents the diremption of the moments, while A, written in the position of the numerator, stands for the persisting unity, so that the formula as a whole symbolizes the "living, actual primal being" mirroring itself in that which it is not (A reflects itself in and as A = B). In itself, Schelling maintains, the primal being (*Urwesen*) is always unity,[16] but in such a way that diremption finds its place in the integral formula. The bond (or copula) thus subsists not merely between the different moments (A and B) but also—and this is what is essential to Schelling's formula of identity—between A and B, on the one hand, and absolute identity (A), on the other. It is in this way that the characteristic doubling of the identity formula is to be understood; this is not the identity of opposites but the identity of itself and that which it is not (in other words, of difference). Only by virtue of this doubling can identity persist in the midst of that which it is not: the finite, relative world.

In this way Schelling distinguishes "the essence in itself" (*das Wesen an sich*)—the as yet unarticulated identity—from this same essence, insofar it is articulated as a play of opposed elements ("the essence in the absolute form," where form means logico-semantic form). This enterprise is guided by a key idea which can only be called "ingenious." In order for absolute (seamless, unarticulated) identity to assert itself in a form (which it articulates propositionally as the opposing of two relata), A *and* B, regardless of their relativity, must each incorporate in themselves the whole unidivided identity—just like the parts of an organism. On the other hand, their separateness must also be capable of making itself felt. This is possible only on condition that both, the comparatively real moment (B) and the comparatively ideal moment (A), double themselves in their opposite number. Henceforth it is no longer B (the infinite real activity) which opposes itself to A (the limiting ideal activity). Rather the identity of A and B (which is expressed by the copula, the identity sign, or the dividing line in the formula) finds itself, under the exponent (or in the "potency") B, opposed to itself under the exponent (or in the "potency") A.

Does this mean that Schelling thinks of his absolute identity as numerical or as qualitative? In contrast to quantitative or relative identity, he does indeed call it "qualitative." But the example that he gives, namely, of the unity of the person beneath the multiplicity of their characteristics,[17] makes clear that he does not mean a qualitative sameness with regard to species or concept in the sense of the Aristotelian tradition. This would be the sameness of two objects a and b with regard to a space of predication P, "when they fall under the same general term as far as this space is concerned."[18] But this is not Schelling's account. "If the idea of the absolute were a general concept [and thus a general term]," Schelling affirms, "then this would not prevent difference from occurring within it, despite the unity of absoluteness."[19] The unity of the concept (for example, 'figure' for all possible circles, rectangles, and polygons) does not exclude the difference of the objects which fall under it. Precisely this difference falls away in the absolute, however,

> because it is essential to the idea of the absolute that in it the particular is also the general, the general the particular, and because of *this* unity form and essence are also one within it. Thus with regard to the absolute, it follows directly from the fact that it is absolute that all differences are absolutely excluded from its essence.[20]

For this reason Schelling bluntly rejects the doctrine according to which the absolute is characterized by identity "in terms of a general or species concept." His talk of "qualitative identity" means the identity of an "individual being"[21] in its numerical selfsameness, regardless of its generality. The fact that the *form* of the proposition asserting identity articulates a duality does not rule out the (numerical) oneness of the entity which is asserted in this form.

Even this minimal information about Schelling's treatment of identity statements is enough for us to reject Hegel's criticism that Schelling's identity is the night in which all cows are black. (It is probable that Hegel is here only taking up a mocking remark which Schelling himself directed in his *Fernere Darstellungen* of 1802 against those who "can make out nothing but empty night in the essence of the absolute and . . . who can recognize nothing in it."[22] For Schelling's identity does not simply identify A and B, as if they collapsed into each other. He had already made this clear in the earliest and least satisfactory version of his *Identitätsphilosophie*, the *Darstellung meines Systems der Philosophie*, which was hastily composed in 1801:

> The indifference of knowing and being is thus not the *simple* identity of A as subject and A as object (Spinoza) but the indifference of A = A as an expression of being and A = A as an expression of knowing.[23]

The bond which gives meaning to talk of identity subsists not between A and B but between the absolute itself (considered as pure unity) and the same absolute (considered as multiplicity). Absolute identity is the "bond between itself as unity and itself as the opposite, or multiplicity."[24] What this difficult formulation really signifies was first illuminated by Schelling when he stopped focusing primarily on its ontological implications, rather than on the question of propositional form. Indeed, it is possible to show that Schelling's philosophy was anchored from the very beginning in considerations of propositional form, a form which—against the mainstream of the epistemological paradigm—functioned as a model for his thinking.[25] This is also evident from the fact that he regularly refers to the binding link in the absolute identity of nature and the subject using a logico-semantic term: the *copula*.

The most illuminating statement on this issue can be found in the first draft of *The Ages of the World* (*Die Weltalter*), dating from 1811.[26] Here the undifferentiatedness of B and A is described under the title of "equiprimordiality" (*Gleichursprünglichkeit*) or "indifference" (*Gleich-Gültigkeit oder . . . Indifferenz*).[27] Indifference means, in this context, mere virtuality of distinction without effective difference.

This indifference, within which distinction is as though anticipated but not yet actualized, should be distinguished from what Schelling calls "one-and-the sameness" (*Einerleyheit*).[28] "One-and-the-same" refers to something whose essence is exhaustively accounted for by the information that it is itself—the case of contentless or tautological identity. This is not so in the case of indifference, where A and B are clearly distinguished conceptually, although not in reality external to each. A is there where B is, so to speak—but both are not a single essence. One-and-the-sameness, by contrast, is a pseudo-relation without distinct terms: one and the same A is posited or affirmed twice. This freedom from contradiction is a strictly analytical principle and does not even touch on the real problem of identity.

The latter, Schelling observes, is always a *relation* of something with something else and accordingly has the structure of a judgement (or assertoric sentence). He claims to have always oriented himself in terms of this structure, in terms of "the nature of the statement or of the predicate."[29] Schelling now argues as follows.[30] The structure of the proposition brings a duality of viewpoints into play. For this reason we can say of someone who utters a tautology that they have not really made a judgement. If I assert in an informative utterance that something is identical with something else, then the second "something" must at least be assumed to be different from the first—otherwise what was affirmed in the subject position would merely undergo a sterile repetition in the predicate position. For Schelling this is the case with analytically true or noncontradictory judgements. According to this terminology is it assumed that a judgement is analytically true when its negation implies a contradiction (Kant's assumption in *Critique of Pure reason*, A 151), or—to put this another way—a proposition is analytically true when its truth is evident from its meaning. Such a statement is uninformative in the sense that it cannot possibly be false, and it thus gives us no knowledge about the world (it would be informative only for those who do not know the meaning of "A'). But Schelling's identity formula is not of this kind. It does not assert the one-and-the-sameness of A and B (which could only signify that the meaning of B is shown to *be* that of A). Rather what is shown is that, in the judgement A = B, A undergoes a real expansion of its content with respect to its being B.

In a way which anticipates Wittgenstein, Schelling reserves the term *knowledge* (*Wissen*) for cases in which the relation of judgement includes information that is not already contained analytically in its first element. Propositions expressing knowledge must be capable in principle of being false. With analytical judgements however the "possibility of the opposite" is excluded a priori, and for this reason it would be peculiar to speak of the acquiring of "knowledge." In a student's transcription of the Munich *Einleitung in die Philosophie* of 1830 we read:

> The expression "knowledge" is used in a broader and a narrower sense. In the former it refers to that knowledge which one can find through mere reflection without any further assistance, or that knowledge whose opposite is impossible. Knowledge in the narrower sense is distinguished from this knowledge through or in mere thought by that fact that its status cannot be decided through mere thought, but only through an actus, a deed; or that it is only present where something can be or not be. For this reason this knowledge is called an emphatic knowledge, or knowledge *cum emphasi*. Thus "is" can be said in every expression with or without emphasis. For example, in the sentence "A clock is a machine"—in which subject and predicate are bound together by mere thought—the copula "is" is posited without any emphasis. If a sentence is to be emphatic, then the subject must be such that is can equally be or not be. A is b, when it could also not be b.[31]

Schelling therefore makes the proposal that we should distinguish between analytical and epistemic relations of identity. In the latter the subject expression as such is not already one and the same as the predicate expression. If we still want to talk of identity in this case, then the identity relation between A and B should not be formalized as a relation between a subject and a predicate, but rather both expressions should be grasped as predicates, which are ascribed to a common subject (= X). This subject would itself be simple (in the sense of analytical one-and-the-sameness:[32] it would be nothing but "itself"), and the predicates would be one only with reference to the subject, not between themselves. One who is in love is in this respect not angry (love and anger are semantically distinct—in Jacob Böhme, whom Schelling is thinking of in this context, these expressions indicate contradictory opposites). But it is entirely thinkable that the person in love and the angry person are the same (like Kafka's *Little Woman*, who sends the first-person narrator entirely contradictory signals, or the woman who gave me signs of love yesterday and today does her best to get rid of me).

Thus the principle of noncontradiction—Schelling insists on this— is in no way impaired by the principle of identity.[33] To give an example: the mind is not the body, and a thought in its mental self-presentation is not a physiological process in my brain. But according to Schelling we cannot conclude from the impossibility of asserting that thought is a neuronal process that it is wrong to say that "the same thing which in one respect is body, is in another mind"[34]— this is the first glimmer fo a theory of identity in the contemporary sense.

I would now like summarize the conclusions of this section. Schelling shows us that the identity of subject and object, mind and nature, cannot be thought in accordance with the model of their total indistinguishability or one-and-the-sameness (as if A *as* A were simultaneously and in the same respect not A). However, Schelling's argument continues, this does not prevent the apparent subject A of the judgement of identity and the apparent predicate B from both turning out to be predicates (which differ from each other) of a subject = X, which is the one and the same as itself in precisely the way that analytical truth or noncontradiction demands. Instead of saying that nature is mind (which would be absurd), one should rather say: There is an X (absolute identity, the copula or the bond), and this X is, on the one hand, nature and, on the other hand, mind (these would be the predicates of X). But this does not make mind, as such, into nature or nature, as such and in the same respect, into mind. One can also reformulate this identity, which is doubled into two subsidiary judgements (X = A and X = B), in the following way: that which A applies to is also that which B applies to, or: $Fa \rightarrow (\exists x)(x=a \wedge Fx)$ or also $[(Fx \rightarrow (\exists y)(Gy \wedge x=y)].$[35] According to this view only X really exists, and it is indistinct and *toto coelo* itself, seamless and without inner reduplication—A and B are *only to the extent* that they are "been" by X. Since B is only a symbolic abbreviation for difference, and A only an abbreviation for the relation of identity (between A and B), the fully developed identity formula asserts: There is an identity which de-differentiates itself, as a relation dominated by its opposite (difference), from itself as a relation posited under the exponent of identity:

$$(A = B)^B \equiv (A = B)^A.$$

Within this relation between two relations which is founded by the identity sign, that which alone *exists* is absolute identity. The relata *exist* only by virtue of it. In their dissolution from the bond of identity they degenerate into Platonic *me onta*, which *are* only in so far as another transitively *is*. In Sartre such a relative mode of existence is referred to as "être été": to be "been" by another.

VI

Looking back over the path travelled so far, let us now enquire what is really going on in these often reckless speculations of the young Schelling. I would say, nothing less than a break with the conceptual scheme which has anchored and moulded the entirety of European thought, from the Greeks up to Fichte and beyond. Even materialism cannot work its way free of it, for in all its variants materialism defends the reducibility of phenomena of consciousness to exclusively physical events. Conversely, idealism makes everything dependent on the sole conditions under which material reality is accessible to us, and these conditions are said to be anchored in consciousness. Whatever the specific contents with which this reductionist schema of interpretation is inscribed may be, they can all ultimately be traced back to the theoretical turning point whose deep structure Martin Heidegger has revealed, and which we began by calling the "schema of representation." According to this schema, to know means to *place* something *in front of* a subject and abandon it to the subject's epistemic and technical will to domination. It is this which explains the "fall" of nature—as the totality of ob-jects—which occurs in the modern sciences and in their legitimating instance, philosophy. From this perspective, the characterization of subjectivity as something to be rescued is indeed suspect. But subjectivity can and must be regarded from another perspective—and Schelling has also provided a valuable stimulus for this task of thought.

In order to justify the violent gesture which inhabits the project of the domination of nature, it was necessary to concoct a pretext by proclaiming nature to be "dead," "inanimate." Only subjects are considered to be living and animate. Even Heidegger, in the *Letter on Humanism*, will provide us with the peculiar information that the gulf between human beings and nature is far greater than that between angels and human beings. No position in modern philosophy has opposed this prejudice more passionately and ingeniously than Schelling's so-called *Identitätssystem*. In this system nature is no mere object, and the human mind is no disembodied spirit. Nature is rather "the absolute subject"[36] under the predominance of the principle of the real. And the human mind is not disincarnate: the predominance of the principle of the ideal within it does not extinguish what Faust, in occidental-melancholic mood, calls "earth's residue, to be borne in pain." To allow nature to appear as subject—and indeed, as absolute subject—means to restore her "natural" rights, of which she was for millenia deprived. If nature appears to us today in the emblem of a ruin, Schelling affirmed in a lecture course of 1832–33, then humanity must be held responsible. Thus philosophy finds itself confronted with the task "of releasing even the realm of nature from the curse which weighs upon it and transforming it back through a rebirth into its primordial, celestial state of being."[37] Here we reencounter not only the central theme of Wagner's *Ring*—the rescuing of the mineral gold from the curse of its coining as tyrannical, loveless money—but also the utopia of the young Marx, who preached the "resurrection of fallen nature,"[38] thereby allying himself with Schelling, who wrote in the first draft of the *Weltalter*:

> Thus at first the mental and the physical agree as the two sides of the same existence, and we can say that the present moment of their highest inwardness is the common birthplace of what will later stand decisively opposed as matter and mind . . . Were there no such point where the mental and the physical are entirely intermingled, then matter would be not be capable of resurrection in the life of the mind, as is undeniably the case. Within the matter of even purely corporeal things there lies an inner point of transfiguration which is only truly unfolded in organic material [gap in manuscript], and in which we recognize the inner identity of the intellectual and physical principle, the site of resurrection, the rebirth of the palingenesis of matter which has fallen under the predominance of the real.[39]

Schelling's commitment to the rehabilitation of a nature so long mistreated (and not only by philosophy) is expressed most clearly and fierily in his 1806 barrage against Fichte. Here Schelling uses the whole range of polemic and romantic irony in order to characterize Fichte as a representative of the Western contempt for, and subjugation of, nature.

Fichte is compared with the character Nestor in Tieck's comedy *Prince Zerbino*, an enlightened arch peti-bourgeois, who considers only the achievements of human intelligence and culture worth mentioning, while nature seems to him merely meaningless, stupid, dead, and alien to mind. Nestor has invested heavily in the Enlightenment and cannot allow himself any indulgence in such stupidities. 'Fichte,' Schelling says,

> this philosophical Nestor, here reminds us unintentionally of another Nestor, the one in *Prince Zerbino*. The latter, returning in a high dudgeon from the groves of poetry, where the forest, the flowers, the breezes had spoken to him, is delighted beyond all measure when he hears the table, the chair, and the rest of the furniture speak. These are no flowers or trees, but natural things which have been animated by rational life, which are glad to be useful conveniences and no longer to have to stand outside and be tossed by the wind like the wretched green trees, which is something no rational being could enjoy.[40]

What Schelling is mocking here is still the most widespread conception of nature: nature is simply the barrier to human—and this means rational, which in turn means technical—activity.[41] This is the "economico-teleological principle"[42] which the romantics nowhere allowed to escape their sharp mockery. This principle, which Fichte defends in a way which undeniably invites laughter, demands "that natural forces be subjugated to human purposes" (Schelling's quotation from Fichte in the same passage)—in other words, to what Kant called an "external purposiveness." This purposiveness can be entirely equated with what we today call the "purposive-rational" or the "instrumental." Instead of releasing nature's own purpose, humanity imposes its own purposes upon her—and thus brings about her fall.

Schelling closes with a severe judgement against the attitude on which this demeaning conception of nature is based:

> We are forced to say it: the origin of spiritual vulgarity of all kinds is the lack of that intuition in which which nature appears to us as self-animating, indeed this deficiency leads sooner or

later to the total extinction of spirit, which no art can further disguise. There is something unwholesome about it, for all power of healing derives from nature. It alone is the true antidote to abstraction. It is the eternally fresh source of inspiration and of a perpetual rejuvenation . . . Where this source dries up we find only a moralization of the whole world, which undermines and hollows out all life, and a real horror of nature and of all vitality, except that of the subject.[43]

Later in the same text, Schelling continues:

But this judgement will be the least significant in the final reckoning. Nature, long misrecognized, will break though to its fulfillment and no book or pamphlet will be able to hold it back, no system in the world will suffice to dam it up. Then everything will be in unison and as one, even in the domain of science and knowledge, just as everything was already from all eternity in unison and as one, in being itself and in the life of nature.[44]

There remains one final perspective, with which I would like to close. Nature not only celebrates its resurrection in Schelling's philosophy— it is also intended to serve as the criterion for a social state free of domination. Just as Schelling defends nature against a way of thinking which declares it to be dead, inanimate, available for exploitation, so also he considers it as the prefiguration of an equality which is to be welcomed, not merely between the real and the ideal, but also among human beings. It is this which connects his philosophy of nature with the inspiration of the French Revolution, which springs from related sources. For Fichte, moral philosophy should constantly aim to penetrate the whole of nature, "his spirit reveals itself to be filled with concepts of limitation, of dependency, of subjugation, of subservience; but never has a free and divine relationship appeared to him in the idea of what is most splendid, of the state, the primordial, nature."[45] This relationship is divine because directly grounded in the absolute, and it is free because it acknowledges the most complete equality of subject and object, the real and ideal world, male and female, without permitting one of the two principles to attain a position of mastery over the other and dominate it.

Those who find this warning, which is indeed full of pathos, too utopian may wish to reflect that no period in the history of human evolution has more bitterly realistic reasons to accord Schelling's idea of a resurrection of nature a unreservedly preeminent value. We have too often forgotten that we belong to the realm of nature—a fact which fits entirely into the tradition of the abstract counterposition of nature and mind. The fearful repression for which humanity in the advanced societies bears the responsibility consists in a blindness to the nature-bound character of our existence as human beings. As a result of this blindness we have come to be included—in an unintended dialectic—among the objects of the technical exploitation of nature. The in-humanity of the image which the natural world mirrors back to us today is only the real reflection of our betrayal of our "primordial compatriotism with nature." There can be no hope that we might return to this original relationship until we become mindful of the fact that humanity is not the purpose of nature and that nature is its own purpose; that it everywhere sets ends for itself; that it is a self-reflexive organism, which regulates itself autonomously through the activities of assimilation and adaptation, just as—*mutatis mutandis*—the self-conscious mind does. This is the lesson which can be drawn, and indeed *must* be drawn, from a sensitized rereading of Schelling.

Eight

The Truth of the Subject
Language, Validity, and Transcendence in Lacan and Habermas

Peter Dews

In a recent conversation with Jacques Derrida, Jean-Luc Nancy suggested that, throughout the period when structuralism and poststructuralism were the predominant philosophical forces in France, Lacan was perhaps the only thinker to insist on keeping the "name" of the subject.[1] Given the climate of the times, in which the concept of the 'subject' was dismissively associated with discredited, supposedly "Sartrian" reveries of autonomy and self-transparency, this was indeed a significant act of intellectual resistance on Lacan's part, in any perspective. Covering his own tracks a little, one might suspect, Derrida responded to Nancy's remark by insisting that other thinkers of the sixties and seventies continued to work on the theory of the subject. Althusser, for example, "seeks to discredit a certain authority of the subject only by acknowledging for the instance of the 'subject' an irreducible place in a theory of ideology," while in Foucault's case "we would appear to have a history of subjectivity that, in spite of certain massive declarations about the effacement of the figure of man, certainly never consisted in 'liquidating' the Subject."[2] However, Derrida's retrospective tends to smooth out the awkward fact of Lacan's uniqueness. For in Lacan's thought, from a very early date, the concept of the 'subject' and the concept of 'truth' are intimately linked, whereas for the other influential thinkers of the period, the influence of Marx, Nietzsche, and indeed Freud, encouraged a view of the subject as the primary locus of (metaphysical) illusion. Althusser insisted, in his famous essay on the theory of ideology, that "all scientific discourse is a subjectless discourse, there is no 'subject of science' except in an ideology of science."[3] Similarly Foucault suggested, in his inaugural lecture at the Collège de France, that "It may well be that the theme of the founding subject permits one to elide the reality of discourse,"[4] while declining to balance this critique with an alternative account of the "nonfounding" subject until much later in his work. The following remarks from the opening of Lacan's first *Seminar* form a striking contrast to such views: "I insist on the fact that Freud was exploring a line of research which is not characterized by the same style as other sciences. Its domain is that of the truth of the subject. The quest for truth is not entirely reducible to the objective, and indeed objectifying, research of the normal scientific method. It is a matter of the realization of the truth of the subject, as a specific dimension which must be detached in its originality from the notion of reality."[5] But what is this truth of the subject for Lacan?

Lacan on Language and Truth

In an essay dating from 1946 Lacan remarks that "no linguist or philosopher could in fact any longer maintain a theory of language as a system of signs doubling a system of realities, the latter defined by the common accord of sound minds in sound bodies."[6] Lacan's reasons for making this claim are similar to those which motivated Wittgenstein's well-known critique of the notion of ostensive definition. Elsewhere Lacan suggests that "there is only one gesture, known since Saint Augustine, which corresponds to nomination: that of the index-finger which shows, but in itself this gesture is not even sufficient to designate what is named in the object indicated."[7] Ostensive definition is inadequate to establish reference, since without commentary it can never determine which *aspect* or *feature* of the ostended context is being isolated, and therefore presupposes the very capacity of language to connect with the world which it is intended to explain. Lacan's conclusion is that "no signification can be sustained other than by reference to another signification: in its extreme form this amounts to the proposition that there is no language [*langue*] in existence for which there is any question of its inability to cover the whole field of the signified, it being an effect of its existence as language that it necessarily answers to all needs."[8] Thus, for Lacan there are no privileged points where language abuts directly onto the real: reference is rather inherent in the functioning of a language—however minimal—as a whole.

However, Lacan does not draw from this insight the conclusion which was popularized by the earlier Derrida, that the very distinction between "signifier" and "signified," or between language and the reality to which it refers, must ultimately be regarded as betraying the "metaphysical appurtenance" of the idea of the sign, an idea which "falls into decay" when the "exteriority of writing in general" is appreciated.[9] Rather, he takes the view that the disclosure of the world involves an indissoluble tension between the prereflexive, linguistic constitution of object-domains and the reflexive assessment of beliefs about the contents of these domains. From such a perspective, as Lacan emphasizes, "the object is not without reference to speech. It is from the very beginning partially given in the objectal, or objective, system, in which must be included the sum of prejudices which constitute a cultural community."[10] This does not entail that the distinction between language and the reality to which it refers is ultimately untenable, as Derrida's notion of the "general text" suggests, since what particular terms are taken to mean cannot be *entirely* separated from the pragmatic success of the beliefs which a linguistic community holds. In other words, there is a continuous interaction between knowledge and meaning, one in which new discoveries—although never unmediated encounters with the real— can destabilize existing interpretations: we are not simply trapped within a specific "disclosure" of the world until some arbitrary shift of perspective occurs. This is no doubt what Lacan is intimating when he claims that the network of the signified "reacts historically" upon the network of the signifier, "just as the structure of the latter commands the pathways of the former."[11]

Lacan's account of this dialectic between the signifier and the signified suggests a divergence from more extreme hermeneutical positions, which are reluctant to admit that the failure of a truth-claim could effect a shift in the linguistic disclosure of the world which framed and made possible the formulation of the claim. But at the same time, Lacan equally opposes a pragmatic reduction of truth to an indicator of instrumental success. In his middle-period writings Lacan often illustrates how language and truth intertwine, in a sense which cannot be instrumentally reduced, by counterposing animal behavior and human communication. He defines a code in terms of "the fixed correlation of its signs with the reality they signify," using as an example the "language of the bees," in which different dance-patterns indicate the direction and distance of pollen-bearing flowers.[12] Although such forms of information transmission cannot simply be reduced to sequences of stimulus and response, we are here operating only at the level of behavioral reactions to perceived patterns and *Gestalten*, a level which Lacan characterizes as the "Imaginary."

The reasons for this choice of term become clear when Lacan refers, as he frequently does in his middle-period writings, to the rituals of rivalry and courtship, and the accompanying forms of parade and display, to be found in the animal world. Lacan does not deny that it may be possible, in this sphere, to find forms of misleading behavior and deception. Animals can lure and intimidate each other, and even fool each other as to their intentions, by creating a disjunction between appearance and reality. (In the human world, an equivalent to such behavior can be found—as he suggests—in the use of diversionary tactics during a battle or of a feint during a boxing match.) But being captivated by an image is not equivalent to being misled by a falsehood—and this is Lacan's crucial point.

The lures of the Imaginary cannot be described as *mendacious*, since lying involves an unjustified claim to truth, and the question of truth does not arise in the domain of disjunctions between (physical) appearance and (psychological) reality. Although animals can produce deceptive *signs* they cannot—to employ Lacan's contrast—produce deceptive *signifiers*, whose misleading character depends on the expectations of the recipient and thus on the manner in which they will be interpreted in a specific situation. As Lacan suggests, an animal "can succeed in throwing its pursuers off the trail by making a false start. This can go so far as to suggest that the game animal is honoring the element of display implied by the hunt. But an animal cannot pretend to pretend. It cannot make tracks whose deception consists in being taken for false, when they are true, in fact indicating the right trail."[13] The animal, in other words, cannot detach the question of truth and falsehood, which depends on intersubjective expectations, from the practice of accurate or inaccurate representation.

Lacan describes this detachment as the passage from "the field of exactitude to the register of truth."[14] He often illustrates it by means of a venerable Jewish joke about an exchange between two passengers on a Polish train: "Why are you lying to me, why do you tell me you are going to Krakow, so that I will believe you are going to Lemberg, when all the time you are going to Krakow?"[15] Superficially, this story suggests that whether a statement functions as a lie is relative to the backdrop of expectations against which it is made, regardless of its "representational" accuracy or inaccuracy. On further reflection, however, it also makes plain that a social world in which the majority of participants habitually lie is impossible on transcendental grounds: the universal expectation of mendacity would simply dissolve into a revision of interpretive schemas aimed at maximizing truth. Thus Lacan is here highlighting a fundamental asymmetry between truth and falsehood: the fact that a lie can function as such only within an intersubjective relation structured by the normative background assumption that the purpose of linguistic communication is to tell the truth. For if a statement considered true at a given time is a statement whose *claim* to truth has been (provisionally) accepted or upheld, a lie is not a claim to falsehood which has been similarly validated but rather a statement made with the intention of raising an unjustifiable claim to truth. Thus the possibility of the lie presupposes a "convention" that the purpose of language is to tell the truth, whereas no such convention is required for the success of a feint or decoy. In Lacan's words: "it is clear that Speech begins only with the passage from pretense to the order of the signifier, and that the signifier requires another locus—the locus of the Other, the Other witness, the witness Other than any of the partners—for the speech that it supports to be capable of lying, that is to say, of presenting itself as Truth."[16]

This insight sharply demarcates Lacan's position from the Nietzsche-influenced dismantlings of truth which have been central to poststructuralist thinking, and continue to play a role in many contemporary "postmodernist" debates. To confirm this, one need only recall the early Nietzsche's account of the origin of the prohibition on lying in "On Truth and Lies in an Extra-Moral Sense." Here Nietzsche suggests that, "out of necessity and boredom," human beings eventually decided to do away with the most glaring manifestations of the *bellum omnium contra omnes:* "This peace treaty brings with it something which appears to be the first step towards the achievement of that mysterious truth-drive [*Wahrheitstrieb*]. Specifically, what is from now on to count as "truth" is fixed at this moment; in other words a regular, valid, and binding denomination of things is invented, and the legislating act of language also gives the first laws of truth: for at this point there arises for the first time the contrast of truth and falsehood."[17] Thus, for Nietzsche, the prohibition on lying is a historically established moral prohibition, motivated by fear of the socially damaging consequences of the practice. He goes on to suggest that it is matched by a parallel prohibition on the utterance of dangerous and disruptive truths.[18]

By contrast, for Lacan the norm of truthfulness has a nonempirical, a priori status. It is not the result of an accord between the partners involved in communication, since for such an accord to be established the truth-telling function of language would have already to be presupposed. The norm of truthfulness is a condition of possibility of any meaningful discussion and, therefore, of the conclusion of any peace treaty. As Lacan states: "I can deceive my adversary by a movement which is contrary to my battle plan, but this movement does not have its deceptive effect unless I produce it in reality and for my adversary. But in the proposals by means of which I open peace negotiations with him, it is in a third locus, which is neither my speech nor that of my interlocutor, that what it proposes is situated."[19] This locus is described by Lacan, from the mid-1950s onwards, simply as the "Other."

Habermas's Consensus Theory of Truth

If the above provides a fair sketch of Lacan's account of the relation between language and truth, it suggests that there may be unexpected parallels between his thought and the philosophical approach to these issues which is currently defended by Jürgen Habermas. For one thing, like Lacan, Habermas has always resisted a naturalistic or pragmatist reduction of truth-claims. In a 1968 essay on Nietzsche's epistemology, for example, he objected to the Nietzschean version of instrumentalism: "The meaning of the empirical accuracy of statements can be explicated with reference to the possibility of transforming them into technical recommendations. But the success of the operations to which these recommendations give rise is not for this reason identical with the truth of the propositions from which these recommendations are deduced, with the aim of achieving certain goals."[20] Thus, from very early on, Habermas was convinced that truth possesses what he has more recently termed a "context-exploding" force, although it took a long time before he was able to formulate this intuition theoretically.

Because of this conviction, Habermas has also argued that the question of truth cannot even be raised at the level of the perception of objects. In Lacan's account of the Imaginary, as we have seen, individuals can react to feints and deceptions with *appropriate* or *inappropriate* behavior, but such actions and reactions cannot be characterized in terms of their truth or falsehood. Similarly, in "Wahrheitstheorien," the founding presentation of his conception of truth, Habermas draws a distinction—even within the domain of language use—between forms of action-related cognition, which are concerned with the adequacy of information about objects of experience, and the dimension of truth. "In an action context," he suggests, "the assertion has the role of information about an experience of objects, but in discourse it has the role of a statement with a problematized validity-claim. The same speech-act can be in one case the expression of an experience, which is either objective or merely subjective, and in another, the expression of a thought, which is true or false."[21] But despite these convergences between Lacan and Habermas, which constitute a somewhat surprising alliance against contemporary forms of contextualism and relativism, it is clear that the transcendental irreducibility of truth is construed rather differently in the two cases.

Habermas's approach gives rise to a "discourse theory of truth," guided by the idea that agreement is the immanent "telos" of language. For Habermas it is part of the pragmatic meaning of making an assertion, that the speaker commits him- or herself to the provision of grounds for what has been asserted, should the validity of the truth-claim raised be questioned. Such a process of questioning and resolving the validity of disputed claims takes place through the form of argumentation, relieved from the immediate pressure of action, which Habermas terms "discourse" (Diskurs). According to this conception, speakers of a language necessarily possess an intuitive knowledge of how to resolve consensually disputed validity-claims, since otherwise language would be unable to fulfill what Habermas takes to be its central function of coordinating action through agreement.

As is well known, this line of enquiry then leads Habermas to the notion of an "ideal speech situation"—of the conditions under which truth-claims could be resolved in a way which would guarantee the objective validity of the outcome. In Habermas's view, this notion is not simply an arbitrary construction, since our capacity to engage in discussion oriented towards the resolution of disputes over validity-claims presupposes an (at least tacit) awareness that conditions of equality and reciprocity between participants in a Diskurs must obtain if the consensus attained is to be true. Otherwise participants would not identify coercion, manipulation, and other structural inequalities as detrimental to the dialogical discovery of truth. The "ideal speech situation" should thus not be understood either merely regulatively, by analogy with Kant's "Ideas of reason," or as a piece of "existing reason" in Hegel's sense. Rather, Habermas suggests, when we engage in discussion, we cannot help but suppose, usually—possibly always—counterfactually, that the conditions of the ideal speech situation have already been at least approximately fulfilled. Thus, the ideal speech situation is neither an empirical phenomenon nor a rationalistic construction, but a "fiction which is operatively effective in processes of communication."[22] In behaving as though it were actual, we help to make it actual, although there can never be any conclusive proof of success, since it is impossible simultaneously to enter into discourse, and to thematize reflectively the structure of this same discourse.

In Lacan, by contrast, there is no attempt to capture the context-transcending force of the claim to truth embodied in our utterances in the nets of an ideal structure of communication. This force is rather revealed by the unavoidability of the presupposition of the witness of an Other who cannot be equated with any possible empirical partner in dialogue. Thus Lacan writes that the "register of truth" is "situated entirely elsewhere [than the field of exactitude], properly speaking at the foundation of intersubjectivity. It is located where the subject can seize nothing except the very subjectivity which constitutes an Other as absolute."[23] It is true that there appears to be an oscillation between an individual and a transindividual characterization of the "Other" in Lacan's thought, for at times Lacan characterizes the Other more impersonally as the "third locus" or the "locus of the signifying convention."[24] However, this oscillation can perhaps be rendered more intelligible by considering the implications of the approach to truth of Karl-Otto Apel, a close colleague and interlocutor of Habermas over many years, who has developed a more explicitly "transcendental" version of the consensus theory.

Apel replies to the "convergence of the poststructuralist, hermeneutic, and pragmatist critique of transcendental philosophy" by arguing that the individual subject must be "more than a point of intersection of historically contingent and structurally anonymous determinations," since as a thinking and reflecting subject he or she participates in an "unlimited community of argumentation" (*unbegrenzte Argumentationsgemeinschaft*) which has the status of a "transcendental subject of redeemable truth-claims."[25] On the one hand, the rules which are discovered by reflection on universal communicative competences are not the *product* of consensus but the necessary preconditions of any attempt to reach consensus. They cannot therefore be equated with any empirically existing discursive conventions, which may in fact be distorted in various ways. In this sense, as Lacan says, the Other is the "locus of the signifying convention" which cannot be equated with any of the participants in communication. But, at the same time, the reconstruction of the transcendental-pragmatic rules makes possible the delineation of an "ideal"—perfectly honest and perfectly sincere—"witness to the truth," comparable to Apel's "transcendental subject of redeemable truth-claims," to whom the incoherences and self-deceptions of my speech would be definitively revealed. Indeed if I could detect all the errors and self-deceptions in the Other's response, I could transform my "real" into an "ideal" partner, in confrontation with whom the illusions of my own speech would be definitively revealed. However, since in order to achieve this I would already have myself to be that ideal partner for another, the true structure of our interaction, and therefore of our stance as subjects constituted by this interaction, is destined to remain "unconscious"—implicit in the dynamic of intersubjectivity but reflectively irretrievable from it.[26]

Truthfulness and Authenticity

But even given these parallels between Lacan's views and "transcendental" or "universal" pragmatics, is not Lacan's conception of truth radically different from that of Habermas? One of Habermas's important innovations is to qualify the traditional centrality of "truth" in philosophy by distinguishing between three "validity-claims," which he categorizes as "truth" (Wahrheit), "rightness" (Richtigkeit), and "truthfulness" (Wahrhaftigkeit). The first of these terms describes the cognitive status of claims about the objective world, the second the normative status of the rules governing interpersonal relations within the social world, and the last the expressive status of claims concerning the subjective experiences of the individual.[27] In Lacan's vocabulary, however, what Habermas understands by truth is rather described as "knowledge" (savoir), whereas what Habermas refers to as "truthfulness" (Wahrhaftigkeit), namely, the accurate self-disclosure of subjectivity, seems at first glance to correspond more closely to what Lacan describes as the "truth of the subject" (la vérité du sujet).

This is the case only "at first glance," because a better suggestion might be that Lacan's vérité in fact corresponds to a category related to, but not identical with, that of truthfulness—namely "authenticity."[28] Whereas truthfulness refers to the honest expression of a particular thought, experience, or feeling, authenticity can be said to concern whether this thought, experience, or feeling, as expressed in a particular context, is in turn a manifestation of what Alessandro

Ferrara has termed "the core of the actor's personality."[29] The function of this concept can perhaps be illustrated by a critical procedure which is central to Charles Taylor's book *Sources of the Self*. Over and over again Taylor shows that a particular philosophical conception was motivated by impulses and implicit convictions which it was incapable of articulating in terms of its own conceptual framework. Thus Taylor writes of utilitarianism that it is "a very strange intellectual position. Built into its denunciation of religion and earlier philosophical views, built into its sense of rationality as an operating ideal, built into its background assumption that the general happiness, and above all the relief of suffering, crucially *matters,* and emerging in the sense that reason liberates us for universal and impartial benevolence, is a strong and at times impassioned commitment to the three goods which I enumerated above [self-responsible reason, the significance of natural fulfillments and benevolence—P.D.]. But in the actual content of its tenets, as officially defined, none of this can be said; and most of it makes no sense."[30] Another way of putting this claim would of course be to say that the utilitarian is "inauthentic": although her expressions of belief and attitude may be *truthful,* these beliefs and attitudes do not in turn truly express the fundamental existential orientation of the person voicing them. Of course, the question of truthfulness may be said to shade into that of authenticity, since if many of a person's beliefs, even if sincerely expressed at the conscious level, do not jell with other things we know of their history, behavior, and attitudes, we will be tempted to claim that they are not her *real* beliefs. Authenticity, in other words, concerns what might be termed the "truthfulness of truthfulness." But this definition in turn raises the question of how we could ever determine what a person's "real" experience is, since inauthenticity can run very deep. It is perhaps because he sees this abyss about to open up that Habermas tends to define truthfulness rather perfunctorily in terms of the faithful expression of subjective experience, although stressing that this inner world should not be understood objectivistically.[31]

The Conflict of Knowledge and Truth

By contrast, from an early date Lacan identified a fundamental conflict between an existentially significant "true speech" (*la vraie parole*), capable of disclosing the being of the subject, and "veridical discourse" (le discours vrai), which might well be truthful. His fundamental thought is that it makes sense to distinguish an authentic self from a construction, however "viable," only if this self exerts the force of a validity-claim. A conflict arises however because, on the one hand, the import of any vocabulary within which a subjective experience is identified and described itself depends on substantive assumptions about the world, including the relation between self and others, thus generating the regress of the "truthfulness of truthfulness": "true speech, in asking veridical discourse what it signifies, will find that a meaning always refers back to another meaning, since nothing can be shown except by means of a sign, and therefore it will make veridical discourse appear doomed to error."[32] On the other hand, if veridical discourse seeks to extract a stable self-description from true speech, thereby detaching it from an evaluation of its context, it will find itself distorting the meaning of this speech: "True discourse, in isolating in the preferred word what is given as a promise, will make it appear mendacious, since it commits itself to a future which, as they say, belongs to no one, and will also make the word appear ambiguous, to the extent that it transcends the being it concerns, in the dimension of alienation where the becoming of this being occurs."[33]

Lacan implies here that because subjective states are not susceptible to a punctual and definitive evaluation, but may always retrospectively acquire a different status and significance within the shifting perspectives of a continuing interaction with others, we are always liable to fall into an objectified construction of the subject's identity. Conversely, objective truth-claims, concerning the nature and significance of specific event in an individual or collective history for example, can scarcely be said to possess a timeless truth which would be independent of the conceptual framework which makes possible the historical interpretation, and which we can readily imagine being superseded in the future. Since the conceptual framework is ultimately an expression of our individual or collective self-understanding and orientation towards the world, the apparent stability of objective truth will be put in question by the intersubjective dynamic which true speech reveals.

In the third Seminar, given around the time of the essay under discussion, Lacan returned to this clash between the claims of objectivity and of subjectivity. He suggested that "disinterested communication is ultimately nothing but failed testimony, or something about which everyone agrees. Everyone knows that this is the ideal of the transmission of knowledge. The entire thought of the scientific community is founded on the possibility of a communication whose limit is defined by an experiment which everyone can agree on. But the very establishment of the experiment is a function of testimony."[34] Thus, for Lacan, scientific knowledge would be impossible without a certain "forgetfulness" of the dimension of subjective experience out of which it emerges. Indeed Lacan goes so far as to suggest, at one point, that the antinomy arising from the clash between subjective and objective dimensions of truth is "that of the meaning which Freud gave to the notion of the unconscious."[35]

In contrast to Lacan, Habermas seeks to avoid the conflict between "knowledge" and "truth" by arguing that the process of rationalization characteristic of modernity has given rise to institutionally differentiated spheres dedicated to the articulation and resolution of the claims specific to one dimension of validity. Habermas admits that objectifying forms of knowledge can "colonize" the life-world, under the pressure of economic and bureaucratic imperatives, thereby inducing reifying distortions into our individual and collective self-understandings. But such colonization could, in principle, be avoided. The identities which locate us as subjects in the life-world are shaped by cultural traditions and inherited practices, and, given favorable political arrangements, these traditions could be drawn on in discussing how to control and orient the development and application of scientific knowledge, including social-scientific knowledge, so as to foster who we (collectively) want to be. There is no hint in Habermas of the thought that the very fact of articulating such a shared self-understanding might be problematic because of the intrinsic difficulties of defining what an adequate revelation of a subject's or community's existential orientation might consist in. These difficulties are, however, implicit in Habermas's account. For he has shifted towards a use of the term *authenticity* to designate something like harmonious self-coincidence, or the redoubled claim to truthfulness "all the way down" discussed above, and he now argues that there can be "ethical-existential discourses" which thematize such individual and collective authenticity-claims.[36] But since the meaning of "discourse" in Habermas is defined by the possibility (however remote) of consensus, this conflicts with his former view that claims to truthfulness cannot be discursively resolved, since their validity or non-validity affects the status of the very discourse in which they are assessed.[37]

Beyond the Social Self

Despite this awkwardness, however, Habermas can feel basically comfortable with his view of authenticity because of his social account of the formation of the subject, an account derived from George Herbert Mead. The implication of this account is that the subject can never detach itself sufficiently from culture and tradition for the question of its relation to this context as a whole to become an issue. According to Mead, the capacity for self-reflection which is taken to be definitive of subjectivity emerges out of the process of identifying with the attitudes of others, a process which helps the individual successfully to negotiate the social environment. The advantage of this account, Habermas contends, is that it enables us to circumvent the "poststructuralist" critique of the subject which understands self-reflection as implying as inevitable self-objectification: to respond to oneself as if from the standpoint of the other is not tantamount to objectifying oneself.[38] Self-reflection appears in this perspective as the internalized version of concrete social processes, not as an ability of the subject to abstract entirely from its empirical social context.

It seems questionable, however, whether Habermas's account of the social and interactive genesis of the self is fully able to account for the capacity for abstraction which is a precondition of the subject's ability to participate in discourses oriented towards the redemption of validity-claims. Habermas is quite clear that such participation requires subjects to take a hypothetical attitude towards their own specific interests—for example, in deciding what norm might be in the interests of all concerned. Similarly, in the discussion of the cognitive claims of the sciences, the participants must abstract from any interest they may have in the outcome other than it that should be objectively valid. Yet Habermas emphasizes that this capacity for reflection on specific problematic issues does not rest on an ability to abstract *entirely* from the life-world context which shapes our identity.[39] However, he also stresses that the notion of rightness or truth which participants orient their contributions to discussion towards is an ideal which transcends any empirical context—indeed Habermas now uses the term "transcendence from within" to describe this "context-exploding" force of validity-claims.[40] And it seems clear that a subject which can orient itself towards such a transcendence must itself transcend any given empirical context, at least in one dimension of its being. Certainly, Apel implies this when he stresses that there is a "transcendental-pragmatic dimension of the self-reflection of the arguing subject" which "cannot be objectivized and formalized," since it consists of insight into the a priori norms of argumentation which arises in the course of argumentation itself, and which presupposes participation in a "transcendental language game."[41] For how could a subject which is merely a precipitate of empirical social interactions, however non-objectifying, participate in such a game? These considerations suggest, at the very least, the need for caution with regard to Habermas's Meadian attempts to reconstruct a purely social and evolutionary genesis of the self.

It can be argued that it is precisely his sensitivity to this nonempirical dimension of the subject which leads Lacan to suggest a conflict between what he terms "knowledge" and "truth." For it is a remarkable feature of Lacan's work that, despite his central emphasis on intersubjectivity, and his reinterpretation of the unconscious itself as an intersubjective phenomenon, he also suggests that there is an irreducible moment of "Cartesian" transcendence which characterizes the subject. Indeed, Lacan draws a close connection between the emergence of modern science and the emergence of the modern subject. In his essay "La science et la vérité," for example, Lacan writes that the distinctive position of modern science can be characterized in terms of "a radical change of style in the *tempo* of its progress, of the galloping speed of its involvement in our world, the chain reactions which characterize what we can call the expansion of its energetic. What seems to be at the root of all this is a modification of our position as subjects, in a double sense: it inaugurates this development, and science reinforces it more and more."[42] Lacan goes on to argue that this modification can be traced to "a historically defined moment which we should perhaps be aware can be strictly repeated in experience, that which is inaugurated by Descartes and which is called the *cogito*."[43]

At first glance, Lacan's claim may seem rather surprising. After all, he begins his celebrated paper on the "Mirror Stage" by suggesting that the experience of this stage "makes us oppose any philosophy directly issuing from the *cogito*."[44] Even here, however, the qualificatory adverb promises further complexities, and in later writings Lacan will stress that the isolation of the "subject" which Descartes undertakes through the suspension of any cognitive relation to the world reveals something decisive about the subject, its "transcendental-pragmatic" status (to use Apel's term) as an indubitable presupposition of all discourse. For Lacan, Descartes's mistake was merely to take the subject which he had discovered for a substantial subject of consciousness. He argues that "it is by taking its place at the level of the utterance [*énonciation*]" that the *cogito* acquires its certainty but that this certainty cannot be translated into the form of a proposition (*énoncé*) expressing a specific self-interpretation: the I *think* is "reduced to this punctuality of being certain only of the absolute doubt concerning all signification, its own included."[45] When viewed in this way, the Cartesian *cogito* "denounces what is privileged in the moment on which it is based, and shows how fraudulent it is to extend this privilege to conscious phenomena, in order to establish their status."[46] For Lacan, in other words, the subject is that moment of nonmundanity, of transcendence, which must be seen as both eluding and making possible the reflexive structure of self-consciousness, even when the emergence of that structure is understood in terms of intersubjective identifications.[47]

We have seen that Lacan argues for a fundamental distinction between "knowledge" and "truth," or between *le discours vrai* and *la vraie parole*. However, the recognition of a difference between the validity-status of truthfulness (or authenticity as a "redoubled" form of truthfulness) and truth does not, taken by itself, imply a conflict between them. Habermas tries to avoid this conflict by suggesting that the reified self-understanding of *le discours vrai* is not inevitable. Within the sphere of the life-world, individuals do not spontaneously relate to themselves and others in objectifying ways. This occurs only when the exclusive orientation to truth characteristic of the sciences is imported back into the sphere of intersubjective communication from the specialized institutional spheres where it legitimately holds sway, in the process which Habermas describes as the "colonization of the life-world." From such a perspective, it is the failure to respect the limits between different types of discourse and their appropriate domains which leads to a disabling of the capacity to ask who we truly are and what we really want—and not to some intrinsic diremption of the modern self.

Authenticity and Truth

It is significant, therefore, that another contemporary representative of the critical theory tradition, Martin Seel, has contested Habermas's view that different validity-claims can be thematized in distinct forms of discourse, each of which can be insulated from other dimensions of validity. Seel suggests that each specialized discourse will necessarily be infiltrated by "assumptions and presuppositions which cannot themselves be thematized with regard to their validity in the current discourse."[48] A moral discussion, for example, will often need to draw on aesthetic and therapeutic claims, just as aesthetic discussions cannot entirely dispense with questions of (cognitive) truth. In consequence, Seel suggests, "The specialization of the expert consists merely in not allowing the different type of validity of the presuppositions to be expressed, and it is on this that his purely immanent, sovereign considerations are based. The *illusion* of specialization, whether it is theoretical, practical or aesthetic, is always the belief in an 'ultimate foundation' of one's own (superior) activity, which separates it from the opaquely determined activity of the dilettantes."[49] If this argument is taken seriously, then it does indeed suggest that no "truth," no cognitive claim in Habermas's sense, can be irrelative to the inextricable interplay of validity dimensions which constitutes the disclosure of a specific life-world, and which provides our "ethical" orientation. The natural sciences may represent an exception in this respect, since here an independent criterion of instrumental success is operative, and may even have *replaced* considerations of cognitive truth.[50] But for most institutionalized domains of knowledge in the social and human sciences, "truth" cannot be quarantined from the wide play and interfusion of validity-dimensions in this way.

Pushing a similar argument somewhat further than Seel would wish to go, Charles Taylor has tried to defuse the conflict between truth and authenticity in the opposite way to Habermas, precisely by not holding them apart. In an extensive series of writings, Taylor has powerfully criticized the representationalism of the predominant conceptions of language within modern European philosophy, suggesting that such views leave what he terms the "expressive," "disclosive," and "constitutive" dimensions of language out of account. By "expression" Taylor means the manner in which language displays the stance of the speaking subject towards a certain reality, or towards others with whom he or she is engaged in dialogue. By "disclosure" he understands the way in which language is capable of "articulating" an issue and thereby first renders it available as a matter of (public) concern. Finally, language is "constitutive" for Taylor because our linguistically articulated self-understandings are not simply a "grid" through which we interpret our experiences and feelings but enter into the moral texture which makes these experiences and feelings what they are.[51]

Taylor's argument is not simply a corrective to the *predominance* of the representationalist view of the self as a detached observer confronting an objective world. He makes the stronger argument that "in some sense, the expressive dimension seems to be more fundamental: in that it appears we can never be without it, whereas it can function alone, in establishing public space, and grounding our sensitivity to the properly human concerns."[52] Moreover, not only is the expressive dimension more fundamental for Taylor, it appears that even the stance of the disinterested observer is itself ultimately the "expression" of a specific self-understanding, rooted in traditions which have acquired predominance in our culture: "My claim is that the ideal of the modern free subject, capable of objectifying the world and reasoning about it in a detached, instrumental way is a novel variant of . . . [a] very old aspiration to spiritual freedom."[53] The implication of this view is that even what is taken to be a cognitive "point zero"—paradigmatically, the detached self of the Cartesian *cogito*—is in fact an expression of a particular value-orientation, so that its apparent value-neutrality is specious. Indeed, Taylor claims that "What you get underlying our representations of the world—the kinds of things we formulate, for instance, in declarative sentences—is not further representations, but rather a certain grasp of the world that we have as agents in it. This shows the whole epistemological construal of knowledge to be mistaken."[54] On similar grounds, Taylor has also argued against Habermas's moral philosophy, suggesting that the commitment to the goal of rational consensus cannot be derived from the normative structure of the speech-situation as such. The implication here is that Habermas's whole conception of a discourse ethics ultimately rests on specific, albeit culturally deep-rooted, commitments to freedom and autonomy.[55]

On closer consideration, however, it seems that Taylor is uncertain whether the modern "disengaged" epistemological and moral standpoint is achievable, but undesirable, or simply not possible at all. He states, for example, that "Even to find out about the world and formulate disinterested pictures, we have to come to grips with it, experiment, set ourselves to observe, control conditions. But in all this, which forms the indispensable basis of theory, we are engaged as agents coping with things."[56] Here Taylor does not seem to dispute the human capacity to formulate "disinterested pictures" merely to resist the overgeneralizing of the ontology which they imply. But if this is the case, it would not be the belief in the possibility of detachment but merely the belief that the "monological observer's standpoint" is "the way things really are with the subject" which would be "catastrophically wrong."[57] Indeed, on this construal, what Taylor terms the "punctual view of the self" must capture at least *part* of "the way things are with the subject," and it is this which he often appears reluctant to admit.

In the light both of these difficulties, and of the complementary difficulties faced by Habermas in distributing the detached and the situated subject between different socio-ontological domains, the philosophical power of Lacan's conception of the subject becomes clearer. For Lacan elaborates a performative, or "transcendental-pragmatic," rereading of the Cartesian demonstration of the existence of the subject, but at the same time he does not consider this subject as a participant in a transparent "transcendental language game" whose distinct structure can be identified (Apel), or—in Taylor's terms—as "ideally disengaged, that is, free and rational to the extent that he has fully distinguished himself from his natural and social worlds."[58] Rather the presupposition of a "subject of the utterance" (*sujet de l'énonciation*), who is the nonempirical subject ultimately responsible for the production of the statement (*énoncé*), is made necessary by the fact that human communication essentially raises validity-claims which transcend all particular contexts. In other words, the subject's speech in its performative dimension raises a claim to "truth" (as authenticity) whose normativity is not grounded in convention, but rather has transcendental force.

Thus, while Lacan would agree with those critics of Habermas who deny that the ideal speech situation can be viewed as the final site of cognitive and moral truth, he would do so not because of a fashionably contextualist constriction of the scope of cognitive truth but rather because of a *de*-limitation of truth as "authenticity" (the truth of the subject). Habermas has claimed that "The individual gains reflexive distance from her own life history only within the horizon of forms of life which she shares with others, and which in turn form the context for different specific life projects."[59] Accordingly, he also stresses that authenticity itself is a culturally specific ideal.[60] For Lacan by contrast, once the Cartesian breakthrough has been made, the subject may always find itself confronted, at the unconscious level of enunciation, with the question of whether *any* contrual of the predominant, culturally accepted ideals would make possible an authentic self-realization.

Undoubtedly, Habermas would be tempted to reject this question as meaningless. For him, the issue of the subject's identity, and thus of what its "good" might be, becomes sheerly unposable once one abtracts from every social and cultural horizon. And here we reach the heart of the divergence between Habermas and Lacan. For Lacan contends that the experience of psychoanalysis reveals a subject who, at the level of the unconscious, obstinately questions his existence beyond any culturally specific horizon of meaning. The subject is engaged in a questioning "not of the place of the subject in the world, but of his existence as subject, a questioning which beginning with himself, will extend to his in-the-world relation to objects, and to the existence of the world, insofar as it, too, may be questioned beyond its order."[61] Lacan does not deny, of course, that this questioning will be formulated in terms of the symbolic repertoire of a specific culture, but his formulations imply that what is at issue is—in part, at least— the relation of the subject to *any* symbolic repertoire in general and thus the problem of the finitude of its self-realization *as* subject.

Support for Lacan's conception can be found in many other currents of contemporary psychoanalysis. The Freudian Oedipus complex, for example, is increasingly coming to be understood by analysts in terms of the child's confrontation with the trauma of having to be *either* male or female, while perverse sexual scenarios are consequently viewed as the outcome of the failure to confront this trauma successfully. Thus Louise Kaplan writes in her recent book *Female Perversions* that "The fundamental wish in perversion is to obliterate all knowledge of the differences between the child and adult generations. The perverse adolescent or adult will arrange his perverse scenario so that he may live forever in the never-never land where there are no real differences between the sexes and no difference between infantile sexuality and adult sexuality."[62] And she concludes that it is "The despair of having to be only one sex, the terror of the finitude of living only one life, ageing, and dying, the infantile anxieties of annihilation, abandonment, separation and castration" which are "held in abeyance by a perverse enactment."[63]

But paradoxically, only a being which is not entirely enclosed by its own finitude can experience the terror of being entirely enclosed by its own finitude. And if the modern subject is not to "forget his own existence and his death, and at the same time to misconstrue the particular meaning of his life in false communication,"[64] this acknowledgement of the limit of truth-as-authenticity must itself be included in the claim to truth-as-authenticity which the discourse of the subject necessarily raises. Recently, Richard Rorty has claimed of

Freud that his "*only* utility lies in his ability to turn us away from the universal to the concrete, from the attempt to find necessary truths, ineliminable beliefs, to the idiosyncratic contingencies of our individual pasts, to the blind impress all our behavings bear."[65] But against this, and in the wake of Lacan, one could rather claim Freud's teaching to be that we experience ourselves as subjects stretched painfully *between* the concrete and the universal, between the idiosyncratic contingency of our pasts and ineluctable truths, indispensable beliefs. Indeed, perhaps it is psychoanalysis, running counter to the deflationist and contextualist trend which Rorty so vividly represents, which has inherited the ancient philosophical task of asking who we are, and what we ultimately desire.

Nine

The Other in Myself

Rudolf Bernet

The phenomenological movement has made a substantial contribution towards new reflection on the nature of the *subject*. However, from Husserl and Heidegger through Merleau-Ponty, Levinas, Ricoeur, and Michel Henry, these new philosophies of the subject are also inclined to be rather anti-subjectivistic insofar as they are motivated by the desire to free philosophical thought definitively from outdated conceptions of the subject. It is perhaps their critical positions regarding psychologism, so-called reism (the subject as a special sort of thing), solipsism, and idealistic spiritualism that have had the greatest effect on present-day philosophy.

All phenomenologists agree that the essence of the subject must be approached through "phenomena," that is, from the "giveness" of all sorts of things. Some phenomenologists even claim that the subject is nothing else than the giveness of things. However, the subject, being "that," or better, "to whom" things are given, cannot itself be a mere thing. It must be added to this determination of the subject that: (1) the givenness of the things and thus also of the subject is not itself given in everyday life; (2) besides being the givenness of things, the subject is also the givenness of itself. The *first* remark refers to the *phenomenological reduction*, which under various names is at work in all phenomenological philosophies. The givenness of things to the subject first appears when these things have lost their overwhelmingly obvious presence. The *second* remark indicates that the givenness of things to the subject is not of the same order as the givenness of the subject to itself. When I am given to myself, when my own life appears to me, I experience myself neither as a thing nor as an object. The following reflections will consider both the circumstances wherein I appear to myself as well as the manner whereby I experience myself in such circumstances.

Before proceeding, a *third* aspect of phenomenology must be mentioned. With the exception of Michel Henry, most phenomenological authors agree that the givenness of the things to the subject and the givenness of the subject to itself are, despite essential differences, inextricably interwoven with each other. That is, though I do not experience myself as a thing, I still experience myself in relation to the experience of things. I experience myself as different from things because, when I experience myself, I remain interested in the experience of things. As Heidegger would put it, even though I experience myself as different from the things which belong to the world, I still experience myself as open for the world. Experience of the self is therefore an experience which goes beyond itself, and the interest in the experience of self is never directed, simply and solely, at my own self.

I shall approach this experience of the transcendence of my own self through three different forms of self-experience: (1) experience of the self as an *ethical* subject that is essentially related to others and to a certain extent also to universality; (2) experience of the self as a *divided* subject; and (3) experience of the self as *difference*. Self-experience in these three sorts of experience of transcendence of the own self is always connected to a certain loss of self. In my concluding remarks, I shall radicalize this insight by proposing that one's own selfhood is ultimately nothing other than the capacity of the subject for loss of the self. *Affectivity*, or better, *the possibility of being touched and moved* is the privileged place for such an experience of self. This affective loss of the contrary, maintains and reveals the self to the self as a tense, changing, and vulnerable self.

Moral Experience of the Self

It is certainly no mere coincidence that in authors such as Augustine, Rousseau, Fichte, and Heidegger, *having a conscience* is presented as the most fundamental form of self-experience. My conscience belongs to me in a most personal manner. Without a doubt, the formation of conscience, moral education, and sometimes large-scale "guilt trips" are aspects of a culture of conscience, but this does not eliminate the fact that I have my own conscience and that this conscience can never be assumed by others. Even if conscience is more than a mere feeling, it is still a way for the subject to feel its own moral obligations. Conscience is one of the few things that belong to me and of which I can never be rid. I can behave unscrupulously or I can try to convince myself that I should not have a bad conscience; but this does not alter the *fact* that I have a conscience and that this is my conscience and not that of somebody else.

On the other hand, it is clear that while having a conscience is a subjective fact, it is not *only* a subjective fact. Conscience is called upon by the experience of the suffering of another, relates itself to a Good that goes beyond the present situation, submits itself to a general law. By having a conscience, the subject experiences itself as somebody that stands open for something that goes beyond the self. More accurately put: there is not a self that must be gone beyond, the self does not precede transcendence; rather, it *is* its own transcendence. Conversely, there is also no ethical transcendence that exists by itself, without requiring personal experience. Moral conscience is therefore a very intimate form of self-experience, wherein the subject feels itself as it loses itself, or if possible, as it forgets itself. In moral conscience the subject experiences itself both as unique and dependent. The self that belongs to the subject, and to the subject alone, is heteronomous.

This determination of the self-experience of the ethical subject sounds provokingly anti-Kantian. Kant's notion of the autonomy of the moral subject should not, however, be taken in too simplistic a manner. According to Kant, the subject which comports itself on the moral level as autonomous lawgiver is, at the same time, *obligated* to do this by the law. The autonomous behavior of the subject does not find its origin in a spontaneous decision of this subject but flows from obedience to the categorical imperative. In other words, the proper autonomy of the subject is imposed upon it. Because of this, Kant claims that even a holy will, that is, a will that is no longer driven by sensuous inclinations, remains subjected to the law and does not coincide with that law. A subjective heteronomy conceived as transcendence is thus not necessarily in conflict with Kant's notion of the autonomous subject of moral action.

Although Kant makes a clear distinction between theoretical and practical reason, his ethics remains essentially connected to the evaluation and judgement of the will of the subject. In making a moral decision, the subject judges the conformity of its will to the general law. The so-called philosophy of value follows closely here the Kantian model, even though it begins with a critique of the purely formal character of Kant's ethics. In both cases, an act receives its moral character by the submission of the subjective will to an objective and universal principle. In order to come to a moral decision, one orients oneself towards the universal law or towards an objective scale or hierarchy of values. I act correctly, therefore, when I do what *one* in the name of the law or of the values must do. Acting in the name of general principles should, however, not be considered the most original form of moral concern. As a suffering subject I find it inadequate that the other respects me solely as an individual representative of general, practical reason. To act simply and solely on the basis of principles is rightly viewed as a form of ethical insensitivity. The ethical subject that acts purely in function of general principles loses at the same time both the sensitivity for the other and the sensitivity for itself. Such a subject risks landing in a form of anonymous objectivism. On the contrary, ethical conscience implies an immediate sensitivity both for the call which comes from the other and for myself as the one who cannot escape from this call.

This is certainly not to say that Kant's moral theory is invalid and takes absolutely no account of the self-experience of the moral subject. Although Kant fails to describe original moral experience in a convincing manner, his ethics makes eminently clear how we—in hindsight—are able to judge and justify our acts as moral. Though we act in most cases on the basis of our conscience, it is unsatisfactory to simply refer to our conscience when we desire to (or must) justify the moral value of our acts. Given the fact that one cannot justify one's own conscience, the attempt to justify a certain act on the basis of conscience is actually a refusal of justification. Those who want to justify their acts as moral are unable to do so without calling upon the general law, ideal values, or good customs and habits. Such a justification also implies a moral self-experience, although, once again, this cannot be considered the most original form of moral self-experience. When an individual subject succeeds in justifying its deeds by means of a reference to general principles without asserting that it has acted solely because of these principles, then this subject appears to itself to have acted coherently and consistently. The subject's various acts conform to the same constant principles, and thus the subject is in conformity with itself. In moral justification, the subject experiences its own identity in the form of what Ricoeur calls "*mêmeté*."[1] In conscience, to the contrary, the subject appears to itself under the form of "*ipséité*."

It is of the greatest importance to distinguish between moral conscience and moral self-justification, and to avoid confusing the experience of self as "*ipse*" with the experience of self as "*idem*." These two forms of self-experience do not, however, necessarily exclude each other; rather, they might be said to compliment each other. A well-conceived self-justification does not annul moral sensitivity for the other. Moral sensitivity for the other does not have to stand in the way of the principled readiness for self-justification. The origin of morality and moral self-justification, however, lies clearly in conscience, that is, in the experience of the loss of self that is unpredictable and can never be wholly justified. Nevertheless, it remains true that the original passivity and heteronomy of conscience is itself not enough to actively engage oneself for the other. Conscience itself does not lead to the deed. There must be a will and a rational principle to lead this will towards the right goal.

The Experience of a Divided Self

In the "Fundamentalontologie" of *Sein und Zeit*,[2] the ontological significance of "conscience" is investigated, and it is interpreted as a fundamental experience of Dasein's own being. In conscience, Dasein confronts its own being as something from which it continually flees. Thus, Heidegger, too, determines self-experience in function of a loss of self. For Heidegger, this loss of self does not so much signify an ethical sensitivity for the needs of the other; rather, the division within the own self is created by mutually irreconcilable interests. In its everyday existence, Dasein enters into all sorts of business that receives its meaning from a pregiven world. The one thing refers to another, and in its restless hustle and bustle Dasein lets itself be caried indefinitely from one task to another. Dasein loses itself in that which concerns it. According to Heidegger, this loss of self means that Dasein loses sight of its own individual self and understands itself in terms of a pseudo-self that is in fact from everybody and nobody. Dasein does what "one" does in a certain situation, takes a position as somebody that without much ado could be replaced by somebody else. Dasein's loss of self is thus linked with the assumption of an anonymous self that is determined solely in function of the mundane task to be accomplished.

Dasein awakes from this loss of its true self only when it is enveloped with a sense of "I don't feel like it any more," when its normal activities lose their meaning, in short, when there is nothing more worth doing. Such a sudden pause or turn-around occurs according to Heidegger in *Angst*; but perhaps as well in aesthetic contemplation, in love, in prayer and forgiveness. In any event, it occurs in a form of affective self-concern that Heidegger calls "*Befindlichkeit.*" Through such an experience, Dasein is brought back to the path towards the unique singularity of its own self, and it deliberately takes this path (*eigens*). Dasein's uncity, that is, its irreplacability, is based on its finitude, which stands in sharp contrast to the unlimited posibilities and infinite activities of the "Anyone" (*das Man*). The overcoming of the loss of self in authentic existence is, therefore, not the recuperation of a self-sufficient and complete self. On the contrary, whenever Dasein confronts its own self and "cares" for the possibilities that belong only to this self, it is confronted as well with its own lack of power and nullity. Such a confrontation cannot be endured for long, and all too eagerly is Dasein willing to surrender this proper self.

Dasein is thus thrown back and forth between the explicit concern for its own self and the escape into the anonymous self of the well-functioning "being-busy." This divided manner of existence belongs irreducibly to the essence of Dasein; Dasein *is* its own dividedness. Having a conscience is therefore also a fundamental form of self-experience, because it relates the two ways of existing to each other without annulling their difference. In having a conscience, the authentic self addresses the anonymous self, but this latter self does not recognize in this voice its own hidden self. On the other hand, it is also true that the authentic self requires the opposition with the anonymous self in order to begin the address. If Dasein were always nothing other than its own self, then the subject would neither speak nor listen, neither gain nor lose, neither give nor receive. Dasein experiences itself as a subject that is divided, that is, as a subject that neither fully coincides with itself nor completely falls apart. Dasein is neither its own self nor the anonymous self; it is both and yet not in the same way.

This division of the subject and this experience of self as confrontation with one's own dividedness is also central to the work of Freud and Lacan. According to Freud, consciousness and the unconscious are cut from the same material, which strangely enough, he calls "thinking." Nevertheless, consciousness and the unconscious differ from each other so much that they are unable to recognize each other. Unconscious representations function best when they do not become conscious, and when they do become conscious, this is a purely qualitative modification which, in principle, alters nothing within the content of these representations. Unconscious representations which do reach consciousness appear to consciousness as something which cannot be accorded a familiar place (*unheimlich*). The logic of the unconscious remains foreign to consciousness. On the other hand, these unconscious representations are mine only when they become conscious, that is, when I recognize them without really recognizing myself in them. For Freud (in opposition to Lacan) there is therefore no real subject of the unconscious; the unconscious becomes subjective only by becoming conscious. The subject is the place where the unconscious becomes accessible to consciousness and where consciousness experiences its own dependence upon the unconscious. The subject is divided and experiences itself only when it is confronted with its own division.

Freud speaks of an "Ichspaltung" and he has summarized his ideas on this notion in an unfinished manuscript from 1938.[3] He makes mention of a "rip" (*Einriss*) in the subject that can never be "healed" (*verheilen*). This rip or cut is due to the following: the ego recognizes something as inextricably linked to itself (Freud gives the example of castration-fear) without the ego being in a position to appropriate it. Given that Freud here points to the "extraordinarily important synthetic function of the ego," it is quite clear that this unity of the ego is not something that precedes the splitting. It is first through the experience of the dividedness of the own self that the synthetic unity of the ego becomes "extraordinarily important." The experience of one's own dividedness is a wound that never heals. The ego of Freud does not invalidate dividedness; it only prevents a psychotic falling apart of the subject. The experience of self is thus for Freud, too, an affective and, more specifically, a painful experience of the dividedness of the self. The unity of the subject is nothing else than the experience of irreducible dividedness. The subject is the possibility of its *own* being touched by the foreign, of its *own* being able to be surprised by the new, of losing *itself* without sinking away.

As a result, it is not surprising that the subject consists not of self-knowledge but of desire, and this desire has a mimetic structure.[4] According to Freud, "one" desires, in the first instance, what others desire. Only in the resulting conflict with others does there arise something like a subjective appropriation of this desire. This appropriation is actually the confirmation of heteronomy of one's own desire. It is only through the imitation and taking over of something from the others that one becomes aware of oneself. In this self-consciousness I experience myself as somebody who coincides neither with the others nor with itself. The experience of this division is that which is most my own.

As is well known, the experience of the dividedness of the self is clarified by Lacan on the basis of the distinction between the "speaking subject" (*sujet de l'énonciation*) and "subject spoken about" (*sujet de l'énoncé*). A subject arises only when something is spoken, and in its speaking the subject appears to itself at the same time as something that is spoken about in a language which has its own rules, independent of the subject. The "first word" of the subject is already a response; as soon as it is spoken, it no longer belongs to the subject. Whoever speaks in his or her own name about himself or herself simultaneously experiences what is said as the effect of a chain of signifiers, of the discourse of others, and of an anonymous language-code. This does not mean that in the case of authentic speaking (*parole pleine*) *only* the others in me speak. The subject speaks neither exclusively in its own name nor exclusively in the place of others. It is a subject only when it speaks in its own name, and when it does so speak, it experiences its dependence on the others.

Speaking is therefore not an experience of the loss of self whereby a self previously possessed by the subject is lost, but rather an experience of the loss of self wherein the own self *first* appears in the experience of the loss. The experience of self in speaking is necessarily connected to the experience that the significance of everything that I say about myself has its origin simultaneously and undecidably both inside and outside myself. Through this tension within the origin of speaking, speaking is set in motion and continues without the subject ever being able to stop it. The subject never gets enough of it because a nonrecoverable lack of being a self always remains. The self-experience of the subject in speaking is thus an experience of dividedness that expresses itself in desire. What prevents the divided self from falling apart is thus for Lacan, not the ego, but desire. Desire is an experience wherein the subject is most itself and simultaneously loses itself the most. Just as for Heidegger death confronts Dasein with an ultimate impossibility, so too according to Lacan does the desiring subject experience itself as driven by a passion for the impossible.

The Self as Difference

Derrida has continually and courageously resisted the temptation to draw premature conclusions from this original dividedness of the subject and the mimetic structure of desire. He has never viewed the phenomenon of an original opposition, of an irreplacable loss, or of an unreachable goal as the possible end of the task of thinking. He has also never accepted the presupposition that every opposition can be reconciled, every loss recovered, or that the impossible must be endured. What inspires Derrida is the interwovenness of disparate elements, the contamination of the medicine by the disease it fights, the impossibility of choosing for the one or the other. His philosophy of difference focuses on the logos of phenomena such as the original supplement, the unwinnable game, the now and its afterwards, postponement and delay, the essential shining-forth, and the necessary going astray.

These phenomena do not appear *to* or *for* a subject; rather, the subject experiences itself as a piece in a game that it did not start, as the trace of a past in which it did not participate, as a "deus ex machina." This "machina" of course does not work without personnel, the game needs actors and authors, the undecidable exists only for those who must decide. It is not sufficient to simply endorse the claim that in place of the subject "die Sprache spricht," that the play plays and that a lecture lectures. Only a subject who wants to say something discovers that this personal speaking is at the same time a type of quotation. Only somebody who must hold a lecture discovers that he or she is continually paraphrasing other authors and speaks as well in the name of colleagues and friends. Yet it would go against the rules of holding a lecture, if he or she were to ask his or her colleagues to respond in his or her place to objections which are raised. Somebody who talks and writes, but also anybody who lives in a human manner, is personally responsible for that which to a great extent lies outside of one's own responsibility. In one's own name, and in one's own name alone, one is responsible for that which one never could have said or done in one's own name. Feeling responsible for a self that never comes simply from oneself is the sort of self-experience which characterizes the finite subject.

Such self-experience, although rather evident, is nevertheless difficult to accept. It is understandable and thus also not "bad" that one tries to escape and is willing to let subjective liability be determined by universal laws. What one may not do is claim that these general laws stand at the origin of the subjective self-experience in the feeling of responsibility. The subjective sense of responsibility is something other than a will that wills itself and in so doing establishes the sphere of right. Self-experience as loss of self is a phenomenon that becomes visible only when one calls into question the notions of a monadological self and of absolute self-consciousness.

Critique of such a conception of the subject plays an important role in Derrida's work. His approach to themes such as absence, exteriority, "alterity," heteronomy, facticity, "spacing," iterability, and so forth, functions clearly in view of a critique of what is called the "metaphysical" concept of the subject. However, Derrida has never allowed this critique to lead him to announce the death of this subject. His deconstructive critique of the metaphysics of presence also yields no occasion for such a pronouncement, insofar as it shows that the metaphysical subject has never existed in the pure form suggested by Heidegger. Hegel, Kant, and Husserl never did succeed in "delivering" the metaphysical subject. In their analyses they often reach at the most unexpected moments the borders of self-consciousness and self-determination. It is for this reason that there is so much to be learned from them about a philosophical description of self-exprience in the loss of self. The philosophies of the absolute subject give an answer to the experience of the loss of self that, at the same time, expresses symptomatically the very structure of this irremediable loss of self.

Derrida's positive contribution to the analysis of self-experience is above all the indication of the necessity of self-*representation* and its *differential* structure. There exists no interior self-consciousness without an exterior appearance of the subject in pronouncements, gestures, activities, and so on. The subject experiences its own self only by means of these expressions. These expressions, though not merely coming from the exterior world, are nevertheless necessarily tarnished by the shortcomings which characterize this world. Thus, for example, it is not possible in a normal, mundane language to say precisely the same thing twice, without changing something in the meaning of what is said. When I look in the mirror, I see myself but also a great many other things that have nothing to do with me. I am happy if someone cites me, but I am often unhappy with the choice or even the content of the citation.[5] On the other hand, it is also the case that when I have something to say, it must be able to be repeated; that without a mirror I would not know that I'm getting older; that the number of citations could be an indication of the value of what I have written. What, then, am I: my first word, my second word, or the anonymous echoes of these words? My youthful feeling, or the middle-aged man in the mirror that ought to see a barber? My writing hand or my signature upon countless diplomas of students who once took a course from me? Derrida's response to each of these questions would be: both and neither! This is indeed the only honest and also the only possible answer.

This is all to say that the subjective self must be understood as *difference*. "Difference" refers to an irreconcilable opposition, an irresolvable tension, the unending postponement of any definitive decision. I am what I now am, and what I now am will only appear afterwards. I am equally what I say as what I do not say. I am what I want to be, but also what others say about me. I only know that I really am because many things refer to me that eventually conflict with each other and which certainly cannot be traced back to one thing. I know *that* I am because I am never certain *who* I am. Given the fact that from time to time I worry about myself, I must be there.

The Self That Can Be Touched

It is therefore easier to describe myself negatively, to say what I'm not rather than to say what I am. Furthermore, I come into contact with myself only by means of the experience of what I am not and what concerns me nevertheless. I remain, to a certain extent, always foreign to myself, though I must at the same time continually rely on myself. I am somebody that can never say with complete lucidity: "I am what I am."

I am certainly able to say of myself, "That's me!" but such a pronouncement does not suffice as an answer to the question "Who are you?" Whenever I say, "That's me!" I usually mean that I recognize myself, for example, on a photograph. This is merely the perception of a formal identity, whereby I ultimately point with my finger to something exterior that in the first instance appears to have nothing to do with me. Whenever I speak about myself as someone with such and such qualities and skills, then I do this mostly in the function of a role pattern, for example, in a job interview. If I am smart enough, then I won't say the same thing to everybody and in different circumstances, and if I'm honest, I won't feel particularly happy with my behavior. I cannot be simultaneously myself and my own impressario. I know all too well that I am not the director of my own qualities nor the owner of my own divided self. To speak *about* myself as somebody with a particular character contradicts the very manner in which I experience myself.

Self-experience also has little to do with a comportment which would suggest that I behave differently with myself than with others. To the contrary! The child that for the first time takes a bath by itself treats its body in the same way as its parents had. Around others, I comport myself in view of how others see and understand my behavior. *Functional* comportment rests upon imitation and is thereby especially impersonal. My comportment becomes truly *expressive* only when it escapes my control, and its meaning is much more accessible for others than for me. Those who purposely comport themselves in a highly expressive and original manner are affected persons, and as a result their behavior comes across as fake and implausible.

It is also not so certain that self-experience is connected with the fact that I am more interested in myself than in others. Malraux begins his *Antimémoires* with the solemn question: "Que m'importe ce qui n'importe qu'a moi?"[6] We call people narcissistic not because they are merely interested in themselves, but rather because they are always trying to get others to be interested in them. In function of what he reads in the look of others, the narcissist is triumphant or depressed. One is not only related to oneself when one is interested in oneself; it is even impossible to be purely interested in oneself. Even when no longer interested in itself and when it appears that neither an univocal self-expression nor an objective self-knowledge is possible, the subject remains related to itself.

The most fundamental self-experience is, however, not situated at the level of a theoretical self-consciousness, of a practical activity and comportment, or of speaking. I am in the most immediate way related to myself in the sensual feeling of myself. This is not to suggest that this *affective self-experience* is better, richer, or less problematic than the other forms of self-experience. The affective form of self-experience is also a form of loss of self. Here, too, there is no feeling for the self that exists independently of the feeling for persons, things, and values. Affectivity rests upon being touched, and the subject is at no time solely touched by itself. Pure self-affection is an invention of philosophers who have been deceived by a metaphysical notion of the subject.

As the capability of being touched, affectivity implies the experience of one's own vulnerability and sensitivity. It is therefore not as if the subject must first stand open for the foreign; rather, from the very beginning the subject is open, something befalls it that is beyond its control. Don't we say that one "falls" in love, or that one "falls" under the spell of something? I can be "struck" by something. I can be struck by a tennis ball, but also by a beautiful face, or by a stirring performance. Human affectivity is thus connected not only to physical touch. It deserves, nevertheless, to be called a "sensuous" capability, for it always concerns a subjective openness and receptivity. One is also open for meaning, and only pedantic teachers claim that it is impossible to feel meanings, ideas, and values. What is definitive for affectivity is not the sort of object that makes an impression on me but the manner whereby I am struck. It should be added that when I am touched affectively, I am not yet intentionally directed at the object that moves me. In affectivity, nothing *appears* to me; there is nothing *in front* of me that is available to me or to which I could direct my view. Although I am completely under the impression of something that comes from outside myself, in the experience of being moved I do not have a representation of something objective.

Whenever I feel "something," I also feel "myself," though the distinction between the two remains unclear. I feel "myself" attracted or repelled by something from which I can no more escape than from myself. Even in the case where my feeling appears to have something to do only with me, I feel neither myself nor my feeling as an objectifiable "something." I feel sick and I call the doctor, but I don't know how to answer his question "How do you feel?" Usually, doctors rather ask "Do you feel this or do you feel that?" and what they intend is not an affective feeling, but the typical way their textbooks tell them a certain organic disruption shows itself in the consciousness of a patient.

How is it, then, that I feel? What sort of self-experience is contained in affectivity? How do I feel myself in joy, hate, pleasure, pain? A possible answer is: I feel myself alive, I feel the energy, the tension, the pulse of my life. Even though I easily lose myself in these feelings, I certainly view these feelings as part of myself. Thus, in affectivity as well, there is no self-concern without loss of self. I lose myself in being in love, and yet, I have never lived so intensely. The affectively determined entanglement of self-concern and self-loss is most evident when one *reflects* upon one's own world of feelings and attempts to describe them. What one then says or writes about oneself is so impersonal and full of worn-out metaphors that one wishes never to have begun. One fails miserably in the effort at self-representation, but still one has with speaking or writing about oneself an intense feeling that causes the voice to quiver and the pen to tremble. Through this new feeling that arises in the description of old feelings, the first disappointment is quickly forgotten. The speaker or writer goes on because the self is once again lost and is driven away by an impossible expectation.

It remains true for affectivity as well that the loss of self remains an experience of self only insofar as no self-destruction takes over. Freud calls the threat of such an affective destruction of the own self "trauma." A trauma arises when the subjective tension caused by the affection is so great that the subject reaches a point of being completely overwhelmed. An impression becomes traumatic when the subject in no way can defend itself against it and can give no meaning to it, when the subject is turned inside out by it and is crushed by it. The subject becomes pure openness with no defense, trace with no reference, a roaring engine with no transmission and exhaust. In trauma, there is the danger that the subject as affective subject will die. Psychotic patients who claim to be dead have frequently undergone an experience of trauma, such as incest or the suicide of a family member.

Intense feelings go together with a degree of self-loss that leads many a feeling subject to build defensive reactions. A feeling always threatens to become a passion that brings about enslavement and self-alienation. Other sorts of people do not defend themselves against their emotions, but feign their feelings and act only as if they feel. They stage-manage an affective loss of self to create a feeling of excitement, which otherwise is so weak in them. One thinks of Don Giovanni, the deceived seducer, who sows all around himself the seeds of passion and whose own self consists of a list of adventures of which his bookkeeper professionally keeps account, subdivided into geographically ordered columns. The uncertain balance between experience of self and loss of self makes the one who feels a continually vulnerable subject. Other people often appear to be less fragile, perhaps because we ourselves are unable to feel their feelings.

However, do we not in fact have an experience of *feeling together*, whereby the indefinite boundary between experience of self and loss of self is even more unclear? In the first place, "feeling together" can mean *feeling the same thing at the same time*. The story is told that the most efficient defense against rugged Swiss mercenaries in an enemy army was let one's own Swiss soldiers sound Alpine horns right before the start of the battle. As soon as the mercenaries heard the sound, they abandoned their usual thoughts of murder, rape, and pillage, were deeply touched, began to cry, and wanted to head for home— together with the Swiss of the enemy army. "Feeling together" can also mean: *feeling one another*. In this case, it is not that we feel the same thing but that one feels the other and its feelings, and feels oneself in the feelings of the other. Here, the partners feeling together experience an affective self-concern in the form of a chiasmus. The best example of this springs immediately to mind: sexuality.

It is not necessary to demonstrate that in sexuality one enjoys oneself and through this has an experience of one's own pleasure. On the other hand, the self-loss which is involved is so great that sexual pleasure has also been called *"une petite mort."* One enjoys oneself, and yet, one enjoys the other more than one enjoys oneself. Or even more accurately, one enjoys oneself in the manner that the other enjoys us and thereby enjoys himself or herself. Sexuality is certainly complicated, and we are never more vulnerable than in our sexual affectivity. Sexual affectivity constantly threatens to derail into an experience of trauma. Sexuality is a form of affective experience wherein the need for a culture of affectivity is most evident. Sexuality without an erotic, without an *"ars amandi"* and the rules which belong to this playful game is an affectivity which threatens to destroy itself. Sexuality implies an incarnate self-experience wherein the subject loses itself in the body of the other and wherein one's own body which is caressed by the other first receives a subjective significance. In erotic play, the flesh is awoken from its unlimited anonymity and becomes a libidinous body that participates in a sensual "In-between" that bonds incarnate subjects in an atmosphere of intimacy.

Besides the libidinous body, there does exist still another form of subjective embodiment whereby, as Husserl says, the body functions as "organ of the will" (*Willensorgan*).[7] In this case, the body is available to an "I" that in its actions makes an almost instrumental use of the body. I use my hands to grasp something, my legs and feet to move somewhere, my eyes to see something that stands far away from me, and so on. Merleau-Ponty has shown well, however, that the "I" that wants to grasp and the grasping hands cannot be distinguished from each other because it is not as if there were first a spiritual subject deciding to grasp and then a hand executing this decision.[8] "Will" and "organ" compose part of the same embodied-sensuous subject. It is the hand that wills and is able to grasp, and the grasping subject is its hand. When the "I" separates itself from its hand and reduces its hand to a mere tool, the hand threatens to mal-function. Only an "I" that has lost itself in the movement of its hands and fingers can properly type into a computer or play the piano.

The hand that caresses and is caressed and the hand that works by grasping something are parts of a subject that is incarnated in a body and that loses itself in its embodiment. Nevertheless, it is difficult to claim that the emobodied subject caresses in the same manner that it drives a truck and that these two types of "hand-ling" harbor the same sort of self-experience. Erotic driving and technical mastery of the game of love lead sooner or later to disastrous consequences. The hand that steers the car forgets its own erotic feeling and the naked hand that caresses knows neither what it could or should do. It is, nevertheless, the same hand. This suggests that there is no sharp distinction between the libidinous body and the working body. The subject that unreservedly gives itself over to the other in the erotic play is in the danger of becoming an object and tool of the other's mastering will. When every form of bodily sensuous proficiency and activity of will disappear in sexuality, the loss of self easily develops into self-alienation. Conversely, the driver of an auto receives the recommendation to develop a feel for the car, to listen to the motor, to drive gently, and so on. Even in the most efficient bodily "functioning" and physical work there remains present a latent erotic significance to the body. Our body never lets itself be reduced to a mere tool without protesting against this through various symptoms. The comportment of the bodily subject is never solely passionately erotic nor solely efficiently goal oriented. In embodied existence, the subject is once again confronted with divergent interests and passions and with the fact that it never fully recognizes itself in its comportment, for it is never certain of the meaning of this comportment.

The subject, insofar as it experiences itself as a self in the form of a partial loss of self, is to be found wherever human beings live. People encounter great difficulty with themselves and dream of being able to forget themselves. Given that their own self is inextricably linked with that which does not belong to the self, they would indeed, together with the forgetting of self, forget as well all other people and the entire world. In doing this, they would surrender their own humanity. Without accepting oneself, one cannot accept others; and without accepting others, one cannot accept oneself. This is not easy. Still, this shared endeavor—which is also called "love"—leads to an experience of self as a gift. In love, this gift of self by the other is experienced as an invitation to lose oneself for the other. Instead of fearing self-loss, the beloved lover is happy to share the burden of his or her own self with the other. The self which he or she gains has lost its unbearable weight.

Ten

Law, Guilt and Subjectivity
Reflections on Freud, Nancy, and Derrida

Philippe Van Haute

Ma liberté n'a pas le dernier mot, je ne suis pas seul.

E. Lévinas

Introduction: Freud and Political Philosophy

In "Why war?" a lesser-known text from—the irony of fate—1932–33, Freud writes that it is a consequence of the innate and irradicable inequality of people that they can be divided into two categories: leaders (*Führer*) and followers (*Abhängige*). The latter are in the majority, they need an authority that they can submit themselves to unconditionally. The average citizen, writes Freud, simply does not have the power to bring his own drives under the control of reason, which would enable him to contribute to the life of the community. In order for him to do so, he has an imperative need for assistance from a ruling class.[1]

The passage mentioned must be read against the background of Freud's more systematic texts on the (political) community. "Group Psychology and the Analysis of the Ego" is a key text as far as this is concerned. In this work, Freud describes the essence of community life. He describes society as an anonymous mass whose members identify with each other on the basis of the fact that they have posited the same object ("the Führer") as their Ego ideal. As a consequence, one can call the love for (the libidinal bond with) the Führer the true cement of society.[2]

Is Freud a totalitarian thinker? Whatever the case may be, we cannot infer from the passages that have just been cited that Freud is supplying a psychoanalytic "imprimatur" to the totalitarian regimes which our century has generated at such an unprecedented rate. Only a peculiar sort of cynic would want to accuse Freud of totalitarian sympathies. But we are not immediately clear of difficulty when we say this. The question still remains whether Freud has, without really being aware of it, developed a theory of the (political) community which does not enable him to reject totalitarianism in a philosophically sound manner. Indeed, if submission to a leader characterizes society as such, what arguments do we have left to reject any form of totalitarianism?

One could of course immediately object that "Group Psychology and the Analysis of the Ego" is meant to be an analysis not of society as such, but of a specific type of society.[3] While writing it, Freud would have had in mind the totalitarian movements whose influence began to be felt in Europe from the early 1920s. But it seems to me that there is only very little textual evidence for such a reading. There is one passage in "Group Psychology" that is particularly revealing for this discussion. After having distinguished between organized and nonorganized masses, Freud proposes to limit his research to organized masses such as the army and the church. Indeed he argues: "We are only attracted by one circumstance, namely that certain facts, which are far more concealed in other cases, can be observed very clearly in those highly organized groups which are protected from dissolution in the manner that has been mentioned" (external force is employed to prevent them from disintegrating).[4] This clearly seems to imply that there are ultimately only organized masses, or at least that we find in each mass an embryonic organization. As far as this "minimal" (embryonic) organization is concerned, all masses are alike. That is precisely why Freud can concentrate on the church and the army to study masses, society, as such. In studying these prototypes Freud is interested only in the minimal organization without which no society can exist, in the (political) relation between a "Führer" and his followers.[5]

So once again, is Freud a totalitarian thinker? We have to tread carefully: "Totalitarian" does not mean that the "Freudian state" would be essentially violent or could be maintained only by means of brutal state violence. On the contrary, I use the term *totalitarian* with the meaning that Claude Lefort has given to it.[6] Two elements of Lefort's concept of totalitarianism are of interest here. According to Lefort, a totalitarian society is first of all characterized by an identification of civil society with the state, an identification which glosses over all real differences within society. Second, there is a division or splitting up of society into "leaders" (possibly a ruling party) and subjects, where the leaders claim that they serve as the mouthpiece for the whole of society. This second characteristic of totalitarian society refers to a logic of identification according to which the people *is* the proletariat *is* the party *is* the leader. This "logic" is sustained and supported, says Lefort, by the phantasy of a homogeneous body whose integrity must be preserved at all costs.

Thus we understand why Jean-Luc Nancy suggests replacing the term *totalitarianism* by that of *immanentism.*[7] The concept of 'immanentism' refers to the idea of a community whose essence would be realized by an uninterrupted communication between its members. This is the true telos of man. In such a community, man would immediately find his true calling. This community is its own achievement (it is its own "work"), bringing itself into being by incorporating or expelling anything which does not immediately belong to its essence. The immanent community progressively tries to reduce all that is other to itself and, in so doing, realizes its own essence.

Freud's description of society seems to correspond perfectly to Lefort's and Nancy's definitions of totalitarianism. Freud does indeed understand society as an intrinsic and finalized political given which does not admit of any significant differences, except for that distinction between the people and their leader (or leaders). On top of this, when Freud describes political society as an organic whole, he repeats the totalitarian phantasy par excellence: the narcissistic phantasy of a homogeneous body that relates only to itself. Or to put it more precisely, a body which does not know of or permit any alterity other than the relation of itself to itself (a self-sufficient body).[8]

Various contemporary authors (Heidegger, Lévinas, Derrida etc.) have wondered whether this phantasy supports the subject-centered thinking of modernity as well. Hegel is often said to bring this subject-centered thinking to its culmination and to its most privileged expression. The subject for Hegel is conceived as that which can contain its own contradiction in itself. For precisely that reason, Hegel can understand the history of philosophy as an attempt at a comprehensive synthesis, a reduction of the whole of experience and everything of significance to a totality in which consciousness encompasses the world, letting nothing else exist outside of it, thereby becoming absolute thought. According to this problematic reading[9] the Hegelian subject is "totalizing" insofar as it progressively reduces all that is other than itself to itself, and realizes its own essence in doing so. By means of the phantasy of the homogeneous body that only relates to itself, we can then understand Freud's description of society as the self-representation of a subject.

Freud has thus succumbed to the unmistakable charms of "immanentism." This is not so interesting in itself. Freud is not the first person to give in to this reduction, and he probably will not be the last one either. Moreover, Freud's importance as a political thinker is at least debatable. And yet his political theories are interesting. Indeed, these theories do not just repeat a number of well known "totalitarian" movements of thought; while doing so, they seem to provide an important impulse for another way of conceiving politics and the political which might enable us to escape "immanentism." Consequently, I would like to read Freud against Freud, in order to chart a few aspects of an "other" conception of politics and the political. This approach will be inspired by the later writings of Derrida; his work and that of his followers orient my reading of Freud.[10] However, the point of departure will be not "Group Psychology and the Analysis of the Ego," referred to above, but rather Freud's "Totem and Taboo."[11]

In both texts, Freud appeals to the myth of a primal horde in which a strong leader possesses all the women. According to Freud, both human history and the emergence of authority have to be understood from out of this primordial situation. "Group Psychology and the Analysis of the Ego" has to do, as we know already, with the origins of political authority. In this book Freud interprets modern mass society as a regressive repetition of the original society. He depicts the leader of this primal horde as an *"Übermensch"*: he is absolutely narcissistic and independent, and his existence does not depend on anyone else.[12] In short, the primal leader is a sort of absolute subject who completely coincides with himself. Freud describes this absolute subject as the model of every political authority.[13] However, this "political" version of the primal myth is actually a repetition and reworking of an earlier version from "Totem and Taboo." In this essay, the central concern is not so much the origin of political authority as that of ethical authority. In "Totem and Taboo" the original ethical authority is not the powerful *Übermensch*, but on the contrary, the guilt-inducing father. The father "culpabilizes," says Freud, because he is dead. The primordial ethical authority is not the authority of anyone personally; in any case, it is not the authority of an absolute narcissus that requires only itself in order to exist.

This reference to "Totem and Taboo" brings us to the center of the discussion I would like to present here. The position I would like to defend is the following: ethical authority always precedes political authority in such a way that it becomes impossible to think of politics or the political community as a ("big") subject. If this is so, how are we precisely to understand this "ethical" authority?[14]

Freud and Nancy on the Origin of the Law and of the Community

"Totem and Taboo" describes the origins of fatherhood. Although Freud calls the leader of the primal horde a "primal father," it is obvious that this qualification does not do justice to the reality. In opposition to the authority of the father, the power of the leader has no legitimacy other than the use of power. Sooner or later, he will be deposed. The sexually deprived sons kill the leader in order to be able to enjoy all his privileges. What is remarkable is that, according to Freud, the sons submit to the leader (accept his command) only after the murder—because they feel guilty.[15] The "dead," writes Freud, become more powerful than the living ever were.[16] The "father" in the true sense—or perhaps it is better to say, as Lacan does, the "paternal function"—becomes established only in and through the collective guilt of the members, and through this they become "brothers." They become "brothers" because they are guilty sons. The sons/brothers do not submit to some external physical power. There is, in any case, no instance left which could exercise this power. The figure of the father who exercises a legitimate power emerges from out of the guilt feelings, and not the other way around. The "guilt feelings" being discussed here are different from and more than mere fear of punishment. According to Freud, this is a moral anxiety with respect to an internal instance, and it is this instance that the subject submits to. In "Totem and Taboo," Freud simply calls this instance "conscience" ("the voice of conscience").[17] He will later designate it with a pair of concepts: 'superego' and 'ego-ideal'.

What is particularly important to remember here is that the "sons" do not submit to a pregiven command or an already existing law. On the contrary: it is out of guilt feelings that they are confronted with the law of the father. Consequently, guilt feelings are what come first: "They thus created out of their filial sense of guilt the two fundamental taboos of totemism."[18] Paradoxically, it is just when there is no longer anyone around to forbid anything whatsoever that the law and guilt, *ex nihilo* so to speak, establish "themselves."

What could this mean? Why do the sons subject themselves to the law just when there seems to be no objective provocation for it? Because they feel guilty, says Freud. But why do they feel guilty? The instance that would have punished them has now disappeared. And one can wonder whether, in a state of nature where brute force rules (the leader takes the women, he has no right to do so), that there is any relevance to talking about a crime in the true sense. The "sons," Freud continues, hate the father because he stands in the way of their own claims to power and their own sexual needs. Nevertheless, they love and admire him at the same time.[19] According to Freud, these reverent and tender inclinations will have the upper hand after the murder, that is, after the sons have already finished putting their hate for and their desire to be the father into practice.[20] Guilt feelings, according to Freud, flow out of this contradiction between the love for, and the murder of, the father: the sons feel guilty because they have done away with their love object.[21] But again, it is as if the "sons" can love the father only after they have eliminated the leader-rival of the primal horde. Before the murder, there is, properly speaking, no father to love. It is only on the basis of guilt feelings and remorse that the sons are to love the leader-rival as a father. In order to love the father (in order to have a father), we apparently have to kill him first.

According to Freud, the leader-rival is not only hated (for understandable reasons) but also, at the same time, cherished and looked up to. The members of the primal horde admire him and therefore want to be just like him. The members of the horde not only challenge the leader's possession of the libidinal objects; they above all want to be as strong and independent as he is. They want to become absolute, self-sufficient *narcissists*, just like the leader. The end point of this narcissistic passion, according to Freud, is the cannibalistic sacrificial meal in which the leader is literally consumed. "The violent primal father had doubtless been the feared and envied model of each one of the company of brothers: and in the act of devouring him they accomplished their identification with him, and each one of them acquired a portion of his strength."[22] What is at stake in this struggle is now quite clear: the acquisition of an identity. Desire culminates in a murder and a cannibalistic sacrificial meal because it is directed towards the acquisition of an identity by means of the assimilation of the other.

And yet, the desire to be like the other has to fail. None of the sons can take over the place of the father. None of the protagonists have their desire fully satisfied. The murder has therefore been in vain. Freud writes: "And as we know, failure is far more propitious for a moral reaction than satisfaction."[23] Guilt feelings spring up, and this is Freud's last word on the subject, from the failure of this identification. None of the sons can occupy the position of the father, the absolute narcissist. Freud explains this by rather factual arguments: the sons will have to take each other into account, and for this reason the steady ascent into the position that the father previously held is impossible.

But perhaps Freud is on the track of something more fundamental here. The identification fails because there is a limit to appropriation. The failure of the identification by the sons already reveals an unbridgeable limit. It discloses an alterity that I cannot appropriate and that makes the assimilation of the other inevitably fail. In the perspective of Freud's story, this alterity can be nothing other than death, the "absolute master," or he who is dead (*Der Tote*).

For the sons, "he who is dead" indeed represents their own inconceivable death. The sons identify themselves with the Father, and they derive their identity from this identification. However, this cannibalistic identification results in the death of the father. The other is dead, but (as a result) they themselves, by virtue of the identification, are also "dead." Or to put it in another way which is probably clearer, the cannibalistic identification confronts them with their being-unto-death according to an inescapable logic.

There are passages in Freud that support this reading.[24] The first moral commandments, Freud writes, originate from the sight of the dead body of a beloved person. The first and most significant prohibition to be awakened in the budding moral consciousness is precisely "Though shalt not kill." According to Freud, this commandment is a reaction to the feelings of hate which lurk behind mourning, feelings which are satisfied seeing the dead body of the loved one. As a consequence, in order for moral consciousness to emerge, the dead body we are confronted with does not have to be that of the father, nor must the dead person actually have to be the victim of a murder. It is sufficient to be confronted with a dead person with whom we identify according to the mode of an all-consuming love. This is how, Freud continues, we are painfully confronted with our mortality: each of these deceased individuals is, by virtue of identification, a part of my own ego (myself).

These remarks go in the direction of our reading of "Totem and Taboo." Following this reading, what the sons subject themselves to is their own proper/improper "death": "I am myself this dead person (proper), but he is still radically other than I am, in as far as I ultimately cannot conceive to myself being dead (improper)." The sons submit to the other (consequently, to themselves) insofar as the other escapes every identification: what the sons are gathering themselves around and what they are submitting themselves to is literally "nothing"—no subject, no Father, no leader—nothing but their own proper/improper inconceivable death, their inability to be an absolute narcissist/subject.[25] The "delayed" (nachträglich) obedience that founds the community is not a submission to a political power, but an ethical respect for what in the subject escapes the subject; it is a respect for what is "beyond the ego" (Über-ich, in the sense of nonassimilable) in the ego. Or again, the community comes into being only on the basis of and as a confrontation with the subject's own proper/improper mortality.

The respect and recognition that is referred to here, and which founds the community, cannot be understood as a speculative logic. It is not as if I recognize myself in the death of the other, but rather that I recognize that there is nothing recognizable in the death of the Other. Death is what we share and what separates us at the same time. The sons are confronted with their own mortality by the figure of the dead father. They are the dead Father himself. But they are the Father in the mode of not being him: no one can die in my place; death is always and inalienably my death. Jean-Luc Nancy expresses this structure in the following way: "Toi e(s)t (tout autre que) moi."[26] The sons are the dead father ("Toi est moi") whose death they can nevertheless never replace ("Toi est tout autre que moi"). The community ("Toi et moi") literally lives off this paradox.

This "delayed" obedience is called a respect for what is "beyond the Ego" in the ego. The superego plays a central role in Freud's theory of psychoanalysis.[27] It is an intrapsychic instance that has to carry out different functions: self-perception, conscience, and the formation of an ideal that I can measure myself against. Freud initially introduces the concept in order to account for certain pathological phenomena: the "Beobachtungswahn" in which the subject feels that an impersonal instance is watching everything it does, thinks and desires; the melancholia in which the sufferer must pay severely for mistakes that he or she never committed; the negative therapeutic reaction or the "refusal" to heal; the neurosis in which the patient suffers from its own incapacity to comply properly with a supreme law which is beyond all doubt.

Freud mainly thematizes the superego out of three metaphors: censor, judge, and inheritance. This last metaphor seems to be the most crucial: the other two are included within it and can be explained by reference to it. The superego is the heir to the Oedipus complex. The establishment of the superego and the "decline" of the Oedipus complex are two sides of the same reality. We could summarize this in a very schematic way by saying that the subject abandons his Oedipal objects by identifying with them. By saying this, Freud is making an appeal to what he has written elsewhere in connection with melancholy. The most standard way the subject successfully abandons his Oedipal objects is by identifying with them in a narcissistic way: the libidinal cathexis of the object is given up and replaced by a libidinal cathexis of the ego that is reshaped according to the model of the lost object. This "cannibalistic" relation to the object permits the ego to remain in the favor of the id, without maintaining the impossible (in the case of death) or forbidden object cathexis (the Oedipal objects, for example). The id now finds its satisfaction in the ego itself. In any case, the superego, according to Freud, originates from an identification with the parental figures, and prototypically with the father figure.

But who exactly is the subject identifying with here? Who is the father (who are the parents) the child is identifying with? This question is less tautological than it looks. Soon after Melanie Klein's critique of the theory of the superego was first published, Freud had to admit that her comments held water.[28] There is no rectilinear connection between the severeness of the superego and the real severeness of the parents. In spite of all the theories of antiauthoritarian education, it is not unusual for children of tolerant parents to have an extremely severe superego. Klein points out that the development of the superego always starts earlier than the Oedipal period in the strict sense, and that the child always identifies with an "image" of its parents and not its real parents.[29] When we combine this thought with Freud's thesis that the little Oedipus identifies with the superego of its parents, then we have to conclude that the formation of the superego at least partially stems from the transformed introjection of the parental commands and prohibitions.

The superego originates not from an identification with the law, but in a transformed (transforming) identification with the representatives of the law (parents, teachers, etc). Therefore, the law is never directly present for us. We always find ourselves, in other words, "before the law,"[30] the law itself continually eluding us. Parents, for example, are not the law: they cannot simply pronounce the law in their own name.[31] The ultimate origin of the law always withdraws. There is no possibility of catching a glimpse of the law itself. Its origin can then be expressed only in a mythical way. In "Totem and Taboo," Freud formulates a mythical story of origins which must supply an answer to the question of the origin of the law. However, Freud's empirical interpretation of this myth is an obstacle preventing him from breaking through to the perspective which I have just formulated.

How is the "delayed" obedience to what is "beyond the ego" in the ego related to the superego that has just been presented? As an intrapsychic instance, the superego represents the law. It is the law as it has been internalized by the subject by means of an identification with the superego of significant authority figures. The superego confronts the subject with a series of sometimes conflicting orders and prohibitions, and it has to adhere to them. On the other hand, the "voice of conscience" that Freud brings onto the scene in "Totem and Taboo" does not seem to say anything definite to us. It provides no specific message about how we ought to behave towards the other (ourselves). So this voice cannot be simply identified with the superego in the strict sense. How are we then to understand this "voice of conscience"?

Following Freud, I have been discussing up to now an "ethical respect" for what places a limit on the (dialectical) assimilation of the other.[32] It is a respect for what prevents us as a community from ever becoming a (super-) subject. Community originates from and on the basis of a respect for what makes totalization (the absolute immanence) impossible. Community is respect for this impossibility. However, how appropriate is the expression "ethical respect"? When the "voice of conscience" hands us no concrete rules of conduct, can we then still call this "moral" or "ethical"? Is what I have referred to up to now as "respect" not rather a sort of primordial affirmation that precedes every concrete moral engagement: a primordial yes to the community as the impossibility of an absolute immanence?[33] In other words, the origin of community is not to be found in the superego as such with all its orders and prohibitions, but rather in the pre-ethical respect for the other, a respect that actually makes the formation of the superego in the strict (ethical) sense possible. This yes can only be understood as an answer to a call: The voice of conscience is perhaps nothing other than the call of a community that we are always already thrown into. What does all this mean?

Intermezzo: Heidegger and Freud

A short reference[34] to Heidegger can clear quite a few things up here. Heidegger also talks about the voice of conscience that calls upon Dasein to assume its characteristic "being-guilty."[35] Heidegger connects this guilt with the impossibility for Dasein ever to be its own ground. Dasein is always already thrown in specific possibilities. The ultimate ground of our existence continually eludes us; Dasein can never definitively justify or ground its existence. It is ultimately groundless. The voice of conscience, according to Heidegger, calls up Dasein to take this nothingness upon itself. The "voice of conscience" is the voice of Dasein itself; it is the voice of "Care" that calls us back from the forgetfulness of the "They." In the "They," Dasein is so caught up in the self-evidence of its everyday habits and certainties that it evades and passes over its ultimate indefiniteness and groundlessness. Primordial "guilt," said Heidegger, does not have to do with the moral responsibility for a lack or a deficiency in the other, nor does the "voice of conscience" offer a practical guide for conducting oneself that guarantees a "good" life. The primordial "guilt" precedes and makes possible every concrete moral guilt.[36]

According to Heidegger, the "voice of conscience" is the "voice" of Dasein itself, which calls upon us to assume our own nothingness. In the light of what has just been said about Freud—while sticking to Heideggerean terminology—one could say that the "voice of conscience" is in a radical way the voice of Dasein as *Mit-sein* (as being-with). It is not unimportant to indicate here what seems to be a major difference between these authors. Even without wanting to make a full comparison, it is obvious that for Freud[37] the confrontation with one's own finitude/mortality is intrinsically linked up with the confrontation with the mortality/finitude of the other. This "confrontation" takes place through a process of identification that plays a fundamental role in the constitution of subjectivity. So, for Freud, "identification" does not have a mere "ontic" value, as Heidegger would probably say, but an ontological (existential) importance. At the same time, it is through the identification with the moral other (the mortality of the other) that we are confronted with our own mortality/finitude. For Heidegger, the death of the other does not confront us with our own uttermost possibility. On the contrary even, Heidegger writes: "death . . . is a possibility in which the issue is nothing less than Dasein's being-in-the-world . . . If Dasein stands before itself as this possibility it has been fully assigned to its ownmost potentiality-for-being. When it stands before itself in this way, all its relations to any other Dasein have been undone. This ownmost non-relational possibility is at the same time the uttermost one."[38] For Freud (and Nancy), however, standing before oneself as mortal seems to be intrinsically relational in a more essential way than it is for Heidegger. Finitude intrinsically, as Freud and Nancy agree on this point, manifests itself as community. Therefore, the community is just like Heidegger's Dasein: a groundless, finite reality. The community, like Dasein, cannot ground itself. The "voice of conscience" calls upon us to assume precisely this groundlessness and finitude. The primordial yes is an answer to a call from the community as an impossible immanence. This yes precedes every factual establishment of a community. It is always already there. The totalitarian deviation also presupposes this yes, even if it does so in the mode of "not-listening." The attempt, in spite of everything, to try to realize an immanent community presupposes that one first submits oneself to the community.

Totalitarianism and Democracy: Freud, Derrida, and Lefort

The call of the community in a certain sense "opens" or "summons" conscience. Through this, we are thrown into a responsibility we did not want to have and whose precise content we do not (cannot) know.[39] The call of the community has, just like the Freudian law (or should I say: as law), no origin which can be demonstrated. Like the law, it constantly withdraws. Just as there is no law of the law, there is no responsibility of responsibility. The origin of responsibility refers back, like the law, to an absolute past that can never be present. We are always already thrown into this responsibility, even when we pass over this call and attempt to forget the primordial yes that goes together with it. Neither the call nor the primordial yes stems from a subject that would have them, as it were, in its possession; or more precisely, the subject cannot give a first-person account of this call and this yes, since it is always already thrown into it. They are rather the dispossession of the subject, establishing the community as an impossible immanence.

Just as the law does not lose its compelling force in having no determinable content, so too is the primordial responsibility void of ultimately determinable content, although we are nevertheless always already subjected to it. Derrida talks about the essential excessiveness of this responsibility. It offers us no handy program that would enable us to determine what we have to do. This responsibility escapes all calculation and lies at the source of all subsequent specific responsibilities.[40] In this sense, this responsibility has the status of a transcendental condition of possibility. Derrida actually refers to it as a quasi-transcendental condition of possibility, because in opposition to the traditional conception, it is not grounded in the subject or in subjectivity.[41]

Both the origin of the law and the origin of responsibility withdraw into an absolute past. Totalitarianism or immanentism is probably nothing other than the attempt to postulate the factual community itself (possibly via the privileged insight of the leaders) as this origin. The totalitarian state accepts no transcendental or external norms that it must comply with. It is a law unto itself, or what boils down to the same thing, it is the tireless representative of the law, whose self-determined responsibilities are fixed, unambiguous, and irrefutable. Here, both the call of the community and the primordial yes are interpreted as the call and the yes of a subject that can pronounce them in its own name.

However, we would be sadly mistaken if we were to characterize totalitarianism as a mere deviation. Totalitarianism is not a kind of *accident de parcours* that we can simply steer our way around. It is not as if we either act and think in a totalitarian way, or we do not. I will first try to clarify what I mean by this in a somewhat intuitive way.

We have to respect the Other as Other. This respect inevitably implies that we try to understand the other in his or her otherness, that we try to grasp the singularity of the motives determining his or her actions, and so forth. For the alternative is indifference, and indifference is obviously not respect. In order to really respect the other in their otherness, I have to really know them as well. At the same time, I must attempt to grasp them in their otherness and let them exist as other. But is not this attempt itself to understand the other in their otherness and to bear (keep) in mind the particularity of their motives simply another way of assimilating the other into my own sphere? If so, then we stand before a paradox: we can respect the other only by not respecting them.

Our reading of Freud teaches us that guilt feelings and conscience are processes in which and through which we try to identify with the other by incorporating them. Therefore, we have always already passed over (in the sense of a forgetting) the call from the community as impossible immanence. The incorporating movement has always already started. Consequently, there is no moment when we are confronted with the other in their pure otherness. The process of cannibalistic identification that is directed towards absolute immanence is always already there from the very beginning. In this sense, totalitarianism as the will to immanence is an indestructible possibility for community.

Heidegger refers to an original "guilt" that we are not able to evade. Via the work of Freud and Derrida, we are now in a position to reformulate this guilt as guilt towards the other. This guilt consists in the fact that we have always already misperceived the other in their alterity. The guilt cannot be removed, seeing that the respect for the nonassimilatable alterity of the other is not possible without such a misperception.

The question then is not so much whether we are able to respect alterity or the impossible immanence of the community. The question is rather this: do we stand (or not) in the tension between the inevitable misperception of the community as impossible immanence and the primordial yes that we have always already pronounced? Every attempt to remove this tension leads to excesses. In the case of sheer misperception, we land in the terror of totalitarianism; sheer respect for the other leads to disintegration and chaos. In the second case there is nothing left to hold us together.

This last remark also makes it possible—and this is my point— briefly to clarify the meaning and importance of the notion of what Lefort calls the "People-as-One" (Le peuple-Un) for democracy.[42] Claude Lefort has pointed out that, in a democracy, no one can claim power as one's own substantial property. In democracy, Lefort says, the place of power remains empty. No single individual or group of individuals is co-substantial with power. This means that no one has privileged access to or knowledge of the will of the people either.[43] This People-as-One—the community as immanent unity—is, after all, a phantasy. It is the phantasy of the total assimilation of alterity in the community. However, we know that this phantasy is always already "at work." There is no community which is not affected by the workings of this phantasy in a primoridal way. Or to put it in another way, without this phantasy, society—democratic society as well—falls apart. Lefort points out in regard to this that the symbolic "void" of the place of power cannot become a real "void." If this were to be the case, society would shatter into a multitude of particular interests, none of which would have any more legitimacy other than that which it could derive out of itself. The phantasy of the People-as-One has to put the brakes on this tendency. So democratic society does not decide for unity, nor for plurality. On the contrary, it stands in the tension between the two.

From this we can understand the democratic principle par excellence: "one man, one vote."[44] The primordial ritual of general elections implies that at the moment when we attempt to recover the one will of the people, we are reduced to mere numerical units, which implies a quasi-dissolution of social relations. The phantasy of a substantial people is, even if only for a moment, literally "dissolved" or put out of play. In contrast to what a whole generation of "social criticism" wanted us to believe, the right to vote is not just a pacifier designed to keep the oppressed masses quiet. Nor is it merely a formal mechanism which remains external to real power relations. Or to put it better, this formal mechanism as such is a permanent recollection of the paradox that grounds and supports democracy.

Conclusion

One might conclude from all this that I am defending what is often called "bourgeois (capitalist) democracy." However, things might be a little bit more complicated. Insofar as capitalist society seems to reduce the whole of reality to objects that can and must be exchanged in a frenetic process of accumulation and appropriation, it is characterized by a misrecognition of what escapes immanentism recalling totalitarian society. But whereas totalitarian society resembles in a strange way the paranoid stance (neither the paranoid patient nor the totalitarian state recognize any external standard for their claims), capitalism reminds us of the pervert or—more precisely—the fetishist position. Just as the fetishist replaces and symbolizes the absent phallus of the mother, the world of commodities seems to replace and symbolize that which cannot be integrated into the social body. They are supposed to fill up—and, in doing so, to hide—the lack that inaugurates the community as an impossible immanence. But the frenetic character of the process of accumulation and the particular kind of "unhappiness" that goes along with it seems to indicate that capitalist society implies at the same time—and also in this it resembles fetishism—a recognition of this lack/impossibility. Both misrecognition and recognition exist next to one another.

However, the problem is that one only very seldom finds fetish-ists going into therapy. Even if they recognize the "pathological nature" of their practices, they are too happy with them most of the time to want to do anything about them. The same might be true of capitalist society. Our incapacity even to consider a possible alterna-tive can be linked to the fact that capitalism gives us too much plea-sure for us to problematize it. But whatever the case may be in this regard, the intrinsic link between capitalism and democracy that con-servative theoreticians expect us to believe in, cannot—in my opin-ion—be accepted without further consideration.[45]

Eleven

Do We Still Want to Be Subjects?

Ute Guzzoni

"Do we still want to be subjects?": a curious title indeed. Is being a subject something which is up to us at all, which we chose to begin at a certain point in time, and which we can bring to an end again of our own volition? And even if we answer in the affirmative, isn't it all too clear that this is merely a rhetorical question, which can be answered with an equally unequivocal yes or no, depending on what we understand by "subject"?

However, I understand the question in my title as a *critical question*—in other words, as a question which marks a threshold. It arises at a crisis or turning point, a point of division and discrimination with regard to a self-understanding which could be meaningful today. This differentiation has perhaps already taken place, or at least its coming has already been announced. If being a human being does not always and inherently mean being a subject, if human beings became subjects only in the course of history, and thus acquired an awareness of their position in the world as knowing and acting subjects, then they must also be capable of leaving this position behind, of abandoning this specific form self-awareness, or at least of thoroughly modifying it.

Every fundamental interpretation of being and of the self raises a specific, unquestioned claim to absoluteness; thus one must already have left such an interpretation some way behind, before one can recognize its relativity and historicity. The question of whether we still want to be subjects becomes possible only when our self-understanding, and our understanding of our being-in-the-world, has already shifted in some way, although perhaps still only implicitly.

I

I will begin by giving a tentative and preliminary explication of my title question, working back from the end and asking in turn what is meant here by "subjects," by "still," by "we," and by "want to be." In the course of this explication a whole series of questions will be left open, and will only subsequently be clarified, and then only partially and in an oblique way.

Subjects

Do we still want to be *subjects*? What is a subject? Or rather, since this word is used in multiple ways, what does the word *subject* mean in my title? According to a formulation of Kant's, the subject is the "ground of thought."[1] This means that the subject is whatever it is that thinks in its capacity *as thinking*, in the sense that this represents the starting point for the thinking relation to an object. Kant emphasized that the subject should in no way be hypostatized, that it is the function or the "form of thought" rather than a thinking substance. And even in Hegel's famous sentence from the Preface to the *Phenomenology of Spirit*—that it is a matter of thinking truth as subject, and not only as substance—this opposition is assumed as self-evident. For modern thought the relation of human beings to objects in the world is paradigmatically a cognitive relation, and the active pole of this relation is the subject, since this subject is more precisely the act of self-relating itself. (Only in the second instance is the autonomous subject of knowledge also equally a subject of action.)

As is well known, the Latin term *subjectum* is a translation of the Greek term *hypokeimenon*, with which Aristotle designates that which underlies a process, a statement, but also any finite being. This Greek "subject" is also a ground of determination, but precisely not as an active ground, not as the "determining" itself, but as that which is determined, that which takes on determinations. It is thus distinguished both from that which thinks the determinations, the human *logos*, and from that which determines as such, the form or the *eidos*, and indeed as their necessary correlate. Only when, at the beginning of the modern age, these two—knowing *logos* and determining *eidos*—coincide, and when the thinking "I" becomes that which forms and determines the materially given, does the concept of the 'underlying' get transferred onto whatever it is which thinks, thereby acquiring its fundamentally active character.

Our understanding of the subject—and correspondingly also the critique of the subject—includes the following two moments, which build on each other: on the one hand, the subject its posited as *autonomously determining* in relation to an object which is determined by it; its autonomy is revealed in a relation of domination over everything which is not itself. The critical question then becomes, Is someone who loves really herself, and thus autonomously, the subject of her desire, someone who thinks the subject of her thinking, someone who acts the subject of her actions? Or is this merely an illusion of the modern philosophy of the subject, or even of modern self-consciousness: "We must not say: *Descartes thinks.* We must say: *it thinks in Descartes.* We must not say *Descartes writes his books.* We must say: *the books of Descartes write themselves under the pen of Descartes.*"[2]

On the other hand, this relation of domination appears as consisting primarily in the subject's *rationality*. However an interpretation and critique of the rational "subject-object relation" can be intended to have a broader or a narrower sense. The first sense can be clarified with the help of a formulation of Wolfgang Welsch's, the second by a characterization from Martin Heidegger's *Holzwege*. According to Welsch, "dominating subjects" are those who "judge everything according to one measure," and consequently he is concerned that other modes of rationality should also be admitted and acknowledged.[3] For Heidegger, subjects are those who set themselves up as the measure. In this connection he speaks of that "way of being human" which "takes over the range of human capacities as the space of measurement and performance for the domination of beings as a whole."[4] Critique is guided in this instance by reference to a mode of being human which is understood as finite dwelling *with* things, and *in* the world.

Still

Do we *still* want to be subjects? Still—this means in an epoch which has already traversed a fundamental critique of the subject-object relation and which almost sees this critique as already belonging to the past. However, it also implies an epoch in which the engagement with the subject and the question of the specificity, role, and meaning of the thinking "I" remains central. It is thus an epoch in which there are many different ways of being concerned with the subject, of merely keeping it within bounds or denying its determining function, and thus generally putting it into question. "Still"—this also means in a philosophical situation which fundamentally sees itself as an "after": after metaphysics, after the developments of modern thought and history, indeed after modernity itself. It always relates itself to the past in a critical way, by fencing itself off, and yet also by establishing conceptual links with what used to be. It confronts the question of whether elements of what once developed over time still penetrate into the present, while certain others have become invalid, or can and must be abandoned to the sedimentations of history. Are we *still* subjects today, or are we subjects *no longer*? Do we in any case no longer want to be such?

We

And yet who are "we"? Do *we* still want to be subjects? For whom, in whose name, on the basis of what experiences do philosophers speak when they try to tell us "what is" and "how it is," in other words, when they concern themselves with the present relation of human beings to their world, to its things, happenings, and states of affairs? The conviction is now widely shared that what is sought for in this questioning can no longer be changeless ontological and anthropological constants. But if it is indeed rather the case that we are here concerned with interpretations of the world and of the self which have developed through historical processes of social recognition, and which can change again in the future, then we are confronted with the question of *who* is bringing strands of argument, insights, intuitions, imaginative constructions, interests, and needs into play—and of what kind these are. Critiques of the fundamental assumptions of a specific worldview will always be guided by differing perceptions and projects. They can be related to what exists in the present, or to a desirable state which can perhaps already be forseen, or may belong to a remote future. Are they based on the fundamental agreement of the majority, or merely on the utopian aspirations of a handful of people? Or is neither one nor the other the case? Who "we" is in this instance is closely connected with the next moment, that of "wanting to be."

Want to Be

Do we still *want to be* subjects? Is there any sense in which what we are concerned with here is something which we can *want to be* or *not* want to be? The contemporary critique of the concept of the subject, above all the postmodern critique, is often based on the conviction that we *cannot* be subjects, that it is merely an illusion when human beings still attribute a fundamental autonomy to themselves in relation to their objects and actions.[5] Isn't it rather a question of being *able* to be, than wanting to be?

To put the problem another way: if the question of our own being-a-subject is not merely to do with autonomy, but with the more fundamental issue of the relation of human beings to their world, is the "other" which we would consequently like to be something which we—some, or many, or all of us—*can be* already in the present? Or is it something which, at best, we *will be*, at some point in an indefinite, utopian future? This would certainly introduce a distinction with respect to "wanting" which would change everything.

And what is it which brings us to the point of wanting to be something other and otherwise than how and what we are, how and what we have become? Is it a matter of logical deductions, experiences, speculations, dreams, or of something else?

II

Do we still want to be subjects? The subject has fallen into disrepute. I have no wish here to add to the multiplicity of critical, sceptical, or pessimistic diagnoses of the times but would simply like to highlight the fact that—and the degree to which—the assumption of an autonomous, rational subject has largely become questionable and suspect today.

The assumption that human beings should autonomously order and dominate the surrounding world, including themselves and other human beings, according to their own criteria and laws, and that, as beings endowed with reason, they are also capable of achieving this has lost its immediate obviousness and plausibility. We have the experience of being powerless in the face of many kinds of objective regularities and compulsions, of organizations and institutions, of powers and interests which essentially transcend and overwhelm us, and which have taken on the character of a second nature. We experience ourselves as externally determined, as merely participating, as integrated and assimilated, not as subjects but as objects, even of our own actions. A triumphalist belief in progress has given way to a profound and widespread resignation.

However, one should not make the mistake of automatically considering every generalized depression to be a significant sign of the times. In the course of the century which is drawing to a close there have repeatedly been all kinds of upswings and downswings, according to the political and economic conjuncture, and the "hole" we are currently in is not necessarily symptomatic of the entire epoch. At the same time, it is fair to claim that, in retrospect, this whole century has been characterized by a gradual decay of authoritative principles and binding values, of religious belief, of self-evident convictions and identities. Today we regard science and technology with a certain scepticism, as we do state power and the possibility of realizing principles such as democracy, solidarity, freedom, and justice. The rational order which modern man wanted to impose upon the world has failed, and to recognize this is neither subversive nor revolutionary. When one appreciates, for example, that the general domination of profit and the interests of power have always already incorporated the needs and interests of the individual, then "capitalism" is no longer a critical-polemical concept.

If we understand by the term *subject* the human capacity for planning, willing, and acting in general, then we must accept that we westerners have in fact succeeded in forming the world in our own image on a planetary scale. The result however is that the natural dimension of our being, independence and initiative, authenticity and qualitative specificity, have to a large extent been suppressed, and that this is one of the reasons for the mood of resignation and the levelling-down of differences which I have just mentioned, and which has been characteristic of recent years and decades. Paradoxically it is precisely the all-embracing consequences and successes of modern planning and agency which have generated from within themselves their own questionable and partly counterproductive effects.

However, the question of human autonomy or of its illusory character can be posed only when one begins with the basic assumption that the self-assertion and self-preservation of human beings is necessary in the face of a world and of an environment which is experienced as hostile and alien. Both the assertion of the autonomous subject, and the domination of powers and forces whose "games" engulf or undermine this subject, operate within the framework of a fundamental confrontation of subject and object. It is through this confrontation that the constellation formed by human beings and reality—including the reality of human beings—seeks to gain control of its own otherness.

But it is not only the actual inversion of supposed autonomy into effective heteronomy, which can undoubtedly be observed in many instances, that has led to a suspicion of the subject as point of departure—just as it is not merely the negative consequences of the destruction of nature which have made necessary a new reflection on nature and the natural. It seems to me that in the concept of auto-nomy, it is just as much—and perhaps even more—the second component, the moment of legislation, that characterizes the subjectivity of the subject—and also ruins it, as it were. For in the regularity of the relation between them, the division between subject and object is cemented in a particular way, a division which can be seen as a belated consequence of the opposition of determining and being-determined which is already to be found in Plato, and especially in Aristotle. All talk about types of rationality and systems of rules remains within a domain of legislation and determination which is always in danger of becoming a realm of abstraction and worldlessness, as is the case not merely for the sciences but also increasingly for the supposed "worlds" of technology and of economic rationality.

Thus there is a fundamental moment in the interpretation of the human being as subject which seems to require even more urgent and decisive transformation than the dubiousness of human autonomy, which taken on its own would certainly not provoke the question of whether we still *want* to be subjects. Talk of a subject-object structure brings the basic attitude of human beings to the world into view, in line with which they believe themselves to have the world over against them, and thus beneath them, as something alien which is to be dominated. In grasping what surrounds them—the things in the world to which, and among which, they belong—as objects, they cut themselves off from these things, oppose them to themselves, make them manipulable and controllable. In becoming objects these things fall out of the system of interrelations which constitutes the world and become something "objective" and calculable. Only by means of this "neutralization" of the localized and the particular can the rationality and functionality of science and technology gain a hold.

What would it mean then, if, confronted with these wider implications of the subject-object relation, we no longer wanted to be subjects? In a fundamental sense, the attitude which seeks to leave being-a-subject behind no longer operates in the domain of being-a-subject, and no longer accepts the content of its determinations from the negation of this way of being. We do not assert our autonomy or even our heteromony, but neither do we doubt them. We neither comprehend beings as a whole from the standpoint of our subjectivity, or as constituted through it, nor do we understand ourselves as merely bearers of functions within one, or an endless plurality of language games. To this extent it is not a question of discovering a new subjectivity, however different this might be, which would avoid the "mistakes" of our inherited form by "evaluating different types of rationality," and would be capable of "transitions from one system of rules to another, the simultaneous consideration of different claims, looking over the conceptual fence."[6]

If I take the view that we can no longer want to remain subjects today, then this is not simply because, in certain situations, we ought behave or interpret our behavior otherwise, perhaps more pluralistically or in a more differentiated way. It is rather because I believe that our being human could be fundamentally different, a being-in-the-world (*In-der-Welt-sein*) or being-out-of-the-world (*Aus-der-Welt-sein*) which would always be concrete.

I can illustrate what this means in a preliminary and approximate way by saying that we would like to be "human beings" and not "subjects." At first this sounds like nonsense. Whereas 'subject' is a *concept* which states what, or of what kind, the thing described as a subject is, for example, something which rationally projects and autonomously determines, we can take "human being" as a *name*, a characterization, which tells us what kind of entity we have to do with, namely with a human being. "Human being" is a name like "tree," "air," "blue," whereas 'subject' is a concept like 'quality', 'finitude', 'opposition'. Thus the question of whether we want to be subjects or human beings does not seem to involve a meaningful alternative. It is obvious that we are human beings, and the only issue which seems open is whether we want to be such as subjects, in the mode of subjectivity, or in another way.

But the question of whether we want to be human beings or subjects can also mean: do we wish to understand ourselves "simply" in terms of our being-human, in our concrete being-in-the-world (for example, in relation both to our concrete capacity for thought and our creatureliness and corporeality), or do we wish to further fix our being in a conceptual determination, that of being a subject? This conceptuality does not so much concern *us* as the generally understood function which human beings perform within the structure of what is—they find their determination in the function of securing the truth and reality of everything which is, and thus in being a subject. The question then addresses the issue of whether the time has not come for us to understand ourselves as something which *cannot* be absorbed by the conceptual characterization of a function, so that we can simply be particular, finite human beings on this earth.

But is this not an all too abstract, "theoretical" demand made on human understanding—despite, or precisely on account of, the fact that it requires the most extreme concretion? Can we really manage without conceptual determinations in the actual process of our self-understanding, including our philosophical self-understanding? Doesn't concretion wind up as something merely tautological, when one seeks to grasp it conceptually? In what follows I would like to attempt an answer to this question which will remain somewhat implicit and indirect.

III

What would it mean, more precisely and concretely, if human beings were no longer subjects? But perhaps at this point we should pose a counter-question, namely, the question of whether they ever were thus, whether being a subject ever really constituted their being human? Were Columbus or Bismarck, Newton or Hegel, the Fuggers or Krupps families, not to speak of the simple farmers, day laborers, townspeople and soldiers, really subjects in the sense that, as the individuals who they were, they were only capable of a calculating, representing, and identifying grasp of entities, that they really only tried to appropriate and master things through reckoning and quantification, and anchored the certainty of the existence of things in their own rationality?

I believe it is one of the greatest—and least considered—difficulties of critical theory, and of the critique of metaphysics in general, that both tend to speak generally of *the* human being and are thus not capable of engaging with the individual in his or her specific sensibility and behavior. Presumably Heidegger and Adorno would not so readily subsume their neighbors and friends, not to speak of themselves, under the characterization of "*das Man*" or of the "externally directed, authoritarian character."[7]

However, we do *also* experience ourselves in many respects as subjects, even when we are on our guard against generalizations. We can constantly observe the fact that we imagine what is as an object in our everyday behavior. We treat our body and the natural features of our being as if they were a mere instrument for rational use. We banish our desire by assigning its origin to the domain of the unconscious, and we discipline our wishes and impulses. We plan our days one by one, and sometimes our whole lives, as if they were problems to be mastered strategically. We manipulate and manage other human beings as if they were mere pieces on a playing board, to be deployed as we wish. We use their needs and interest for our own purposes. And when it is no longer a question of specific individuals who are bound to us by personal ties, but of the distant inhabitants of different countries and cultures, then we often regard them merely as the inventory of an alien world, and in various ways we treat them simply as fodder for statistical operations.

For us the things around us are for the most part only inconspicuous and indifferent elements of our environment, either as merely present-to-hand or as ready-to-hand, as materials or tools, or as building blocks for our material and ideal constructions. They are awkward or useful, to be employed or thrown away, without any life or meaning of their own. Whether in the cycle of production, of distribution or of consumption, things acquire their meaning almost entirely from our nexus of purposes and from their function for us. And even the natural and historical events and process which we perceive outside of us have usually already been related to us and to our interests. We have always tended to make ourselves, the others, and what is other, into objects of our subjectivity.

There is however another aspect to all this. We have experiences of ourselves, of other human beings, of things and events, which elate us or cast us down, which we enter into or which we refuse. We are drawn into movements and currents. Relations to people and things can be formed in which we are not one-sidedly determining but capable of being attentive to what occurs between the other and us. We let ourselves be swept along, or we protect ourselves. We stand in astonishment, or transported, or full of anxiety in the face of what we encounter. And the fact that we encounter it means that it comes to us of its own accord, that it strikes us and moves us and says something to us. We can even listen to ourselves and allow ourselves to be. We are always involved in a being-with-one-another, we enter into relation with ourselves, with the others, with what happens and what brings things about. The other of any particular moment does not *have to be* an object, and we do not *have to be* subjects of our experiences and actions.

The aim of these last remarks is not to evoke some ideal image. Rather it is to name something which each of us has always already encountered over and over again, some of us perhaps more and others less, at times more faintly and at others more intensely, sometimes almost unremarked and at others with a fulfilling and joyous awareness. Human beings in general may be other-directed and alienated, and indeed we are certainly like this ourselves for most of the time. But why do we deny that other which we *also* are, when we try to say what we are? Why do we define ourselves one-sidedly from the standpoint of what is levelled down and indifferent, and not also just as much in terms of that which truly moves us and addresses us in one way or another? A new self-understanding of human beings, one that aims to go beyond an actual or desired identification with a supposedly autonomous subject, can have recourse to these aspects of being human, which are already present and which must now be perceived and taken seriously in a new way.

If we interpret the question "Do we still want to be subjects?" from this standpoint, then this also means that we should be sceptical about the contemporary assertion, correlative to the subject-centred approach, that we are in fact merely objects, both in our relation to the multiple forms of second nature and—in general—in relation to everything which we merely imagine we have under our control. Starting from the way in which we perceive and experience ourselves, we might pose the question of whether this diagnosis is really accurate, when we consider things honestly—in other words, when we do not simply gaze from the outside at the roles which human beings play in the world today. Do we experience *ourselves* truly and exclusively as objects? Can we actually realize the idea that we are merely objects or moments of our desire, as the quotation I used at the beginning suggests—can we verify it in our own bodies? Do we really *experience* ourselves as a moment of language games, and so forth? Why should our sense of being able to will of our own accord, and our way of knowing ourselves not count? Is it not the case that a mere theory, even one which raises the claim to be close up to reality and remote from "Grand Theories," has won the upper hand against what we are actually aware of in ourselves and in others?

Among other things, it seems to me that an unperceived holding on to the criterion of being a subject is responsible for this diagnosis; the interpretative schema of subject-object remains in force, except that the former subjects are now on the side of the object. Thus, for example, it is not the individual subject but the language-game, the lawlike regularity, or history which becomes the real agent and, therefore, the authentic subject; but this merely displaces—and even intensifies—the function of the subject, rather than putting it into question. Thus the function of the subject continues tacitly to embody the claim against which the being of the individual must be measured. But do we still *want* to be subjects at all, so that it would still be relevant to ask whether we actually are capable of being such?

Some will perhaps object that my list of symptoms is too empirical and loses sight of the transcendental subject, by contrast with the empirical subject. But the transcendental project is valid only when we *want* to be subjects. If we abandon the basic metaphysical question of the principles and general structure of nonhuman being, why should we continue to hold onto the question of the subject, even of a deconstructed one?

Once again: we *are* not subjects, but human beings in a world, together with others on the earth and under the sky, as man and as woman, as youth or elderly person, as one who is sick or healthy, in a southerly or northerly, flat or mountainous, rural or urban landscape. We *are* not subjects but rather are defined by the fact that we are born and die, love and are indifferent, work and learn and celebrate.

The question of whether we want to be subjects concerns ourselves. It is not the abstract question of whether the "being" of human beings consist in being a subject but whether we wish to continue interpreting ourselves as subjects. It is not a question which is aimed at human beings from the outside in an analyzing, defining, and determining way, in order to identify them in one way or another as human. It is a question posed from the inside, of our own accord, about whether we actually discover our being-in-the-world as subjects.

To put this the other way around: The thesis of being a subject derives essentially from an external perspective. Those who philosophize speak not of themselves but of the "subject" which they are not and can never themselves be. This is because the subject as such does not live and experience, is not born and does not die, and can feel neither pain nor joy.

IV

One could however object to the direction these reflections are taking with the question, Do we not need certain fundamental principles and maxims, which can be founded only in a universal subjectivity, in order to address the "great problems of ethics and of our common social life?" Do we not need something constant and certain, which we can hold onto and which we can agree about, and which will enable us to orient our doing and acting? Must we not therefore seek to win back a generally recognized site where a subject could be placed with which we could identify individually and collectively, thereby "establishing a common measure?"

I do not believe so. Such an apparent need seems to me to rely on a misunderstanding. It relies on the belief that we can attempt to counter our mortality and finitude and contingency, and the multiplicity and mutability of the others and what is other, by a recourse to the universal, fundamental, and identical which functions as a compensation and sublimation—and thus ultimately as a denial. Neither in theory or practice has a general maxim or a general principle ever been able to guarantee appropriate and "human" behavior and action. Concepts and theorems are in my view essentially ill-suited for solving concrete problems. In order to come to terms with problems and conflicts, and to find the way which is appropriate for the given situation and for "human" purposes, we need instead a *sense* for the fleeting, an *eye* for the others and their needs and interests, and *ear* for our own voice and insights.

Theoretically this does not seem to amount to very much. But there are no general a priori yardsticks and criteria, and rationality can always be found both on one side and the other. Instead of insisting perversely on a counter-factual rationality or authoritative criterion of justice we should practice the patience of the "long and tranquil gaze upon the object,"[8] even when this gaze does not lend itself to the construction of an overarching theory.

We may indeed characterize that which comes "after" the subject as "subject" or "subjectivity" once again. I find this misleading and clumsy because of the conceptual features of these terms, as I have already described them, but this is of no ultimate significance. What is decisive is whether we succeed in leaving behind the fundamental constellation of the "opposed," the constellation of confrontation. The most diverse thinkers of the century which is currently coming to a close—from Heidegger and Adorno to Derrida, Lyotard, or Sloterdijk—have emphasized the significance of the accepting, receptive, indeed passive moment in human doing, over against the modern preference for activity, performance, and making happen. Some of these thinkers have pointed to the fact that the feminine way of relating to the world has begun to take on a paradigmatic significance in this context. Because of the specific historical forms of its development, this way of relating finds listening and entering into the situation of the other, rather than wanting to control and master, to be the more obvious attitude to take up.

Such a listening and answering attitude can be also be guided, although perhaps not entirely, by a subterranean knowledge of the relevant needs and expectations of the other. From this perspective it may perhaps become clearer why I am convinced that an "ethical way of relating," a caring human social life, in which one is attentive both to the other and to oneself, is not dependent on a rationally oriented subject with a strong ego and on the norms which correspond to this subject, indeed necessarily correspond insofar as they are norms. When being-in-the-world understands itself in terms of the world and its interrelations, and is ready to listen to and take notice of the relevant facts and factors, then it will act and relate on the basis of this attitude, and not on the basis of pregiven norms.

To put this in another way: we may ask the question of how intersubjectively binding rules can the thought, when no a priori obligations deriving from common maxims, principles, or codes can be assumed, and when the universal stipulations of rationality and reason have disappeared. But this seems to me to be a sophistical or illusory question that refuses to take on board the presuppositions of the approach I have outlined. The "new form of subjectivity"—if that is what we want to call it—which this approach is aiming for is based on trust in a world which is indeed not a priori, which is frail and fragile, temporary, and transitory, and yet remains in existence as a shared world. Heidegger characterized it as the fourfold of heaven and earth, mortals and immortals. One might also call it the being-together of human beings in the plurality of their times and locations on this earth, or in this world. It is the manifold interweaving of the experiences of human beings, who all stand between birth and death, amid the changing of day into night and summer into winter, experiences which are entwined with each other and imply each other.

If one orients oneself to reality from an external standpoint as a judging subject, and grasps reality in terms of the model of a subject relating to objects, then it is quite consistent to assume that binding rules and criteria must be found within the multiplicity of relations which lie open to one's gaze. From such a standpoint, only thus can order and a meaningful life in common be guaranteed. But this standpoint also presupposes many abstractions, and the real interplay "functions" in a completely different way. If this interplay is good and successful, then this is as a result of a willingness to listen to each other and engage with each other shown by those who must do things and achieve things together.

But even if ethical behavior does not require a determining subject, are not the sciences, advanced technology, law-making, and in part also government dependent on codified presuppositions? I would not seek to deny this. But I also believe that Adorno was right when he claimed that even if the subject is only partly put in question, it is thereby entirely put in doubt. As I have already implied in the foregoing, being in the center and not being in the center are mutually exclusive. If we want to be precise, then human beings can only be entirely subjects, or not subjects at all. Thus I believe that the "relative" subject-object structures which constitute scientific and technological activity have a completely different character, because of this relativity, from those which preceded them. Abstraction, reduction, schematization, and even conceptualization then become operational procedures but are no longer structures which can claim the dignity of being. We can make use of them in order to direct attention away from ourselves and our concrete being-in-the-world. But we need to be aware of what we are doing in this case, and above all *that* we are doing it. As philosophers we should try to find a path which would permit us *not* to abtract from our worldliness.

V

Do we still want to be subjects? In my view, no. As subjects Europeans discovered and colonized foreign continents, Christians converted other peoples, men disciplined their wives, and husbands and wives disciplined their children. As subjects individuals have suppressed their own inclinations and needs, while generalities have excluded those elements which could not be incorporated. I believe that we can longer want to be subjects. But this does not mean that we can renounce questioning ourselves and asking what things would be like, were we to learn to accept ourselves as fallible and not all-determining mortals.

This is not a question of morality. It is a question of which ontology we wish to acknowledge, once we have grasped that the metaphysics of infinite principles, intended to compensate for our own finitude, has played itself out. Perhaps things were different at an earlier time. But I believe that today we have probably achieved the insight that it is up to us which ontology we choose. We *are* not merely playing pieces in a gigantic game which is being played we know not why, by we know not whom. Neither *are* we simply free beings, who can organize the world at will through the power of their reason, or of an anticipated reason. We are neither merely objects, nor merely subjects. But we *are* not simply something in between, or some completely different thing. We "are" what we allow ourselves to be, every hour and every day, in our responsive interplay with whatever arises and occurs around us and within us.

Notes

Chapter 1

1. See below, p. 107.

2. Dieter Henrich, "The Origins of the Theory of the Subject," in *Philosophical Interventions in the Unfinished Project of Modernity*, ed. A. Honneth, T. McCarthy, C. Offe, and A. Wellmer (Cambridge MA, 1992), pp. 75–76.

3. F. W. J. von Schelling, *On the History of Modern Philosophy*, trans. A. Bowie (Cambridge, 1994), p. 174.

4. Ibid., p. 116.

5. Odo Marquard, *Transzendentaler Idealismus, Romantische Naturphilosophie, Psychoanalyse* (Cologne 1987), p. 235.

6. F. W. J. Schelling, *Stuttgarter Privatvorlesungen*, in vol. 4 of *Augewählte Schriften*, ed. M. Frank (Frankfurt am Main, 1985), p. 82.

7. See below, p. 198.

8. Martin Heidegger, *Being and Time*, trans. J. Macquarrie and E. Robinson (Oxford, 1962), p. 323.

9. See below, p. 90.

10. See below, p. 52.

11. See below, p. 55.

12. See below, p. 99.

13. See below, p. 170.

14. See below, p. 178.

15. Emmanuel Levinas, *Otherwise than Being; or, Beyond Essence,* trans. A. Lingis (The Hague, 1981).

16. See Michel Henry, *Phénoménologie matérielle* (Paris, 1990).

17. 'Eating Well,' in *Who Comes After the Subject?* ed. Eduardo Cadava, Peter Connor, and Jean-Luc Nancy (New York, 1991).

18. Ibid., p. 105.

19. Ibid., pp. 102–3.

20. See below, p. 215.

Chapter 2

1. See, for example, *Metaphysics,* 1028b33–1029a13.

2. "*Obiectum* signified that which was thrown before, held against our perceiving, imagination, judging, wishing and intuiting. Subiectum, on the other hand, signified the *hypokeimenon,* that which lies present before us from out of itself (and not brought before us by representation), whatever is present, e.g., things" (Martin Heidegger, 2nd ed. *Wegmarken* [Frankfurt am Main, 1978], p. 72). See similar remarks by Heidegger in "Die Zeit des Weltbildes" in *Holzwege,* 6th ed. (Frankfurt am Main, 1980), pp. 86, 103–4.

3. Cf. *The Shorter Oxford English Dictionary,* S.V.V. Subject, subjected, subjective, subjectivity, subject matter.

4. For a list of these words for Being, see the 1962 lecture "Zeit und Sein", in *Zur Sache des Denkens,* 3rd ed. (Tübingen, 1988), pp. 7, 9, translated by J. Stambaugh under the title *On Time and Being* (New York, 1972), pp. 7, 9.

5. Cf. *Prolegomena zur Geschichte des Zeitbegriffs,* Gesamtausgabe vol. 20, 2nd ed. (Frankfurt am Main, 1988), pp. 184, 187–88. (Hereafter cited as *PGZ*); translated by T. Kisiel under the title *History of the Concept of Time* (Bloomington, 1985), pp. 135, 138 (hereafter cited as *HCT*).

6. See Gadamer's remarks in a 1981 interview with *Le Monde,* republished in *Entretiens avec "Le Monde,"* vol. 1, *Philosophies* (Paris, 1984). p. 238; Derrida's "Envoi," in *Psyché: Inventions de l'autre* (Paris, 1987), pp. 109–43.

7. Heidegger, "Die Zeit des Weltbildes," p. 108.

8. Ibid., p. 124.

9. A point made by Etienne Balibar in "Citizen Subject," *AS* 23/*WC* 33.

10. Cf. Frederick Neuhouser, *Fichte's Theory of Subjectivity* (Cambridge, 1990).

11. Immanuel Kant, *Critique of Pure Reason*, trans. N. Kemp Smith (London and Basingstoke, 1929), B 135.

12. David Hume, *A Treatise of Human Nature*, ed. P. H. Nidditch (Oxford, 1978), pp. 251–63 and appendix, pp. 633–36.

13. Edmund Husserl, *Cartesian Meditations*, trans. Dorian Cairns (Dordrecht, 1960), pp. 1–26.

14. Edmund Husserl, *Ideas*, trans. W. R. Boyce Gibson (New York, 1976), paras. 46–50, pp. 143–55.

15. Emmanuel Levinas, *The Theory of Intuition in Husserl's Phenomenology*, trans. A. Orianne (Evanston, 1973); Jean Paul Sartre, *The Transcendence of the Ego*, trans. F. Williams and R. Kirkpatrick (New York, 1972).

16. PGZ 178–80 / HCT 128–30.

17. Maurice Merleau-Ponty, "The Philosopher and his Shadow," in *Signs*, trans. Richard McCleary (Evanston, 1964), pp. 159–81.

18. *PGZ* 170 / *HCT* 123.

19. *PGZ* 168 / *HCT* 121.

20. Deleuze and Guattari emphasize that the subject is a philosophical concept, and that the task of philosophy as a discipline is that of "creating concepts" (*Qu'est-ce que la philosophie?* [Paris, 1991]). Consequently, the return to the subject in contemporary philosophy might simply show the incapacity of current thinking to live up to the demands of its history, that is, the demand to create new concepts. In lieu of the word *subject*, Deleuze proposes the concepts of *"pre-individual singularities and non-personal individuations"* (*AS* 90 / *WC* 95). In his conversation with Jean-Luc Nancy, Derrida makes a similar point about the need for new names for the "subject," such as *subjectile* that occurs in Derrida's discussion of Artaud (AS 100 / WC 104).

21. Rene Descartes "Meditations on First Philosophy," in *The Philosophical Writings of Descartes*, vol. 2, trans. John Cottingham, Robert Stoothoff, and Dugaid Murdoch (Cambridge, 1984), p. 17.

22. Kant, *Critique of Pure Reason*, B 134.

23. For examples of such an argument, see Mikkel Borch-Jacobsen, "The Freudian Subject: From Politics to Ethics" (AS 53–72 / WC 61–78); Philippe Van Haute, "Psychanalyse et existentialisme: A propos de la théorie lacanienne de la subjectivité," *Man and World* 23 (1990): pp. 453–72.

24. On the concept of the subject in Schelling, see, in this volume, Andrew Bowie's "Re-thinking the History of Subjectivity: Jacobi, Schelling, and Heidegger" (pp. 105–126) On Schleiermacher, see Maciej Potepa "Die Frage nach dem Subjekt in der Hermeneutik Schleiermachers," in *Die Frage nach dem*

Subjekt, Manfred Frank, Gérard Raulet, and Willem van Reijen ed. (Frankfurt am Main, 1988), pp. 128–43. See also Manfred Frank's remarks on Schleiermacher and Sartre in *What is Neostructuralism?* trans. Sabine Wilke and Richard Gray (Minneapolis, 1989).

25. Cf. *PGZ* 17–21, 41–46 / *HCT* 16–18, and 32–36.

26. Cf. Martin Heidegger, "Seminar in Zähringen 1973," in *Seminare* (Frankfurt am Main, 1986), pp. 379–80.

27. Martin Heidegger, *Der Begriff der Zeit* (Tübingen, 1989), p. 12; translated by William McNeill, under the title *The Concept of Time* (Oxford, 1992), pp. 7–8.

28. Heidegger, *Der Begriff der Zeit*, p. 13; *The Concept of Time*, pp. 8–9. And see Philippe Lacoue-Labarthe's exploration of the theme of nobody (*personne*) in relation to Heidegger in "The Response of Ulysses" (*AS* 153–60 / *WC* 198–205).

29. In this volume, see Jean-Luc Marion, "The Final Appeal of the Subject" and Dominique Janicaud, "The Question of Subjectivity in Heidegger's *Being and Time*"; see also on this topic, Michel Haar, *Heidegger et l'essence de l'homme* (Grenoble, 1990).

30. "Letter on Humanism," in Heidegger, *Wegmarken*, pp. 346–47; translated by F. Capuzzi and J. Glenn Gray, in *Martin Heidegger: Basic Writings*, ed. D. F. Krell (New York, 1977), pp. 228–29.

31. Heidegger, *Seminare*, p. 383.

32. Heidegger, *Wegmarken*, p. 338; *Martin Heidegger: Basic Writings*, p. 221.

33. Heidegger, "Zeit und Sein," pp. 20, 45; *On Time and Being*, pp. 19, 42.

34. Friedrich Nietzsche, *Also Sprach Zarathustra* (Leipzig, 1930), pp. 359–63; translated by R. J. Hollingdale under the title *Thus Spoke Zarathustra* (Harmondsworth, 1961), pp. 333–36.

35. Jacques Derrida, *La voix et le phénomène* (Paris, 1967), pp. 78–97; translated by D. Allison under the title *Speech and Phenomena* (Evanston, 1973), pp. 70–87.

36. Jürgen Habermas, *The Philosophical Discourse of Modernity*, trans. F. Lawrence (Cambridge, 1987), see esp. pp. 294–326.

37. Ludwig Wittgenstein, *Tractatus Logico-Philosophicus*, trans. C. K. Ogden (London and Henley, 1922), proposition 5.6ff., pp. 148–53.

38. Heidegger, "Zeit und Sein," pp. 8–9; *On Time and Being*, pp. 8–9.

39. Cf. *Martin Heidegger*, "Überwindung der Metaphysik," in *Vorträge und Aufsätze*, 6th ed. (Pfullingen, 1990), pp. 67–95.

40. Jacques Derrida, *L'écriture et la différence* (Paris, 1967), p. 132; translated by A. Bass under the title *Writing and Difference* (London, 1978), p. 88.

41. Theodor W. Adorno, *Negative Dialectics*, trans. E. B. Ashton (New York, 1973), p. 380.

42. Emmanuel Levinas, *De l'existence à l'existent*, 2nd ed. (Paris, 1986), p. 19; translated by A. Lingis under the title *Existence and Existents*, (The Hague, 1978), p. 19.

43. Cf. Luc Ferry and Alain Renaut, *La Pensée 68: Essai sur l'antihumanisme contemporain* (Paris, 1985); translated by M.H.S. Catani under the title *French Philosophy of the Sixties: An Essay on Antihumanism* (Amherst, 1990). See especially, Ferry and Renault's final chapter, "Return of the Subject" (pp. 263–85; trans. pp. 208–27). The argument of *La pensée 68* is continued, with particular reference to *l'affaire Heidegger*, in Ferry and Renaut's *Heidegger and Modernity*, trans. F. Philip (Chicago, 1990).

44. Cf. "L'état du sujet aujourd'hui," in *Le monde morcelé: Les carrefours du labyrinthe* III (Paris, 1990). It should be noted that Castoriadis has always argued for a conception of subjectivity inseparable from the project of individual and collective autonomy.

45. For a fascinating discussion of this work, see a late interview with Foucault, "The Ethic of Care for the Self as a Practice of Freedom," in *The Final Foucault*, ed. J. Bernauer and D. Rasmussen (Cambridge, 1988), pp. 1–20.

46. It seems to me that if the question of the subject is to be reformulated today, then it must proceed from the question of sexual difference and from the feminist critique of gender neutral subjectivity; that is, male subjectivity. If Irigaray is justified, as I believe she is, to claim in *Speculum of the Other Woman* (trans. Gillian C. Gill [Ithaca, 1985], pp. 133–46) that any prior theory of the subject has always been appropriated by the masculine, then any reopening of the question of the subject must show how subjectivity is inevitable marked, traced, and coded by gender. Anticipating an analysis given below and in relation to Levinas, this has a double consequence: on the one hand, in the final footnote to "Violence and Metaphysics," Derrida writes that "it would be impossible, essentially impossible, for *Totality and Infinity* to have been written by a woman" (*L'écriture et la différence*, p. 228; *Writing and Difference*, p. 321). Levinas speaks as a man in his philosophical discourse, which, as Derrida notes, is a remarkable phenomenon in the history of philosophical writing. Why remarkable? Because Levinas gives up the pretension to neutrality that is so characteristic of philosophical discourse. Although this would have to be traced textually, I believe it can be claimed that Levinas's notion of the subject is gendered and gendered male, even if it describes itself in feminine metaphors (like maternity) and even if its justified object of critique is the virility and potency of the supposedly neutral philosophical ego. However, on the other hand, in Levinas's descriptions of the dwelling, eros, and fecundity, Levinas maintains the feminine not as something apprehended in relation to itself and acknowledged as an other, otherwise sexed, but as something seen

from the point of view of man. Thus, the feminine is, in Irigaray's terms, "the other of the same," and not radically other. By defining the alterity of the feminine in terms of "modesty," "effacement," and "shunning the light," woman is fixed as the other for man in the most traditional terms. Thus, Levinas's description of the feminine, combined with his continual subordination of the claims of sexual difference to ethical difference and his insistence upon the son as the means for the achievement of plurality and the break with Parmenides, mean that after having come so far in the acknowledgment of the alterity of the other sex, Levinas, as Irigaray puts it, "clings once more to this rock of patriarchy in the very place of carnal love" (see "Questions to Emmanuel Levinas," in *The Irigaray Reader*, ed. M. Whitford [Oxford, 1991], pp. 178–89, esp. p. 183).

47. Cf. Mikkel Borch-Jacobsen, *Lacan: The Absolute Master* (Stanford, 1991); Phillipe Van Haute, "Psychanalyse et existentialisme"; and, in this volume, Peter Dews, "The Truth of the Subject: Language, Validity, and Trascendence in Lacan and Habermas."

48. See Andrew Bowie, *Aesthetics and Subjectivity: from Kant to Nietzsche* (Manchester, 1990); Terry Eagleton, *The Ideology of the Aesthetic* (Oxford, 1990).

49. Cf. P. Lacoue-Labarthe, et al., *Le retrait du politique* (Paris, 1983), p. 203–4.

50. Frank, *What is Neostructuralism?* p. 6.

51. Cf. Bernhard Waldenfels, "Jenseits des Subjektprinzips," in *Der Stachel des Fremden*, Frankfurt am Main, 1990), pp. 72–79.

52. Levinas, *De l'existence à l'existent*; idem, *Le temps et l'autre* (Paris, 1983), which has been translated into English by R. Cohen (Pittsburgh, 1987).

53. Both included in Emmanuel Levinas, *Humanisme de l'autre homme*, Livre de Poche ed. (Montpellier, 1972), pp. 73–91, 95–113; hereafter *HAH*. Trans. A. Lingis in *Collected Philosophical Papers* (Dordrecht, 1987), pp. 127–39, 141–51 (hereafter cited as *CPP*).

54. A precursor for Levinas's notion of ethics might perhaps be found in Rousseau's concept of 'compassion' or 'pitié', a prereflective, prerational basic mood (Heideggerian *Grund-Stimmung*) which disposes me towards the other and takes place at the level of sensibility. See *A Discourse on Inequality*, trans. M. Cranston (Harmondsworth, 1984), p. 70.

55. "Signature," in *Difficile Liberté*, Livre de Poche ed. (Paris, 1976), p. 499.

56. Cf. Merleau-Ponty, "The Philosopher and his Shadow."

57. Maurice Merleau-Ponty, *The Visible and the Invisible* (Evanston, 1968), p. 23.

58. Cf. "The Constitution of Psychic Reality in Empathy," in *Ideas*, bk. 2, *Studies in the Phenomenology of Constitution*, trans. R. Rojcewicz and A. Schuwer (Dordrecht, 1989), p. 175.

59. See Merleau-Ponty's remarks in the working notes to *The Visible and the Invisible*, pp. 175–76, 183, 200.

60. Merleau-Ponty, "The Philosopher and his Shadow," p. 168.

61. On Levinas's critique of Merleau-Ponty, see the two short essays (which are essentially two difference drafts of the same essay), "Merleau-Ponty: Notes on Intersubjectivity" and "Sensibility" in *Ontology and Alterity in Merleau-Ponty*, ed. G. Johnson and M. Smith (Evanston, 1990), pp. 54–66.

62. Ibid, pp. 58–59.

63. I am here following Peter Dews's interpretation of Lacan, given in this volume in "The Truth of the Subject: Language, Validity, and Transcendence in Lacan and Habermas." For me, the comparison between Levinas and Lacan raises the fascinating, speculative question as to whether one can read the Levinasian account of the constitution of the subject in psychoanalytical terms; that is to say, as a developmental account of the formation of subjectivity in an infant.

64. Fyodor Dostoevsky, *Notes from Underground* (Harmondsworth, 1972), p. 123.

65. *HAH* 111 / *CPP* 150.

66. See Frank's discussion of Sartre's *L'idiot de la famille* in *What is Neostructuralism?* pp. 364–65.

67. Emmanuel Levinas, *Ethique et infini*, Livre de Poche edition (Paris, 1982), p. 95.

68. Cf. Martin Heidegger, "Brief über den 'Humanismus,' " *Wegmarken*, p. 327: "Humanism is opposed because it does not set the *humanitas* of man high enough."

69. Emmanuel Levinas, "Tout autrement," in *Noms Propres* (Montpellier, 1976), p. 87; translated as "Wholly Otherwise," by Simon Critchley in *Re-Reading Levinas*, ed. R. Bernasconi and S. Critchley (Bloomington, 1991), p. 6.

70. Levinas, "Tout Autrement," p. 98; "Wholly Otherwise," p. 7.

71. Cf. Friedrich Schleiermacher, *The Christian Faith*, Trans. H. R. Mackintosh and J. S. Stewart (Edinburgh, 1989).

72. Cf. Emmanuel Levinas, *Autrement que savoir* (Paris, 1988), p. 72.

73. Frank, *What is Neostructuralism*, p. 10.

74. For a discussion of this text, see the essays collected in *Of Derrida, Heidegger and Spirit*, ed. D. Wood (Evanston, 1993).

75. Cf. Derrida's "Nombre de oui," in *Psyché: Inventions de l'autre*, p. 646.

76. The problem that is left hanging here, and which would disrupt this happy homoiosis between Derrida and Levinas—although it is the only explicit criticism that Derrida makes of the Levinasian conception of the subject—concerns the limits of responsibility in Levinas. To whom am I responsible on a Levinasian view? Who is my neighbor? Derrida claims that, for all its novelty and force, the Levinasian conception of the subject conceives of responsibility as an obligation only to other human beings and not to animals and living things in general (*AS* 107–8 / *WC* 112–13). Therefore, although Levinas engages in a critique of traditional humanism, his thinking (like that of Heidegger) remains humanistic insofar as ethical obligation is limited to other humans (*AS* 100 / *WC* 105). To employ Derrida's neologism, Levinas would remain within the sphere of what Derrida calls "carno-phallogocentrism," where carnivorous sacrifice is essential to the constitution of subjectivity. John Llewelyn has devoted an extended study to this question of whether an ecological ethics is derivable from Levinas (cf. *The Middle Voice of Ecological Conscience* [London and Basingstoke, 1991]). I would argue that it is indeed true that language is the condition of possibility for ethical obligation in Levinas and that one therefore has obligations only towards linguistic beings. However, what or who counts as a linguistic being? Are human beings alone capable of language and ethics? I think it can be shown that what Levinas means by language can be extended to include nonverbal as well as verbal communication, and therefore it could be claimed that insofar as animals and living things in general are capable of nonverbal language—i.e., that the language employed by living things does not necessarily have to conform to human intelligibility—a Levinasian ethics would still have obligations towards nonhuman sentient beings. The criterion for obligation would be sentience. However, in making this argument, I realize that I am perhaps taking Levinas where he would not want to be taken. (For a discussion of Levinas and humanism, see my *The Ethics of Deconstruction* (Oxford, 1992), pp. 176–82.

77. Within a contemporary French context, one would also have to consider the work of Philippe Lacoue-Labarthe, *Le sujet de la philosophie: Typographies I* (Paris, 1979); Alain Badiou, *Théorie du sujet* (Paris, 1982); Bernard Sichère, *Éloge du sujet* (Paris, 1990).

78. A position outlined in the opening pages of Lacoue-Labarthe's *La Fiction de Politique: Heidegger, l'art et la politique* (Paris, 1987), pp. 13–20; translated by C. Turner under the title *Heidegger, Art and Politics* (Oxford, 1990), pp. 1–7.

79. Cf. Llewelyn, *The Middle Voice of Ecological Conscience*, p. ix.

80. Heidegger, "Zeit und Sein," p. 28; *On Time and Being*, p. 26.

81. See, in this volume, Dominique Janicaud, "The Question of Subjectivity in Heidegger's *Being and Time*."

82. Emmanuel Levinas, "L'ontologie est-elle fondamentale?" *Revue de Métaphysique et de Morale*, 56, no. 1 (1951): pp. 89–98; translated by P. Atterton

under the title "Is Ontology Fundamental?" *Philosophy Today,* summer 1989, pp. 121–29.

83. Emmanuel Levinas, "Transcendence et Hauteur," *Cahiers de l'Herne,* ed. M. Abensour and C. Chalier (Paris, 1991), p. 112. One finds a similar evaluation of the end of philosophy in Deleuze and Guattari: "we have never had any problem concerning the death of metaphysics or the overcoming of philosophy: this is useless and tiresome drivel . . . Philosophy would willingly yield its place to any other discipline that could better fulfill the function of creating concepts, but as long as that function subsists, it will still be called philosophy, always philosophy" Deleuze and Guattari, *Qu'est-ce que la philosophie,* p. 14.

84. On *Seiendheit* in Heidegger, see, for example, "Einleitung zu: 'Was ist Metaphysik,' " in *Wegmarken,* p. 373.

85. Cf. Jacques Derrida and Pierre-Jean Labarrière, *Altérités* (Paris, 1986), p. 71; on this topic, see Critchley, *The Ethics of Deconstruction,* pp. 13–20.

86. Levinas, *Theory of Intuition in Husserl's Phenomenology,* pp. 155, xxxiii.

87. Ibid, pp. 155–58.

88. Cf. Emmanuel Levinas, *En découvrant l'existence avec Husserl et Heidegger,* 3rd ed. (Paris, 1974), pp. 53–76.

89. Emmanuel Levinas, "Éthique comme philosophie première," in *Justifications de l'éthique,* ed. G. Hottois, (Bruxelles, 1984), pp. 41–51; translated by S. Hand and M. Temple under the title "Ethics as First Philosophy," in *The Levinas Reader,* ed. S. Hand (Oxford, 1989), pp. 75–87.

90. Levinas, "Éthique comme philosophie première," p. 49; "Ethics as First Philosophy," p. 84.

91. Levinas, "Éthique comme philosophie première," p. 49; "Ethics as First Philosophy," p. 82.

92. Levinas, "Éthique comme philosophie première," pp. 50–51; "Ethics as First Philosophy," p. 85.

93. Cf. the penultimate epigraph to *AE / OB.*

94. Levinas, "Éthique comme philosophie première," p. 51; "Ethics as First Philosophy," p. 86.

Chapter 3

The translator would like to thank Simon Critchley for his advice on resolving certain problems that arose during the course of the translation. Note that all translator's remarks are in square brackets and, in the case of footnotes, clearly marked.

1. Martin Heidegger, *Being and Time*, trans. John Macquarrie and Edward Robinson (Oxford, 1962), H. 1. [All page references to *Being and Time* are to the eighth German edition, as reprinted in the English translation.—*Trans.*]

2. Title of para. 1 of *Being and Time*.

3. Heidegger, *Being and Time*, H. 7. Let us take advantage of the opportunity presented by this quotation for a brief clarification concerning the question of the translation (or nontranslation) of *Dasein*—which shall be left as it is or be translated as Existent (*Existant*). Doubtless it seems better to leave the term untranslated than to resort to nonsensical translations, such as "human reality" (*réalité humaine*). or "being there" (*être-là*). But to do so lends a false sense of security. To refuse *systematically* to translate *Dasein* turns it into something inexpressible, an absolute *hapax* that is nevertheless repeated over the course of many pages. Heidegger wanted to preserve this common German word from its *ontic usage*, not from intelligibility. Untranslated, *Dasein* becomes at times a strange "object": untouchable, distant, almost sidereal. We nearly forget that it concerns man in his existential reality, the being which is care for self (*souci de soi*), "which in each case we ourselves are, and which we call 'man' " (*Being and Time*, H. 196–97). "*Das 'Wesen' des Daseins liegt in seiner Existenz*" (*Being and Time*, H. 42). This short sentence, emphasized by Heidegger and corroborated by other passages (e.g., H. 212) seems to justify translating *Dasein* by Existent or Ek-sistent (*Existent, Ek-sistent*), to distinguish it from the existent in merely ontic usage (a usage that is occasionally found in Sartre). To translate or not to translate? It is the text that must speak in its context.

4. See Hildegard Feick, *Index zu Heideggers Sein und Zeit*, (Tübingen, 1961), p. 75.

5. Heidegger, *Being and Time*, H. 25.

6. Ibid., H. 25.

7. Ibid., H. 188.

8. Ibid., H. 322–23.

9. Alluding to paras. 17 and 18.

10. Heidegger, *Being and Time*, H. 95.

11. Ibid., H. 96. [This translation, as well as the one preceding, have been modified slightly.—*Trans.*]

12. Ibid., H. 47.

13. Ibid., H. 189.

14. Ibid., H. 329

15. [Janicaud himself opted for "wrenching" to translate *arrachement*, the basic meaning of which is a forceful or violent tearing or pulling away. It is to be understood here in connection with ecstasis.—*Trans.*]

16. Ibid., H. 53.

17. Ibid., H. 41.

18. Ibid., H. 188. [Janicaud emphasizes the "itself" (Sich-selbst)—Trans.]

19. Ibid., H. 287.

20. See Ibid., H. 307.

21. Ibid., H. 336, H. 339, H. 343.

22. Ibid., H. 323.

23. Ibid., H. 322. [The translation has been modified slightly to reflect the emphasis given in the French translation; Macquarrie and Robinson translate *Vereinzelung* as "individualization," whereas the French translation given reads "*solitude*."—Trans.]

24. [There is as yet no English translation of this text, but see Heidegger, *Vier Seminare* (Frankfurt am Main, 1977), 137. The seminar has also been republished in vol. 15 of the *Gesamtausgabe.*—Trans.]

25. These nevertheless cannot be reduced to their metaphysical sense, according to Heidegger.

26. See in particular the commentary to the thirteenth paragraph in Heidegger, *Hegel's Concept of Experience* (New York, 1970), 102–12. [Originally published in *Holzwege* (Frankfurt, 1957), 159ff.]

27. See Heidegger, *Being and Time*, H. 322.

28. Heidegger, "Time and Being," in On *"Time and Being,"* trans. Joan Stambaugh (New York, 1972), 24. [Originally published in *Zur Sache des Denkens* (Tübingen, 1969), 25.]

29. Heidegger, *Being and Time*, H. 146.

30. See Dominique Janicaud, "Haute Solitude," *Nouvelle Revue de Psychanalyse* 36, (autumn 1987): p. 19.

31. See Dominique Janicaud, "L'apprentissage de la contiguïté" in *Critique* 1976: 664–76; also, Janicaud, *La puissance du rationnel* (Paris, 1985), pp. 280ff.

32. N.b.: My agenda intersects that of Ricoeur insofar as I think, as does he, that the question of the Self in Heidegger (and its preservation, in spite of its displacements) is deepened by the oscillation "backward and forward in the inquiry" between that which is asked about (Being) and that which does the asking (*Dasein*) (see Paul Ricoeur, "Heidegger and the Question of the Subject," in *The Conflict of Interpretations*, ed. Don Ihde [Evanston, 1974], p. 227. [Originally published in *Le conflit des interprétations* (Paris, 1969), pp. 222–32.]) On the other hand, if it is true that Heidegger's ontological fundamentalism does not manage to free itself completely from the aporias of

subjectivity, I believe that Habermas pushes his refutation of this fundamentalism to a point of extreme schematisation when he reduces the advances made by Heidegger to a "mere inversion of the thought-patterns of the philosophy of the subject" (see Jürgen Habermas, *The Philosophical Discourse of Modernity*, trans. Frederick Lawrence [Cambridge, 1987], p. 160 and all of lecture 6).

Chapter 4

1. M. Heidegger, *Vom Wesen der Wahrheit: Zu Platons Höhlengleichnis und Theätet* (Freiburg lecture, winter term 1931/32), *Gesamtausgabe* 34, p. 82 (hereafter cited as *GA* 34).

2. Following Levinas I will write "essance" to refer to the verbal character of Heidegger's "Wesen."

3. Page references in the text are to the Macquarrie and Robinson translation of *Being and Time* (Oxford, 1988) with the German pagination (15th ed. [Tübingen 1979]) given after the slash. When necessary, the English translation has been changed.

4. M. Heidegger, *Der Begriff der Zeit: Vortrag vor der Marburger Theologenschaft, Juli 1924* (Tübingen, 1989), p. 13.

5. Alphonse de Waelhens *La philosophie de Martin Heidegger* (Louvain and Paris, 1971), p. 115.

6. See especially her "Was ist Existenz-Philosophie?" in H. Arendt, *Sechs Essays* (Heidelberg, 1948), p. 73 and Jacques Taminiaux' interesting remarks in his "Arendt, disciple de Heidegger?" in *Études Phenomenologiques* 1985 no. 2: pp. 111–36.

7. E.g., "In the end, idle talk is even indignant that what it has surmised and constantly demanded now *actually* happens. In that case, indeed, the opportunity to keep on surmising has been snatched away (*Ist ihm ja doch damit die Gelegenheit entrissen weiter zu ahnen]*" (*BT* 218 / 174).

8. M. Heidegger, "Phänomenologische Interpretationen zu Aristoteles (Anzeige der hermeneutischen Situation)" (1922), in *Dilthey-Jahrbuch* vol. 6 (1989): p. 238.

9. See Richard Rorty, "Moral identity and private autonomy," in his *Philosophical Papers: Essays on Heidegger and Others*, vol. 2 (Cambridge, 1991), pp. 193ff.

10. Eugen Fink, "Philosophie als Überwindung der 'Naivität,' " in *Nähe und Distanz. Phänomenologische Vorträge und Aufsätze* (Freiburg and Munich, 1976), p. 116.

11. Ibid.

12. J. Derrida, introduction to E. Husserl, *L'origine de la géometrie* (Paris, 1974), p. 98 (hereafter cited as *OG*).

13. Although it should be noted that *Being and Time* at times engages in a discourse on the will that should be analyzed carefully with respect to its position in the economy of Heidegger's argument (e.g., p. 237 / p. 193 where "to comport oneself *unwillingly* [*unwillentlich*] towards one's possibilities" is equated with the inauthentic [*uneigentlich*]; also, of course p. 316 / p. 271, "The call reaches him who *wants* to be brought back" [my emphasis] and p. 334 / p. 288 [*Gewissen-haben-wollen*]).

14/ Cf. J. Derrida, *Ulysse gramophone: Deux mots pour Joyce* (Paris, 1987), p. 89 ("*téléphone intérieur*").

15. J. Derrida, *De la grammatologie* (Paris, 1967), p. 33.

16. Ibid., p. 36.

17. For Husserl's views on linguistic incarnation and its role for the constitution of ideality, see the clear exposition by Derrida in *OG*, e.g., pp. 86–87.

18. As is well known, Heidegger left this question unanswered in *Being and Time*: "Is [language] a kind of equipment ready-to-hand within-the-world, or has it Dasein's kind of Being, or is it neither of these? What kind of Being does language have, if there can be such a thing as a 'dead' language?" (p. 209 / p. 166).

19. A full analysis of the problem of (un-)truth in *Being and Time* would have to confront the remarks one finds in sect. 44, where untruth seems clearly linked to the vocalization of *Rede* (e.g., pp. 262, 264 / pp. 219, 222), with earlier passages where it was suggested that truth and falsity already characterized *Rede* before it is expressed. I will come back to these issues on a different occasion.

20. Alphonse de Waelhens, *La philosophie de Martin Heidegger*, op. cit. p. 194.

21. Rudolf Bernet, *La vie du sujet* (Paris, 1994).

22. M. Heidegger, "The End of Philosophy and the Task of Thinking," in *Basic Writings*, p. 390.

23. I owe the distinction between a first and a second reduction to R. Bernet (see n. 21).

24. M. Heidegger, *Grundfragen der Philosophie: Ausgewählte "Probleme" der "Logik"* (Freiburg Lecture, winter term 1937/38), *G.A.* 45, p. 147.

25. My attention was drawn to this passage by a footnote in E. Tugendhat's *Der Wahrheitsbegriff bei Husserl und Heidegger* (Berlin, 1970), p. 316.

26. See my "From Foucault to Heidegger: A One Way Ticket?" *Research in Phenomenology* 21 (1991): p. 116–40.

Chapter 5

1. Martin Heidegger *Sein und Zeit*, para. 65, p. 323, ll. 28–29. I shall quote from the 11th ed. (Tübingen, 1963).

2. Ibid., para. 9, p. 41, ll. 28–29.

3. Ibid., para. 60, p. 297, ll. 2–3.

4. Ibid., para. 40, p. 186, ll. 39.

5. Ibid., para. 56, p. 273, ll. 25–28.

6. Ibid., para. 51, p. 252, ll. 26–27.

7. Aristotle, *Metaphysics, Z,* 13, 1039 a 7.

8. Heidegger, *Sein und Zeit*, para. 54, p. 267, ll. 32–33.

9. Ibid., para. 64, p. 322, ll. 24–33.

10. Ibid., ll. 24–29. One should be astonished by the categorical formulation of this proposition, which is attenuated only by a somewhat reserved negation ("not yet").

11. In this sense, see Paul Ricoeur, "Heidegger and the Question of the Subject," in *The Conflict of Interpretations* (Paris, 1969); Dominique Janicaud: "If, therefore, the Self is not erased but stripped of its import as soon as the existential analytic is deployed, one must yield to the observation that subjectivity is neither destroyed nor emptied of content by Heidegger. It is metamorphosed, but nevertheless preserved and even revived through the fundamental role of the *Selbst*." (See in this volume, "The Question of Subjectivity in Heidegger's *Being and Time*," p. 52); and Jacques Derrida: "there is an analogy (to deal with this very prudently) between the function of Dasein in *Being and Time* and that of the subject in an ontologico-transcendental or even ethico-juridical disposition. For sure, Dasein is irreducible to subjectivity, but the existential analytic still conserves the formal characteristics of any transcendental analytic. Although it displaces many phenomena, Dasein and that which responds to the question 'who?' comes to occupy the place of the 'subject,' of the *cogito*, or of the classical *'ich denke."* Dasein retains many of the essential traits of subjectivity (freedom, resoluteness, self-presence or self-relation, the 'call' *(Ruf)* that leads to moral conscience, responsibility, imputability or originary culpability *(Schuldigsein)*, etc. And whatever might have been the movements of Heidegger's thinking after *Being and Time* and 'after' the existential analytic, it leaves nothing 'liquidated' 'behind' it" (" 'Il faut bien man-

ger," ou le calcul du suject," in *Cahiers Confrontation* no. 20 (Paris, 1989) p. 93; see also p. 99). In what is essential, these three positions are in agreement and, in what is essential, we assume them.

12. Heidegger, *Sein und Zeit,* para. 83, p. 436, ll. 34–37.

13. Ibid., para. 57, p. 277, ll. 31.

14. René Descartes, *Passions de l'Ame,* para 53.

15. Littré, *Dictionnaire de la langue francaise,* vol. 3, p. 133; O. Bloch & W. von Warburg, *Dictionnaire étymologique de la langue francaise* (Paris 1932, 1989), p. 343

16. This is why we can, or rather must, withdraw ourselves from the dichotomy that F. Laruelle proposes to us in a discussion which is, in other respects, as generous as it is lucid: either to found the call or appeal through a novel recourse to transcendence, or to found it upon itself in radical immanence. For, with respect to the "identity of the reduction with the donation or giving," nothing is less self-evident than to claim that "it is necessary to found this identity, and to give it an absolute reality." Indeed, the call or appeal does not in general necessitate either an absolute foundation or reality, because it is already completely accomplished from the moment that it has resounded, and thus from the moment it has disappeared; in brief, from the simple fact of giving itself and losing itself. Or better, it only interpellates insofar as it resounds without reason or fundament and immediately disappears without trace or name.

17. See the definitive work of J. L. Chrétien and, in particular, *L'effroi du beau* (Paris, 1987), chap. 3, and *L'Antiphonaire de la nuit* (Paris, 1989).

18. Augustine, *Confessions,* 3.7.11.

Chapter 6

1. See Andrew Bowie, *Schelling and Modern European Philosophy: An Introduction* (London, 1993), and F. W. J. Schelling, *On the History of Modern Philosophy,* translated with an introduction by Andrew Bowie (Cambridge, 1994), for the alternative conceptions, some of which will be considered below. The classic critique of Hegel's position in this respect is Sartre's in *Being and Nothingness.* As I show in *Aesthetics and Subjectivity: From Kant to Nietzsche* (Manchester, 1990; reprinted in 1993), Sartre's basic position was common currency in German Romantic philosophy.

2. Martin Heidegger, *Die Grundbegriffe der Metaphysik* (Frankfurt am Main, 1983), p. 30.

3. It may well be that Fichte's insight into the problem of "reflexivity" (see Dieter Henrich, *Fichtes ursprüngliche Einsicht* [Frankfurt am Main, 1967] and my remarks below on the regress of reflection) was actually influenced by

Jacobi, given that the two knew each other's work well and the underlying problem has the same structure.

4. Heinrich Scholz, ed., *Die Hauptschriften zum Pantheismusstreit zwischen Jacobi und Mendelssohn* (Berlin, 1916), p. 52.

5. Cited in Dieter Thomä, *Die Zeit des Selbst und die Zeit danach: Zur Kritik der Textgeschichte Martin Heideggers. 1910–1976* (Frankfurt am Main, 1990), p. 232.

6. The creator God, who is seen as "personality," creates out of his own freedom, rather than simply embodying the harmonious structure of the universe, as Spinoza's God does. The complexities of this conception are best worked out by Schelling from the time of the *Freiheitsschrift* onwards. See *Schelling and Modern European Philosophy: An Introduction*, particularly chaps. 5 and 6.

7. In the *Concluding Unscientific Postscript* Kierkegaard uses the excuse of the *salto mortale* to dismiss Jacobi, even though it is clear that he actually owes much to Jacobi's contentions in the *Letters*. The same can be said of Schelling in his 1812 polemic against Jacobi (Friedrich Wilhelm Joseph Schelling, *Sämmtliche Werke*. ed. K. F. A. Schelling, pt. 1, vol. 10 [Stuttgart, 1856–61], pp. 19–136). The disturbing aspects of what Jacobi maintains form the core of many of Schelling's later philosophical insights, not least of his separation of "negative" and "positive" philosophy. This issue is too large and complex to consider here: see Birgit Sandkaulen-Bock, *Ausgang vom Unbedingten: Über den Anfang in der Philosophie Schellings* (Göttingen, 1990).

8. *Morgenstunden*. p. 319, quoted in Dieter Henrich, *Der ontologische Gottesbeweis* (Tübingen, 1967), p. 4.

9. Scholz, *Hauptschriften zum Pantheismusstreit*, p. 51.

10. Henry E. Allison, *Benedict de Spinoza: An Introduction* (New Haven, 1987), p. 64.

11. Scholz, *Hauptschriften zum Pantheismusstreit*. p. 271. Martin Heidegger, *Der Satz vom Grund* (Pfullingen, 1957), points out at great length the significance of the difficulty involved in translating "Nihil est sine ratione." The argument of Heidegger's book is initially identical with Jacobi's key argument.

12. Ibid., p. 90. The roots of the division between "explanation" and "understanding" (*Verstehen*), which Dilthey will make into a central theme of twentieth-century philosophy, and which has played a key role in debates in the social sciences, are already present here. The irreducibility of understanding to what can be explained in causal terms remains one of the key themes of hermeneutic philosophy, particularly in Heidegger's account of *Verstehen*. Even Jacobi's choice of words is reminiscent of Heidegger's concern with "world-disclosure," as that which must precede cognitive truth claims.

13. Heidegger makes an analogous point in *Being and Time* when he suggests that *all* interpretation and *all* cognitive claims inherently involve cir-

cularity, because we must already have initially understood that which we wish to interpret, so that "The decisive thing is not to get out of the circle but to get into it in the right way" (Martin Heidegger, *Sein und Zeit* [Tübingen, 1979], p. 153).

14. Fichte will claim something similar in relation to Kant's theoretical philosophy, while making the I into the prior ground. This is what links Jacobi's position to Fichte's "insight," in that Fichte realizes that consciousness itself can be led into a regress by reflecting upon itself, which entails being conscious of being conscious etc., which in turn means the undeniable fact of consciousness cannot be explained by reflection (see Henrich, *Fichtes ursprüngliche Einsicht*).

15. Hermann Timm makes the link to Heidegger in *Friedrich Heinrich Jacobi*, ed. Klaus Hammacher (Frankfurt am Main, 1971), but does not substantially develop it.

16. Frederick C. Beiser, *The Fate of Reason: German Philosophy from Kant to Fichte* (Cambridge, Mass., 1987), pp. 89–90.

17. Donald Davidson, *Inquiries into Truth and Interpretation* (Oxford, 1984), p. 223.

18. Ibid., p. 267.

19. Scholz, *Hauptschriften zum Pantheismusstreit*, p. 274.

20. Friedrich Heinrich Jacobi, *David Hume über den Glauben oder Idealismus und Realismus: ein Gespräch* (Breslau, 1787), p. 225. Whether this is an adequate criticism of Kant can be and has been disputed. Jacobi's most powerful statement on Kant is the following, on the relationship between the phenomenal and the noumenal:

> For even if according to [Kantian philosophy] it can be *admitted* that a transcendental something *may* correspond as cause to these merely subjective beings [Wesen], which are only determinations *of our own being*, it yet remains hidden in the deepest obscurity *where* this cause and what the nature of the relation it has to its effect is. (Jacobi, *David Hume*, p. 224)

21. Donald Davidson, "The Structure and Content of Truth," *The Journal of Philosophy.* 87, no. 6 (1990): p. 303.

22. I am assuming here that Davidson's objections to the idea of a "conceptual scheme" are compatible with Jacobi's notion of "the true," described below, which is prior to any attempt at a systematic account of knowledge.

23. Friedrich Heinrich Jacobi, *Jacobi an Fichte* (Hamburg, 1799), pp. 10–11.

24. The argument here already suggests Nietzsche's position with regard to modern science in *The Birth of Tragedy*, where Nietzsche suggests that following the principle of sufficient reason leads to the abyss.

25. Jacobi, *Jacobi an Fichte*, p. 14.

26. Jacques Derrida, *La voix et le phénomène* (Paris, 1967), p. 115.

27. Hegel wrote a long piece disagreeing with Jacobi, but ultimately the key argument of Jacobi is developed in the work of the late Schelling into the most influential early critique of Hegel, whose ideas were repeated in Kierkegaard, Feuerbach, and others. See Bowie, *Schelling and Modern European Philosophy*.

28. Ernst Tugendhat, *Der Wahrheitsbegriff bei Husserl und Heidegger* (Berlin, 1970), p. 277.

29. Jacobi, *Jacobi an Fichte*, p. 27.

30. J. G. Fichte, *Werke*, vol. 1 (Berlin, 1971), p. 95.

31. See Bowie, *Schelling and Modern European Philosophy*.

32. Jacobi, *Jacobi an Fichte*, p. 30.

33. Schelling, *Sämmtliche Werke*, pt. 1, vol. 1, p. 167.

34. Hölderlin, who espoused a similar position to Jacobi, was a decisive influence on Schelling in this respect. See Manfred Frank, *Der unendliche Mangel an Sein* (Frankfurt am Main, 1975); idem, *Eine Einführung in Schellings Philosophie* (Frankfurt am Main, 1985); Bowie, *Aesthetics and Subjectivity*, chap. 3; idem, *Schelling and Modern European Philosophy*, chap. 1.

35. Heidegger, *Die Grundbegriffe der Metaphysik*, p. 414.

36. See Bowie, *Aesthetics and Subjectivity*; idem. *Schelling and Modern European Philosophy*.

37. On these issues in more detail, see also the essay by Manfred Frank in this volume. To avoid repetition I have tried to compress my analysis, which relies heavily on that of Frank anyway. The reader might at this point be advised to read Frank's essay before returning to mine.

38. Schelling, *Sämmtliche Werke*, pt. 1, vol. 7, p. 17.

39. Ibid., p. 148.

40. John D. Barrow and Frank J. Tipler, *The Anthropic Cosmological Principle* (Oxford, 1986), p. 4.

41. Wolfram Hogrebe, *Prädikation und Genesis: Metaphysik als Fundamentalheuristic im Ausgang von Schellings "Die Weltalter"* (Frankfurt am Main, 1989), p. 54.

42. Martin Heidegger, *Nietzsche*, vol. 2 (Pfullingen, 1961), p. 194.

43. Ibid., p. 200.

44. Ibid., p. 256.

45. Ibid., pp. 208–10.

46. As Frank shows in the essay in this volume Schelling alters the statement into A = B, in order to express the crucial aspect of his theory of identity.

47. Schelling, *Sämmtliche Werke*, pt. 1, vol. 6, pp. 146–47.

48. Ibid., vol. 3, p. 506.

49. I suggest the link of this to Heidegger's *The Origin of the Work of Art* in Bowie, *Schelling and Modern European Philosophy*, chap. 3; for a detailed account, see Manfred Frank, in this volume.

50. See Bowie, *Schelling and Modern European Philosophy*, chaps. 4 and 6, for an extensive account of Schelling's Hegel-critique.

51. Schelling, *Sämmtliche Werke*, pt. 1, vol. 6, p. 198.

52. Ibid., p. 220.

53. Ibid., p. 142.

54. Martin Heidegger, *Schellings Abhandlung Über das Wesen der menschlichen Freiheit* (Tübingen, 1971), p. 75.

55. I have briefly considered the theological aspect of the *FS* in Bowie, *Schelling and Modern European Philosophy*, chap. 5; for reasons of space I have omitted this aspect here.

56. Martin Heidegger, *Die Metaphysik des deutschen Idealismus (Schelling)* (Franfurt am Main, 1991), p. 137.

57. Ibid., p. 135.

58. Peter Dews has suggested to me in conversation that this prefigures the basic structure of the *Dialectic of Enlightenment*.

59. Schelling, *Sämmtliche Werke*, pt. 1, vol. 7, p. 468.

60. Heidegger, *Schellings Abhandlung*, p. 227.

61. Ibid., p. 231.

62. Ibid., p. 232.

63. Heidegger, *Die Metaphysik des deutschen Idealismus*, p. 185.

64. Heidegger, *Nietzsche*, vol. I, p. 478.

65. Thomä, *Zeit des Selbst und die Zeit danach*, pp. 166–75.

66. I have translated and introduced the Munich lectures *On the History of Modern Philosophy* for Cambridge University Press.

67. Schelling, *Sämmtliche Werke*, pt. 1, vol. 10, p. 10.

68. Ibid., p. 11.

69. On this see Bowie, *Aesthetics and Subjectivity*, chap 3.

70. Schelling, *Sämmtliche Werke*, pt. 1, vol. 10, p. 11.

71. Schelling does admittedly then try to restore an essentially idealist system in his *Philosophy of Revelation* by trying to make real developments in the history of thought square with his philosophical model, but the failure of his philosophical theology does not affect his arguments against Hegel.

72. Manfred Frank shows the untenability of some of Heidegger's arguments concerning subjectivity in *Derrida: A Critical Reader*, ed. David Wood (Oxford, 1992), pp. 218–34. See also Thomä, *Zeit des Selbst und die Zeit danach*.

73. The recent work of Hilary Putnam can suggest this. See the conclusion of Bowie, *Schelling and Modern European Philosophy*. The links of German idealism and romanticism to American pragmatism have hardly been explored, even though Peirce, Royce, and Dewey in particular were familiar with the work of Schelling and Hegel. I shall be looking at this connection in a later publication.

74. See my "Reflections on Aesthetics and Truth" in the proceedings of the University of Bradford Colloquium, *Perception and Understanding* (forthcoming).

75. F. W. J. Schelling, *Philosophie der Offenbarung*, ed. Manfred Frank (Frankfurt am Main, 1977), p. 166.

76. Ibid., p. 170.

77. Schelling, *Sämmtliche Werke*, pt. 1, vol. 10, p. 101.

78. See my " 'Non-Identity': The German Romantics, Schelling and Adorno," in *Intersections: Nineteenth-Century Philosophy and Contemporary Theory*, ed. T. Rajan (Albany, N.Y.: 1993).

Chapter 7

1. René Descartes, *Oeuvres et lettres*, ed. Andre Bridoux (Paris 1953), p. 168.

2. F. W. J. Schelling, *Einleitung in die Philosophie*, ed. Walter E. Ehrhardt, Schellingiana vol. 1 (Stuttgart-Bad Cannstatt 1989), p. 63.

3. Schelling, *Einleitung in die Philosophie*, p. 52.

4. Letter from Marx to Ludwig Feuerbach, 3 Oct. 1843, in *Marx-Engels Werke*, ed. Institute for Marxism-Leninism of the Central Committee of the SED, (Berlin 1964–1968), vol. 27, pp. 419–21.

5. Gottfried Wilhelm, Leibniz, *Die philosophische Schriften von Gottfried Wilhelm Leibniz*, C. I. Gerhardt ed., vol. 7, 1875–90, (Hildesheim, 1960–61), pp. 219, 228; idem, *Opuscules et fragments inédits*, ed. Louis Couturat (Paris 1903), pp. 240, 362 ff., 519 ff.

6. Leibniz: "It is not true that two substances can be entirely alike (that is, in all their determinations) and differ only in number" (*Discours de Metaphysique*, para. 9; cf. *Monadologie*, para. 9).

7. Michael Wolff, *Der Satz vom Grund, oder: Was ist philosophische Argumentation?* in *neue hefte für philosophie* 26 (1986): pp. 89–114, citing here p. 100.

8. Ibid., pp. 100–101.

9. Schelling, *Einleitung in die Philosophie*, p. 49.

10. Cf. F. W. J. Schelling, *Sämmtliche Werke*, ed. K. F. A. Schelling, pt. 1, vols. 1–10, pt. 2, vols. 1–4 (Stuttgart 1856–61), pt. 1, vol. 4, p. 113 and pt. 2, vol. 1, p. 317.

11. Schelling, *Sämmtliche Werke*, pt. 1, vol. 1, p. 386.

12. Ibid., p. 42.

13. Cf. the outstanding *Habilitationsschrift* of Michael Heidelberger, *Die inner Seite der Natur: Gustav Theodor Fechners wissenschaftliche-philosophische Weltansicht* (Göttingen 1989).

14. Schelling, *Sämmtliche Werke*, pt. 1, vol. 6, pp. 500–501. Cf. pp. 538–39 and 548–49.

15. Ibid, vol. 7, p. 425.

16. Cf. ibid.

17. Cf. ibid., vol. 6, p. 501.

18. E. Tugendhat and U. Wolf, *Logisch-semantische Propädeutik* (Stuttgart, 1983), p. 169.

19. Schelling, *Sämmtliche Werke*, pt. 1, vol. 4, p. 374.

20. Ibid., p. 375.

21. Ibid., vol. 7, p. 438, n. 2.

22. Ibid., vol. 4, p. 403.

23. Ibid., p. 134n.

24. Ibid., vol. 7, p. 55.

25. Cf. ibid, vol. 4, paras 15–16, pp. 120–21.

26. F. W. J. Schelling, *Die Weltalter*, ed. Manfred Schröter, version 1, (Munich 1946), pp. 26–29.

27. Ibid., p. 27.

28. Ibid., pp. 26–27; Schelling, *Sämmtliche Werke*, pt. 1, vol. 7, pp. 421 ff.

29. F. W. J. Schelling, *Initia philosophiae universae* (Erlangen lecture course, winter semester 1820–21), ed. Horst Fuhrmans, (Bonn 1969), p. 69.

30. Cf Schelling, *Die Weltalter*, version 1, pp. 26–27.

31. Schelling, *Einleitung in die Philosophie*, pp. 17–18; cf. also idem, *Initia philosohiae universae*, p. 50.

32. "The true meaning of the judgment, for example that A is B, can only be the following: that which is A is that which is B, or that which is A and that which is B are *one-and-the-same* [*einerlei*]" (Schelling, *Sämmtliche Werke*, pt. 1, vol. 8, p. 213 [my emphasis on the decisive expression—M.F.]). "The true meaning of that unity asserted at the beginning is thus: one and the same = x is both the unity and the opposition" (ibid., p. 217).

33. Cf. Schelling, *Die Weltalter*, version 1, p. 27.

34. Ibid., p. 28.

35. Cf. Wolfram Hogrebe, *Prädikation und Genesis. Metaphysik als Fundamentalheuristik im Ausgang von Schelling's "Die Weltalter"* (Frankfurt am Main, 1989). p. 81.

36. Schelling, *Sämmtliche Werke*, pt. 1, vol. 7, 457.

37. Ibid., p. 473.

38. *Marx-Engels Werke*, supp. vol. 1, p. 538.

39. Schelling, *Die Weltalter*, version 1, pp. 32–33.

40. Schelling, *Sämmtliche Werke*, pt. 1, vol. 7, pp. 18–19.

41. Ibid., p. 10. Fichte goes so far as to speak of "so-called nature"; "because it does not fit with his views, he does not even grant the poor thing the right to be called nature: she is only a phantom, an inert precipitate of the original, transcendental activity of the I." (ibid., p. 11).

42. Ibid., p. 17.

43. Ibid., p. 19.

44. Ibid., p. 126.

45. Ibid., p. 51.

Chapter 8

1. " 'Eating Well,' or the Calculation of the Subject: An Interview with Jacques Derrida," in *Who Comes after the Subject?*, ed. Eduardo Cadava, Peter Connor, and Jean-Luc Nancy (London and New York, 1991), p. 97.

2. Ibid.

3. Louis Althusser, "Ideology and Ideological State Apparatuses," in *Lenin and Philosophy and Other Essays* (London 1971), p. 160.

4. Michel Foucault, *L'ordre du discours* (Paris 1971), p. 49.

5. Jacques Lacan, *Le séminaire*, bk. 1, *Les écrits techniques de Freud* (Paris, 1975), p. 29.

6. Jacques Lacan, "Propos sur la causalité psychique," in *Écrits* (Paris, 1966), p. 166.

7. Jacques Lacan, *Maurice Merleau-Ponty* (pirate edition) (Paris, n.d.), p. 13.

8. Jacques Lacan, "L'instance de la lettre dans l'inconscient," in *Écrits*, p. 498.

9. Jacques Derrida, *Of Grammatology* trans. Gayatri Chakravorty Spivak (London 1976), p. 14.

10. Lacan, *Le séminaire*, bk. 1, p. 126.

11. Jacques Lacan, "La Chose Freudienne," in *Écrits*, p. 414.

12. Jacques Lacan, "Fonction et champ de la parole et du langage en psychanalyse," in *Écrits*, p. 297.

13. Jacques Lacan, "Subversion du sujet et dialectique du désir dans l'inconscient freudien," in *Écrits*, p. 807.

14. Jacques Lacan, "Le séminaire sur 'La Lettre volée,' " in *Écrits*, p. 20.

15. Ibid.; cf. also *The Four Fundamental Concepts of Psychoanalysis* (Harmondsworth 1979), p. 139.

16. Lacan, "Fonction et champ de la parole et du language," p. 252. The complete quotation runs: "Même s'il ne communique rien, le discours représente l'existence de la communication; même s'il nie l'évidence, il affirme que la parole constitue la vérité; même s'il est destinée à tromper, il spécule sur la foi dans le témoignage." Cf. "Position de l'inconsicent," in *Écrits*, p. 839 ("L'autre est la dimension exigée de ce que la parole s'affirme en vérité"), and many other passages in Lacan's work.

17. "Dieser Friedenschluß bringt etwas mit sich, was wie der erste Schritt zur Erlangung jenes rätselhaften Wahrheitstriebes aussieht. Jetzt wird nämlich das fixiert, was von nun an 'Wahrheit' sein soll, das heißt es wird eine

gleichmäßig gültige und verbindliche Bezeichnung der Dinge erfunden und die Gesetzgebung der Sprache gibt auch die ersten Gesetzte der Wahrheit: denn es entsteht hier zum ersten Male der Kontrast von Wahrheit und Luge" (Friedrich Nietzsche, "Über Wahrheit und Luge im aussermoralischen Sinne," in *Sämtliche Werke: Kritische Studienausgabe*, vol. 1, ed. Giorgio Colli and Mazzino Montinari (Berlin and New York, 1967–77), p. 877.

18. "Die Menschen fliehen dabei das Betrogenwerden nicht so sehr, als das Beschädigtwerden durch Betrug . . . In einem ähnlichen beschränkten Sinne will der Mensch auch nur die Wahrheit: er begehrt die angenehmen, Leben erhaltenden Folgen der Wahrheit, gegen die reine folgenlose Erkenntnis ist er gleichgültig, gegen die vielleicht schädlichen und zerstörenden Wahrheiten sogar feindlich gestimmt" (ibid.).

19. Lacan, "L'instance de la lettre," p. 525.

20. Jürgen Habermas, "Nietzsches Erkenntnistheorie," in *Kultur und Kritik: Verstreute Aufsätze* (Frankfurt am Main 1973), p. 255.

21. Jürgen Habermas, "Wahrheitstheorien," in *Vorstudien und Ergänzungen zur Theorie des kommunikativen Handelns* (Frankurt am Main, 1984), p. 134.

22. Ibid., p. 180.

23. Lacan, "Le séminaire sur 'La Lettre volée,' " p. 20.

24. Lacan, "L'instance de la lettre," p. 525.

25. Karl-Otto Apel, "Das Problem einer philosophischen Theorie der rationalitätstypen," in *Rationalität: Philosophische Beiträge*, ed. Herbert Schnädelbach (Frankfurt am Main 1984), pp. 27–28.

26. An important consequence of this account, of course, is that for Lacan the unconscious is essentially an intersubjective phenomenon: "The unconscious is that part of the concrete discourse, in so far as it is trans-individual, that is not at the disposal of the subject in reestablishing the continuity of his conscious discourse" ("Fonction et champ de la parole et du langage," p. 258).

27. Cf. Jürgen Habermas, "Handlungen, Sprechakte, sprachlich vermittelte Interaktionen und Lebenswelt," in *Nachmetaphysiches Denken* (Frankfurt am Main, 1988), pp. 63–104.

28. I realize that the equation between Lacan's "truth of the subject" and the concept of 'authenticity' will seem to many an "existentialist" betrayal of Lacanian psychoanalytical insights. However, Lacan himself makes use of the category of the authentic up until the mid-1950s (cf. "Each time that a man speaks to another in a full and authentic manner there is, in the proper sense, a transference, a symbolic transference . . ." Jacques Lacan, *Le Séminaire*, bk. 1, p. 137). And even after this date, the notion of passing beyond illusion to confront that which ultimately defines the being of subject, in the form of the

objet petit a, is retained. What else can the result of this confrontation be but authenticity?

29. Cf. Alessandro Ferrara, "Authenticity and the Project of Modernity," in *European Journal of Philosophy* vol. 2, no. 3 (December 1994): p. 243.

30. Charles Taylor, *Sources of the Self: The Making of the Modernity Identity,* (Cambridge, 1989), p. 332.

31. "In acts of self-presentation I do not assert anything about inner episodes, I make no statement at all, but rather I express an experience" (Habermas, "Wahrheitstheorien," p. 157).

32. Jacques Lacan, "Variantes de la cure-type," in *Écrits*, p. 352.

33. Ibid., p. 351.

34. Jacques Lacan, *Le séminaire,* bk. 3, *Les psychoses* (Paris, 1981), p. 49.

35. Lacan, "Variantes de la cure-type," p. 353.

36. Cf. Jürgen Habermas, "On the Pragmatic, the Ethical, and the Moral Employments of Practical Reason," in *Justification and Application* trans. Ciaran Cronin (Cambridge 1993), pp. 1–17. In earlier writings Habermas reserved the term *authenticity* primarily for the distinctive claim to expressive validity of the work of art. More recently, he has corrected this overly subjectivist account of the aesthetic and has reimported the resulting concept of 'authenticity' as the achieved metaphorical interplay of validity claims back into the ethical-existential domain. Here it seems to connote an absence of aesthetic, moral or cognitive one-sidedness or 'reification.'

37. Cf. Habermas, "Wahrheitstheorien," pp. 182–83.

38. Cf. Jürgen Habermas, *The Philosophical Discourse of Modernity,* trans. Frederick Lawrence (Cambridge, Mass. 1987) chap. 11.

39. Cf. Jürgen Habermas, "Treffen Hegels Einwände gegen Kant auch auf die Diskursethik zu?" in *Erläuterungen zur Diskursethik* (Frankfurt am Main, 1991), pp. 33–36.

40. Cf. Jürgen Habermas, "Exkurs: Transzendenz von innen, Transzendenz ins Diesseits," in *Texte und Kontexte* (Frankfurt am Main, 1991).

41. Cf. Karl-Otto Apel, "The Problem of Philosophical Foundations in Light of a Transcendental Pragmatics of Language," in *After Philosophy: End or Transformation?* ed. K. Baynes, J. Bohman and T. McCarthy (London 1987), pp. 272–83.

42. Jacques Lacan, "La science et la vérité," in *Écrits*, pp. 856–57.

43. Ibid., p. 857.

44. Jacques Lacan, "Le stade du miroir," in *Écrits*, p. 93.

45. Lacan, *Four Fundamental Concepts of Psychoanalysis*, pp. 140–41.

46. Jacques Lacan, "Position de l'inconscient," in *Écrits*, p. 831.

47. For further discussion of Lacan's relation to Descartes, cf. Bernard Baas and Armand Zaloszyc, *Descartes et les fondements de la psychanalyse* (Paris, 1988), esp. chaps. 1–3.

48. Martin Seel, "Die zwei Bedeutungen 'kommunikativer' Rationalität," in *Kommunikatives Handeln*, ed. Axel Honneth and Hans Joas (Frankfurt am Main, 1986), p. 57.

49. Ibid., p. 58.

50. In *Reason, Truth and History* (Cambridge 1981), Hilary Putnam suggests that "according to the watered-down operationism which seems to have become the working philosophy of most scientists, the content of the scientific theory consists in testable consequences, and these can be expressed in statements of the form *if we perform such and such actions, then we will get such and such observable results*" (p. 178).

51. Cf. Charles Taylor, "Theories of Meaning," in *Human Agency and Language: Philosophical Papers* 1 (Cambridge 1985).

52. Ibid., p. 269.

53. Charles Taylor, "The Concept of a Person," in *Philosophical Papers 1*, pp. 112–13.

54. Charles Taylor, "Overcoming Epistemology," in *After Philosophy*, ed. Kenneth Baynes, James Bohman and Thomas McCarthy (Cambridge, Mass. 1987), p. 477.

55. Cf. Taylor, *Sources of the Self* pp. 85–87.

56. Taylor, "Overcoming Epistemology," p. 476.

57. Cf. Taylor, *Philosophical Papers 1*, p. 258.

58. Taylor, "Overcoming Epistemology," p. 471.

59. Habermas, "On the Employments of Practical Reason," p. 11.

60. "My identity is only responsive to—even at the mercy of—the reflexive pressure of an altered self-understanding if it observes the same standards of authenticity as ethical-existential discourse itself. Such a discourse already presupposes, on the part of the addressee, a striving to live an authentic life—or the suffering of a patient who has become conscious of the 'sickness unto death'" (ibid., p. 12).

61. Jacques Lacan, "D'un question préliminaire à tout traitement possible de la psychose," in *Écrits*, p. 550.

62. Louise Kaplan, *Female Perversions* (Harmondsworth 1993), p. 128.

63. Ibid., p. 361.

64. Lacan, "Fonction et champ de la parole et du langage," p. 282.

65. Richard Rorty, *Contingency, Irony and Solidarity* (Cambridge 1989), p. 34.

Chapter 9

1. Paul Ricoeur, *Soi-même comme un autre* (Paris, 1990).

2. Martin Heidegger, *Sein und Zeit* (Tübingen, 1927); *Being and Time*, trans. J. Macquarrie and E. Robinson (New York, 1962).

3. Sigmund Freud, "Die Ichspaltung im Abwehrvorgang," G. W. vol. 17, pp. 55–62; James Strachey, ed. *Standard Edition* (London 1953–1974) vol. 23, p. 271.

4. M. Borch-Jacobsen, *Le sujet freudien* (Paris, 1982).

5. Samuel IJsseling, *Mimesis: Over schijn en zijn* (Baarn, 1990).

6. André Malraux, *Antimémoires* (Paris, 1967), p. 10.

7. Edmund Husserl, *Ideen zu einer reinen Phänomenologie und phänomenologischen Philosophie*, bk. 2, *Phänomenogische Untersuchungen zur Konstitution*, Husserliana 4 (The Hague, 1952); *Ideas Pertaining to a Pure Phenomenology and to a Phenomenological Philosophy*, bk. 2, *Studies in the Phenomenology of Constitution*, trans. R. Rojcewicz and A. Schuwer (Dordrecht, 1989), section 38.

8. Maurice Merleau-Ponty, *Phénoménologie de la perception* (Paris, 1945); *Phenomenology of Perception*, trans. C. Smith (London, 1961).

Chapter 10

1. S. Freud, *Standard Edition* (hereafter cited as *S.E.*), vol. 22, pp. 212–13.

2. Freud, *S.E.*, 18, pp. 69–143 (especially pp. 122ff.).

3. Cf. for instance J. Lacan, *Écrits* (Paris, 1966), pp. 474–75.

4. Freud, *S.E.* 18, p. 88

5. For this interpretation cf. M. Borch-Jacobsen, "Le sujet freudien: du politique à l'éthique," *Cahiers Confrontations* 20 (1989): pp. 53–72. Cf. also T. Adorno, "Freudian Theory and the Pattern of Fascist Propaganda," in A. Arato and E. Gebhardt eds., *The Essential Frankfurt School Reader* (Oxford, 1978), p. 134.

6. C. Lefort, *Eléments d'une critique de la bureaucratie* (Geneva, 1971); Idem, *Un homme en trop: Réflexions sur "L'archipel du Goulag,"* Coll. Combat (Paris, 1976); Idem, *L'invention démocratique*, Coll. politique. XIX_e—XX_e siècles (Paris, 1986).

7. J-L. Nancy, *La communauté désoeuvrée* (Paris, 1986).

8. C. Lefort, "L'image du corps et le totalitarisme," in *L'invention démocratique*, pp. 166–84.

9. For a different reading of Hegel cf. L. Devos, "Absolute Knowing in the Phenomenology," in *Hegel on the Ethical Life, Religion and Philosophy*, ed. A. Wylleman, Louvain Philosophical Studies 3 (Leuven, 1989), pp. 231–70.

10. P. Lacoue-Labarthe and J.-L. Nancy, "La panique politique," *Confrontations*, 2 (1979): pp. 33–57. My interpretation of Freud, however, is especially dependent on the work of M. Borch-Jacobsen; cf. M. Borch-Jacobsen, *Le sujet freudien* (Paris, 1982); idem, "Le sujet freudien: du politique à l'éthique," *Confrontations* 20 (1989): pp. 53–72; idem, *Le lien affectif* (Paris, 1991).

11. S. Freud, *S.E.* vol. 13, pp. 1–162.

12. "He, at the very beginning of the history of mankind, was the 'superman' whom Nietzsche only expected from the future . . . The leader himself need love no one else, he may be of masterful nature, absolutely narcissistic, self confident and independent" (Freud, *S.E.* vol. 18, pp. 123–24).

13. Ibid., p. 127.

14. What follows should of course be carefully compared to the thought of E. Lévinas. I hope to do that in another article.

15. Freud, *S.E.* vol. 13, p. 143.

16. Ibid.

17. Ibid., pp. 67ff.

18. Ibid., p. 143.

19. Ibid., pp. 141–42.

20. Ibid., p. 143.

21. Ibid.

22. Ibid., p. 142.

23. Ibid., p. 143 (in note).

24. For what follows of Freud, see ibid., vol. 14, p. 295.

25. M. Borch-Jacobsen, "Le sujet freudien: du politique à l'éthique," p. 69.

26. "You a(nd)re (completely different from) me." Nancy, *La communauté désoeuvrée*, p. 74.

27. Cf. on the Freudian "superego" J. Florence, *Ouvertures psychanalytiques*, Publications des Facultés universitaires Saint-Louis (Bruxelles, 1985).

28. M. Klein, "Symposium on Child-Analysis," *International Journal of Psychoanalysis*, vol. 8 (1927).

29. M. Klein, "Early Stages of the Oedipus-Conflict," *International Journal of Psychoanalysis*, vol. 9 (1928); idem, "A Contribution to the Psychogenesis of Manic-Depressive States," in *Essential Papers on Object Relations*, ed. P. Buckley (New York, 1986), pp. 40–70; idem, "Notes sur quelques mécanismes schizoides," in *Développements de la psychanalyse*, ed. M. Klein et al. (Paris, 1980), pp. 274–300.

30. Cf. J. Derrida, "Préjugés, devant la loi," in *La faculté de juger*, J. Derrida et al., (Paris, 1985), pp. 87–140.

31. This is why Lacan always distinguishes between the real and the symbolic father.

32. In what follows I am very much dependent on some later texts of Derrida; cf. among others " 'Il faut bien manager' ou le calcul du sujet," *Confrontations*, 20 (1989): pp. 91–114; "Nombre de oui," in: *Psyché: Inventions de l'autre* (Paris, 1987), pp. 639–50.

33. For a good commentary on the meaning of this primordial yes in the work of Jacques Derrida, cf. G. Bennington and J. Derrida, *Jacques Derrida* (Paris, 1991), pp. 176–90, 212–22.

34. Actually it is too short and sketchy; the relation between Heidegger and what has just been said about Freud, is much more complex than I can develop here.

35. M. Heidegger, *Being and Time* (Oxford, 1980), pp. 312–48. For a brilliant comment on these passages, cf. J.-Fr. Courtine, "Voix de la conscience et vocation de l'être," *Confrontations* 20 (1989): pp. 73–88.

36. Heidegger, *Being and Time*, pp. 329.

37. Or, more precisely, for Freud as we presented him.

38. Heidegger, *Being and Time*, p. 294.

39. Derrida, " 'Il faut bien manger" ou le calcul du sujet," p. 105.

40. Ibid., p. 103.

41. It is also important to note here that the primordial yes cannot be a matter of a sort of one-off act. It belongs on the contrary to the structure of this yes to call forth its own repetition. Cf. J. Derrida, "Nombre de oui," pp. 639–50.

42. Lefort, "L'image du corps et le totalitarisme," p. 173.

43. C. Lefort, *Essais sur le politique: XIX$_e$–XX$_e$ siècles*, (Paris, 1986), p. 265.

44. Ibid., pp. 266–67.

45. These last two paragraphs are the result of a discussion with Michael Newman.

Chapter 11

1. Immanuel Kant, *Critique of Pure Reason*, B 429.

2. Vincent Descombes, "A propos of the 'Critique of the Subject' and of the Critique of this Critique," in *Who comes after the Subject?*, ed. Eduardo Cadava, Peter Connor and Jean-Luc Nancy (London and New York, 1991), p. 125.

3. Wolfgang Welsch, *Unsere postmoderne Moderne* (Weinheim 1991), p. 316.

4. Martin Heidegger, *Holzwege* (Frankfurt am Main, 1957), p. 84.

5. Cf. Descombes, "Critique of the Subject."

6. Welsch, *Unsere postmoderne Moderne*, pp. 316 ff.

7. The statement attributed to Heidegger concerning the rooms of the old castle which houses the Neske publishing firm, "Hier wird noch gewohnt" (This place is still a dwelling), speaks for itself in this context.

8. Theodor W. Adorno, "Anmerkungen zum philosophischen Denken," in *Gesammelte Werke*, vol. 10, pt. 2, *Stichworte* (Frankfurt am Main, 1977), p. 602.

Notes on Contributors

Rudolf Bernet (1946) is Professor of Philosophy at the University of Leuven and Member of the Board of Directors at the Husserl Archive. He is editor of Husserl's *Collected Works* and author of *An Introduction to Husserlian Phenomenology* (1993) and *La vie du sujet* (1994).

Andrew Bowie (1952) is Professor of European Philosophy at Anglia Polytechnic University, Cambridge. He is author of *Aesthetics and Subjectivity: From Kant to Nietzsche* (1990), *Schelling and Modern European Philosophy: An Introduction* (1993), and has translated and edited Schelling's *On the History of Modern Philosophy* (1994).

Simon Critchley (1960) is Reader in Philosophy at the University of Essex. He is editor, with Robert Bernasconi, of *Re-Reading Levinas* (1991), with Robert Bernasconi and Adriaan Peperzak, of *Emmanuel Levinas: Basic Philosophical Writings* (1996), and *Blackwell's Companion to Continental Philosophy* (1996). He is author of *The Ethics of Deconstruction* (1992) and *Very Little ... Almost Nothing* (1996).

Peter Dews (1952) is Senior Lecturer in Philosophy at the University of Essex. He is author of *Logics of Disintegration: Post-Structuralist Thought and the Claims of Critical Theory* (1987) and of *The Limits of Disenchantment: Essays on Contemporary European Philosophy* (1995). He has also edited a book of interviews with Jürgen Habermas, *Autonomy and Solidarity* (rev. ed., 1992) and is the editor of *Habermas: A Critical Reader* (forthcoming).

Manfred Frank (1945) is Professor of Philosophy at the University of Tübingen. He is author, among other works, of *Der kommende Gott* (1982), *Was ist Neostrukturalismus?* (1983; English translation, *What is Neostructuralism?*, 1989), *Eine Einführung in die frühromantische Asthetik* (1989), and *Conditio Moderna* (1993).

247

Ute Guzzoni (1934) is Professor of Philosophy at the University of Freiburg. She has published numerous essays, particularly on the work of Heidegger and Adorno. She has also written several books, including *Veränderndes Denken* (1985) and *Werden zu sich* (1963), an interpretation of Hegel's *Science of Logic*.

Dominique Janicaud (1937) is Professor of Philosophy at the University of Nice. He is author of *Hegel et le destin de la Grèce* (1975), *La puissance du rationnel* (1985; English translation, *Powers of the Rational*, 1995), *L'ombre de cette pensée* (1990), *A nouveau la philosophie* (1991) and *Le tournant théologique de la phénoménologie française* (1991).

Jean-Luc Marion (1946) is Professor of Philosophy at University of Paris X (Nanterre) and is Visiting Professor at the University of Chicago. He is author of *Sur la théologie blanche de Descartes* (1981), *Dieu sans l'être* (1982; English translation, *God without Being*, 1992), *Sur le prisme métaphysique de Descartes* (1986) and *Réduction et Donation: Recherches sur Husserl, Heidegger et la phénoménologie*.

Philippe Van Haute (1957) is Professor of Philosophy at the University of Nijmegen, Scientific Director of the Dutch-Flemish Research School in Philosophy and Member of the Belgian School for Psychoanalysis. He is author of *Filosofie en Psychoanalyse* (1990) and editor, with Peg Birmingham, of *Dissensus Communis: Between Ethics and Politics* (1995).

Rudi Visker (1959) is Senior Research Fellow at the Institute of Philosophy, University of Leuven, under the auspices of the Belgian National Fund for Scientific Research, and has been a Visiting Fellow of the University of Essex. In addition to several publications in the philosophy of economics and in modern and contemporary philosophy, he is author of *Michel Foucault: Genealogie als Kritik* (1991; English translation, *Michel Foucault: Genealogy as Critique* Verso 1995).

Index